Validity in the Identification and Interpretation of Literary Allusions in the Hebrew Bible

Validity in the Identification and Interpretation of Literary Allusions in the Hebrew Bible

DAVID R. KLINGLER

☙PICKWICK *Publications* · Eugene, Oregon

VALIDITY IN THE IDENTIFICATION AND INTERPRETATION OF LITERARY ALLUSIONS IN THE HEBREW BIBLE

Copyright © 2021 David R. Klingler. All rights reserved. Except for brief quotations in critical publications or reviews, no part of this book may be reproduced in any manner without prior written permission from the publisher. Write: Permissions, Wipf and Stock Publishers, 199 W. 8th Ave., Suite 3, Eugene, OR 97401.

Pickwick Publications
An Imprint of Wipf and Stock Publishers
199 W. 8th Ave., Suite 3
Eugene, OR 97401

www.wipfandstock.com

PAPERBACK ISBN: 978-1-6667-2452-3
HARDCOVER ISBN: 978-1-6667-2023-5
EBOOK ISBN: 978-1-6667-2024-2

Cataloguing-in-Publication data:

Names: Klingler, David R. [author]

Title: Validity in the identification and interpretation of literary allusions in the Hebrew Bible / David R. Klingler.

Description: Eugene, OR: Pickwick Publications, 2021 | Includes bibliographical references.

Identifiers: ISBN 978-1-6667-2452-3 (paperback) | ISBN 978-1-6667-2023-5 (hardcover) | ISBN 978-1-6667-2024-2 (ebook)

Subjects: LCSH: Allusions in the Bible | Bible.—Old Testament—Criticism, interpretation, etc. |Allusions | Bible as literature

Classification: BS1184 K55 2021 (paperback) | BS1184 (ebook)

10/12/21

Contents

1	**Introduction**	1
	Need for the Study	3
	Presuppositions of the Study	11
	General Method of Inquiry	16
2	**The Historical Progression of Hermeneutical Thought**	18
	Current Philosophical Hermeneutics and the Postmodern Turn	19
	Origin, Progression, and Impact of Continental Philosophy	27
	A Response to Continental Philosophy	58
3	**What Is a Literary Allusion?**	60
	Need for a Definition	60
	Brief Survey of Current Proposals and Problems	62
	Developing a Definition: The Necessary Categories and Components	69
	Defining the Terms of Literary Reference	89
	Conclusion	93
4	**How Do We Identify an Allusion?**	94
	Current Proposals and Problems	95
	Current Approaches to Classification	113
	Unaddressed Issues	116
	Conclusion	127
5	**Validation of and Disagreements over Literary Allusions**	128
	Validation of Literary Allusions	128
	Disagreements over Literary Allusion	146
	Conclusion	153
6	**Illustrations in the Identification and Validation of Literary Allusion in the Old Testament**	154
	Allusion in Narrative: Genesis 19 in Judges 19	156
	Allusion in Law: Genesis 19 in Deuteronomy 29:23?	176

	Allusion in the Prophecy: Genesis 19 in Isaiah 1:9–10?	180
	Allusion in Poetry: Genesis 19 in Psalm 11:6?	184
	Conclusion	188
7	**Conclusion**	190

Bibliography 193

1

Introduction

NOT TOO MANY YEARS ago readers and hermeneutical theorists alike believed that it was possible to read a text in order to understand what it was that the author had to say. In fact, it was the very reason that people used to read—or so at least they thought. Many of today's literary theorists and philosophers however have informed us (ironically through writing) that we were in fact not reading the author's words for the purpose of understanding his intended meaning but instead importing meaning into the text from our own horizon (i.e., presuppositions, prejudgments, and prejudices). Therefore, it is not the author who was speaking to us, but we were, at least in part, speaking to ourselves. However, in spite of all the recent technical jargon and extended treatises concerning horizons, historicism, presuppositions, prejudgments, prejudices, intertextuality, and the like (i.e., one's situatedness) coming from all of the experts in the fields of hermeneutics, philosophy of language, philosophy of mind, epistemology, metaphysics, and so on, one haunting logical inconsistency remains: those who insist that *we* are all so biased by our own situatedness that *we* are incapable of objectively correct interpretations emphatically insist that *their* conclusions concerning this fact are objectively correct interpretations of the evidence. Obviously, this line of reasoning is a self-defeating contradiction on par with the statement, "There are absolutely no absolutes!"

That this brand of philosophy has overtaken secular literary studies is undeniable. Unfortunately, it has also managed to overtake and dominate the discussions in nearly *every* field of inquiry, even the field of biblical studies, with the effect that this postmodern mindset now rules the day. Truth is a matter of one's perspective. "Everything is hermeneutics" is now the postmodern battle cry. However, what will be argued below emanates from the belief that how one responds to the question of meaning and hermeneutics is everything. For, as Vanhoozer rightly states, "The fate of hermeneutics and humanity alike stand or fall together."[1] In summary then, on the one hand recent philosophers have argued that we are all so controlled by our situatedness (i.e., our presuppositions, prejudices, prejudgments, etc.) that we are not, in fact *cannot be*, objective; on the other hand they have been able to shape and mold the presuppositions, prejudices, and prejudgments of the western culture to the extent that *we* now naively believe the assertion (i.e., objective interpretation) that there are no objective interpretations.

This philosophical approach has led to devastating results for interpretation of texts. Not only has the death of the author been declared in literary studies[2], but so also has the death of the Author been declared in philosophical studies.[3] Meanwhile, most Christian scholars have avoided these philosophically driven hermeneutical discussions, which assume the death of both the author and God, while at the same time unknowingly operating according to their hermeneutical conclusions. It is for this reason that Christian scholars can no longer sit on the philosophical sidelines and wait for an exegetical discussion over a particular text to arise. Instead, a lack of engagement in hermeneutical theory means that the game has already been played and its outcome determined *before* the text to be interpreted is even considered. This is not an option for the Christian scholar or the Church that this brand of philosophy sets out to destroy. These philosophical hermeneutical issues *must* be settled *before* we approach a text lest what ensues is not the "playing of the game," but simply the "reading of the box scores!" For, if the philosophical underpinning which guide a hermeneutical approach assume that God is dead then no conclusion derived from that hermeneutical approach would be able to resurrect him. It is for this reason that, while the primary focus of this study is on validity in the identification and interpretation of literary allusions, much will have to be said about the philosophical theories and conclusions that undergird much of the present day hermeneutical approaches in order to tear down the fallacious arguments and expose the power play that have undermined the belief that an author, or the Author, can speak and be understood.

1. Vanhoozer, *Is There a Meaning in This Text?*, 22.
2. Cf. Barthes, "The Death of the Author," 125–30; Foucault, "What Is an Author?," 141–60.
3. Nietzsche, *The Gay Science*, 119–20.

NEED FOR THE STUDY

There are two main reasons why a theoretical work on the interpretation of literary allusions is needed. First, the simple fact is that to date there has been no comprehensive theoretical work that adequately addresses the topic of literary allusion. Irwin explains, "whereas there is no shortage of theoretical work on subjects as irony and metaphor, there is a scarcity of theoretical work on allusion, a small number of articles, and no books."[4] Second, there is a need both to reestablish and reopen discussions concerning the discernment of authorial intention as well as the means by which authors convey meaning (i.e., literary devices such as allusions) since the rejection of authorial intention in current hermeneutical discussions are intentionally in direct contradiction to both basic logic and the orthodox Christian faith. The result of this rejection renders the Bible a non-authoritative, historically situated collection of writings with no *correct or incorrect* interpretation.

Lack of Theoretical Works

Once the topic of literary allusion is considered two things become quickly apparent. First, there is a plethora of interpretive works that claim the presence of literary allusions in the texts they examine.[5] Second, while there are an overwhelming number of interpretive works on allusion, there is almost a total lack of theoretical works dealing with the topic. What is not clear is why the lack of theoretical works on the topic of literary allusion exists. While there may be several potential reasons for this void, three seem most probable.

---

4. Irwin, "What Is an Allusion?," 287. Irwin qualifies his statement in his footnote by stating, "No books in English, that is." He does go on to cite one book written in Italian (Conte, *Memoria die poeti e sistema letterario*) which was translated into English (Conte, *The Rhetoric of Imitation*) and one notable article written in Polish (Pasquali, "Arte Allusiva," 11–20). That article later appeared in a book (Pasquali, *Pagine stravananti*, 2:275–83). Irwin did not mention an unpublished dissertation by Ben-Porath (Ben-Porath, "The Poetics of Allusion,") as well as portions of a few works that begin to address the issue of literary allusion (most notably, Kellett, *Literary Quotation and Allusion*). Since his article (published in 2001), more articles and books have appeared, mostly addressing the question of how one identifies literary allusions. These will be discussed below. In addition to these, there is one work published in Estonian that has been overlooked in the current discussion (Mihkelev, *Vihjamise Poeetika*). However, his statement serves to make the point that work in this area is still lacking and is in need of attention.

5. Cf. Hebel, *Intertextuality, Allusion, and Quotation*. Hebel chronicles more than two thousand works in nearly two hundred pages of bibliography.

Straightforward

One reason for the lack of a comprehensive theoretical work on the topic of literary allusion is that, at least at first glance, literary allusions seem quite straightforward. This would explain the myriad of interpretive works that claim the presence of various literary allusions in the literary texts that they set out to examine. In fact, the list of works making such claims is so long that it would be nearly a lifelong endeavor for one to undertake the task of interacting with all of them. This is true not only in the field of literary studies, but of biblical studies as well.[6] Further, even if one were to undertake such a monumental task, several troubling observations would immediately arise after examining only a few examples. First, while all of these authors are claiming the presence of one or more literary allusions in a text, almost none specify what they mean by the term "allusion" resulting in a lack of clarity concerning what they are claiming to be present in the text.[7] Second, many of these works are contradictory. What one interpreter claims is an allusion, another either rejects or claims is instead an allusion to a different text.[8] Third, interpreters regularly declare via fiat the presence of a literary allusion without providing a defense that validates their claim. This lack of validation makes any effort to reconcile differences in interpretations either difficult or impossible.

Together these three observations lead to the conclusion that there is a significant need for a theoretical treatment of the topic of literary allusion that clearly defines "literary allusion," precisely identifies the working parts of literary allusions, carefully explains how literary allusions function, methodically sets forth a means by which the interpreter can validate his claim for the presence of a literary allusion as intended by the author of a text, and adequately explains why so many interpreters disagree about the presence of a literary allusion in a given text. This work will seek to do just that.

Philosophical

A second possible reason for the lack of a comprehensive theoretical work on the topic of literary allusion is that both in the broader field of literary studies and more specifically in the field of biblical studies there has been a

---

6. Just a few simple searches on theological databases on the topic of allusion, echo, citation, quotation, reference, and intertextuality turns up thousands of works.

7. Cf. Irwin, "What Is an Allusion?," 287.

8. Cf. Paulien, *Decoding Revelation's Trumpets*. Paulien's dissertation evaluates ten major commentaries on Rev 8:7–12. These works proposed 288 allusions to the Old Testament with the startling finding that all ten works agreed on only one allusion.

paradigm shift in hermeneutical theory over the past several decades. Since a work on the interpretation of literary allusions is obviously only a small part of the larger endeavor of the interpretation of texts (or said more succinctly, a work in the field of hermeneutics), the study of literary allusions has been dramatically affected by this paradigm shift as well. Therefore, in order to understand the significance of the change that has occurred as it relates to the specific topic of literary allusion, one must first be familiar with the shift that has occurred in the broader field of hermeneutics. Today's hermeneutical theory is built upon several centuries of philosophical thought presented in technical jargon. Unfortunately, this reality effectively removes the contemporary discussion from the popular forum and places it firmly inside the academy.

Unnecessary

A third reason for the lack of a comprehensive theoretical work on the topic of literary allusion is directly related to the previous one: many current hermeneutical approaches hold that there is no objective and therefore "correct" interpretation of a text. In arguing such a hermeneutical approach, Thomas Howe summarizes the logical argumentation of this viewpoint in the following eight assertions: (1) Everyone comes to the world with his own framework of understanding; (2) No particular framework of understanding is universally valid; (3) But, universal validity is precisely what is implied in the notion of objectivity; (4) Therefore, no interpreter can be objective in interpretation; (5) But, if no interpreter can be objective, then no interpretation is universally valid; (6) But, if no interpretation is universally valid, then the concept of a "correct" interpretation is at best relative or at worst empty; (7) Since there is no such thing as a correct interpretation, there is no means of adjudicating between interpretations; (8) In fact, the very idea of adjudicating between interpretations is at best relative and at worst empty.[9]

The ramifications of this line of thinking utilized by many contemporary hermeneutical approaches has effectively led to the death of the author as the controller of meaning since, so the argument goes, the author's intended meaning is not recoverable. Hence, no reader is therefore capable of

---

9. Howe, *Objectivity in Biblical Interpretation*, 458. It is with statements 4 and 5 that this line of argumentation breaks down. The transition from "is" in statements 2 and 3 to "can" in statements 4 and 5 produces the problem. Surely it is possible for a situated subject (i.e., coming to the world with one's own framework of understanding) to recognize both contingent truths and necessary truths. If not, how else could statements 1 and 2 be asserted as necessary truths?

arriving at either a "correct" (or "incorrect") interpretation of it. This philosophical shift has had the effect that theoretical works on the interpretation of texts in light of the author's intention have come to a virtual standstill. For, if the author's meaning is not recoverable then why waste time and effort in writing another book addressing the hopeless task of correct or valid interpretation? In fact, some have even gone so far as to suggest the concept of an "author" of a text is a western construct. Vanhoozer observes, "Behind the innocuous figure of the author as determiner of textual meaning, according to Derrida, lies the whole edifice of Western philosophy, together with its metaphysical scaffolding. In challenging the traditional picture of what an author is and does, Derrida attempts nothing less than an undoing of the central ideas of philosophy and theology alike."[10]

Therefore, it turns out that once considered, the topic of literary allusion is more involved than one might first think.[11] William Irwin understands the problem well:

> One might suggest that the reason for the scarcity [of theoretical work on allusion] is that it is just not a very important or interesting topic, but surely this is not the case. Allusion is bound up with a vital and perennial topic in literary theory, the place of authorial intention in interpretation, and in literature itself allusion has become an increasingly pivotal device . . . allusion is a difficult and elusive topic. Still, difficulty alone cannot explain the lack of attention to allusion, and thankfully, it is not the purpose of this paper to explain this lack of attention.[12]

So while Irwin acknowledges the lack of attention in these areas, his brief article sets out only to develop a workable definition of allusion. Still, his statement raises two key points. Irwin correctly points out that one cannot separate literary allusion from authorial intention. As will be seen below, if one tries to separate these two, then literary allusion ceases to be a literary device utilized by the author to convey meaning and instead turns

---

10. Vanhoozer, *Is There a Meaning in This Text?*, 48. Surely philosophers such as Nietzsche, Heidegger, Gadamer, Derrida, Fish, and Rorty see the contradiction in their argumentation. After all, they are writing to argue that there is no meaning in the written word except that which the reader places there. Yet, they clearly set out to win the reader over to their side of the argument. Thus, at the core of this issue is not the *meaning* of a text, but the *authority* of a text. These men are in essence arguing that no text or interpretation of a text has any authority over a reader! At its core, there is a colossal power play at work here with enormous ramifications for the Church.

11. Irwin, "What Is an Allusion?," 287.

12. Irwin, "What Is an Allusion?," 287.

Introduction   7

into a creation of the reader. Additionally, Irwin correctly points out that literary allusion has become a pivotal device within literature itself.

Upon completion of this study it will be seen that the elusiveness of allusions is produced by a lack of adequate attention being given to several simple but contributing factors. First, there is no widely agreed upon definition for literary allusion. While a few definitions have been proposed, they are either too simplistic or fail to realize the rhetorical nature of allusions. A definition of an allusion must clearly delineate what an allusion is and what it is not. Further, a good definition must distinguish it from other similar literary devices. As will be seen below, other literary devices such as echo, reference, citation, quotation, and paraphrase are often intermingled producing a lack of precision in the discussion. Therefore, clear definitions of similar literary devices must be spelled out as well so that the necessary distinctions are made clear.

Second, the fact that allusions are rhetorical literary devices utilized to import meaning into an alluding text from the text alluded to has been neglected. This point needs to be delineated and emphasized. Even though two texts may contain the same terms, themes, or structures, these items alone or even in tandem are not proof enough that a literary allusion exists. There *must* be a distinguishable rhetorical purpose for an allusion to exist since allusions are utilized by the author to assist in the conveyance of his intended meaning.

Third, there is little agreement on how one recognizes an allusion in a text. As will seen below, several have presented different list of identifying criteria. However, if these criteria were decisive, then all disagreements would have been put to rest; yet disagreements still abound.[13] This raises the question, how can the reader tell if potential allusion was intended? The answer to this question lies in the recognition that an allusion is not simply a matter of similarity of texts but of the importation of meaning for the purpose of making a rhetorical point. If one only sees similarities yet cannot specifically explain the rhetorical relation between the two texts or the meaning to be imported, then it is quite probable that an echo or literary reference, not an literary allusion, is present. Therefore, if one is to argue for the presence of an allusion then one must be able to explain the rhetorical point being made by explaining the "working parts" of the allusion.

Fourth, there has been a lack of recognition concerning the rhetorical function of an allusion because there has been a lack of attention given to exactly how allusions work. All allusions have the same *working parts* that

---

13. See Jauhiainen, *The Use of Zechariah in Revelation*. For a summary of his findings in chart form, see pp. 100, 130, 134–35. See also Paulien, *Decoding Revelation's Trumpets*.

the author utilizes to rhetorically connect two texts. These parts are as follows: (1) the developing textual meaning of the alluding text, (2) the stable textual meaning of the alluded text, (3) the alluding literary marker(s) that serve to make the connection of the two texts, (4) and rhetorical function of the allusion and the meaning to be imported from the alluded text into the alluding text.

Fifth, the need to validate one's claim that an allusion is present in a text has been neglected. In order to do this, the interpreter must be able to defend his understanding via explaining the working parts of the allusion as well as the rhetorical point being made by the author through the use of the allusion. Ben-Porath spells out the process by which the reader "actualizes" an allusion.[14] Unfortunately, her work does not try to explain how one knows that an allusion was intended (it appears that Ben-Porath falls in the camp of those who ascribe to "reader-response" interpretive model) but instead assumes that an allusion is really "there" to be actualized. This work has gone largely unnoticed to the detriment of the ongoing discussion on the topic of literary allusion.

Re-establishment of Authorial Intention

The second reason why the present study is needed is that there is an urgent necessity for the re-establishment of authorial intention in the field of hermeneutics. Recent and current hermeneutical landscapes have produced a plethora of reader-response interpretive methodologies that reject the role of the author as the controller of meaning. Because of this turn in hermeneutical philosophy, it is now commonly argued that it is the reader who controls the meaning of a text. However, the full ramifications that follow the adoption of such literary approaches have yet to be realized. One example of such shortsightedness is the fact that these interpretive philosophies effectively render literary allusions as textual phenomena explainable only by what the reader sees in the text instead of strategically and intentionally constructed literary devices utilized by an author for the conveyance of intended meaning. Therefore, not only would a discussion on an author's use of a literary allusion to convey meaning be of no value, but so also would any discussion about the author's use of *any* literary device or strategy such as characterization, point of view, satire, irony, plot, rhetoric, aesthetics, etc. for the purpose of conveying meaning to the reader. For if in fact it is the reader and not the writer who controls the meaning of a text, then most literary study up to this time has been in vain.

14. Ben-Porath, "Poetics of Allusion," 1–18.

Consider the following definition of literary allusion by Ziva Ben-Porath: "In a literary text allusion is a device by which the reader links one or more elements in a given text with other independent and not identical elements in an evoked text."[15] Two points should be made at this juncture. First, her definition is at best an example of a reader-oriented approach to the text. Second, it should be noted that the reader-oriented direction of literary studies, led by, among others, Stanley Fish (one of Ziva Ben-Porath's readers on her doctoral dissertation), would logically end with such a conclusion. For, if the author's intended meaning is not recoverable, yet the reader sees an allusion in a text, then who ultimately is doing the alluding? If it is not the author of a text who alludes, then who does? The only other option available is the reader. However, if it is in fact the author that alludes, then why does he allude if not but to assist in the conveyance of his intended meaning? In fact, is that not exactly why authors utilize *all* literary devices? What is at issue here is not just the isolated topic of literary allusion. Instead, all literary devices stand or fall on the central issue of who controls the meaning of a text.

The importance of this point is as follows. Literary allusions (along with all other literary devices) have traditionally been thought to be literary devices utilized by an author to convey his intended meaning. However, if authorial intention is irrecoverable, then any theoretical, analytical, or interpretive work on any literary device would be a trivial and meaningless endeavor. But, if it can be demonstrated that the conclusions of modern hermeneutical philosophers are guilty of breaking the law of non-contradiction and are thus nothing more than power plays constructed for the purpose of rejecting authority, then the possibility of reading for authorial intention and arriving at a valid and correct interpretation has not been overturned at all. In addition, the need for a study of the author's utilization of literary devices for the conveyance of his authorial intention is restored as well. Therefore, the question that will arise in this study is not whether it is the author or the reader who controls meaning, but rather, *how* does the author control meaning?

While reader-response interpretive philosophies defend the notion that it is the reader who brings meaning to the text, it is most ironic that those who claim to be interpreting under the rubric of authorial intention often appear to be engaged in the same offense as their adversaries since they too regularly disagree over the meaning of a text. In fact, when disagreements arise among those who defend the notion of authorial intention, each interpreter commonly believes that it is the other who has failed to

---

15. Ben-Porath, "Poetics of Allusion," 1.

recognize the original author's intended meaning rather than himself. As will be seen below, there is no area where this is more apparent than in that of literary allusions. Here, agreement is the exception rather than the rule.

The result of these disagreements among those who hold that meaning is controlled by the author's intent has served to embolden hermeneutical pragmatists such as Fish to conclude that the two camps are really no different in that both are simply *users* of texts.[16] In other words, whether one is willing to admit it or not, texts are "used" in that they are filled with meaning by the reader rather than sought to have the original author's intended meaning revealed. The resulting hermeneutical milieu appears to be one in which interpretive freedom is the rule so long as this freedom is *not* used to make any claim regarding the original author's intent since it is a foregone conclusion that the original author's intention is unknowable and therefore cannot be appealed to for a defense of a "correct" interpretation. Instead, there are no correct or incorrect interpretations but only different individual and communal readings and trajectories. The result then is that the only meaning that cannot be sought by the interpreter is the author's intended meaning. In effect, every text means only what it means to the individual interpreter or interpreting community. That is, every individual interpreter or interpretive community provides a meaning of a text for itself. Every reader (or interpretive community) is an author unto himself and only to himself since he can speak for no other, *especially the author*.[17] Every interpreter reads according to what is "right in his eyes" and in doing so appoints himself as god over the text. The result of this current situation is that the author is stripped of his authority to speak.[18] Even more troubling is that while the removal of the author's right to speak is problematic for most works, it has catastrophic ramifications for work that claims to be authoritative.

Therefore, hermeneutical pragmatists like Fish argue that it is irrelevant whether one aligns himself with a reader-response approach or an authorial-intent approach, and that it is ultimately the reader (or reading community) that provides the meaning to a text. Or by implication in the case of literary allusions, it is the reader who is discovering (i.e., inventing) connections between texts that may never have been intended by the author.

The resulting crisis in literary studies (and more importantly, in biblical studies) is that the scholars from both camps have become caught up

---

16. Fish, *Is There a Text in This Class?*, 338–55.

17. Notice the effects of the power play resulting from the philosophical argumentation introduced above. As will be seen below, this rejection is at its core a theological one directed most specifically at the Bible and the Church it creates.

18. As has been pointed out repeatedly, those who argue for this view do so adamantly with the demand that their words be heard and followed.

in allusionomania with few giving an adequate defense of their claims. Therefore, discussions today often center on the pragmatic equivalent of "what the text means to me" rather than "what the text meant to the author who wrote it" with the result that neither reader-response interpretive approaches nor author-intent interpretive approaches have produced any agreement concerning what allusions are and how they work. However, this ought not to be the case. Instead, those who argue that a text should be read for the author's intent *must* be able to defend their position.

PRESUPPOSITIONS OF THE STUDY

Every study begins with certain presuppositions upon which its argumentation will be based. This one is no different. The presuppositions of this study can be divided into three categories: (1) the "otherness" of texts, (2) clarity concerning subjectivity and objectivity, and (3) knowledge of the difference between veracity and validity.

Rejection of Hermeneutical Relativism

This study rejects the assertion of Hermeneutical Anti-realists who argue that there is nothing "there" in the text to be interpreted.[19] From the beginning it has been commonly understood that the author is the controller of the meaning of his words. However, because there has been a shift in the philosophical underpinnings of the hermeneutical endeavor, this is no longer the case. Today the view that the author is the determiner of meaning has been deemed simple and naive. Over the last century, literary scholars have sought to replace such "hermeneutical realism" (i.e., the belief that there is something "there" in the text to interpret, also often pejoratively referred to as "hermeneutical naivety") with "hermeneutical anti-realism" (i.e., the belief that the only thing "there" in the text is what the reader places there). Today's hermeneutical anti-realist has evolved from Kant's *Critique of Pure Reason*, through Nietzsche's declaration of the death of God, to Derrida's declaration of the death of the author as the controller of textual meaning.

The obvious problem that arises from such a line of reasoning is that if meaning is not put in the text by the author, then an allusion would not be placed in the text by the author either. Therefore, it is not the author who alludes but the reader who makes arbitrary connections from within his

---

19. For an extended discussion on this subject, see Vanhoozer, *Is There a Meaning in This Text?*, 15–196.

interpretive horizon or reality. If this theory were true then one would expect to find many different opinions concerning whether or not an allusion exists; and in fact, this is exactly what one finds when the scholarly work in this area is evaluated. However, while the current plethora of opinions concerning the presence of allusions in texts may be an accurate portrayal of the present situation, one who holds out hope for the author's rights does not have to give up hope by succumbing to some brand of hermeneutic non-realism. For, if the literary device of allusion is simply a creation of the reader, then what about all other literary devices and writing strategies? In fact, one is left wondering why college professors who embrace hermeneutical non-realism hand out syllabi to their students or demand that papers be handed in by those same students. Further, how can one write to convince others that hermeneutic non-realism is correct unless it is in fact false?

This study rejects the conclusions of hermeneutical non-realism and seeks to return to a more consistent, stable, objective, and intellectually honest option which holds fast to the belief that it is the author's right to speak (i.e., provide and control the meaning of the text) and be heard (i.e., have the reader understand the meaning that the author intended). This applies to all authors in all places at all times-even those who would use this right to argue in self-defeating fashion to the contrary.

Problems with Hermeneutical Anti-Realism

Once considered, several logical shortcomings in current hermeneutical philosophies are exposed. For example, if all that is in a text is what the reader (subject) puts there (i.e., his interpretation is totally subjective), then how does a text (object) have the ability to "change" the reader (subject)? Further, then how can two readers (different subjects) with two different "horizons" agree on an interpretation (view of an object)? How can two different readers (different subjects) with the same "horizon" disagree on an interpretation (view of an object)? How can a reader (subject) disagree with the author of a text's (object's) conclusions? Why do those who argue for hermeneutic non-realism write (create objects)? How can a reader's mind (subject) be persuaded concerning what the text (object) "says"? In fact, if all that is in a "text" (object) is what the reader/interpreter (subject) puts there, *then how is communication at any level even possible?*

The response to these questions can lead only to the acknowledgment of both the "otherness" of the author (creator of the object) and the meaning that his words contain (object/text). For, if the conclusions of current hermeneutical philosophies are correct then Stanley Rosen's observation is most appropriate: "if reading is writing, then writing is scribble."[20] Surely, this whole line of thinking violates the law of non-contradiction.

Logical Fallacies of Pragmatism

This study sets out to expose the reality that the pragmatism of the "fusion of horizons" crowd has run amok. Just because the concept of the fusion of horizons may account for what often *does* happen, it does not adequately account for what *must* happen, or even what authors *intend* to happen. In fact, before one can even argue the claim that a fusion of horizons has occurred, one must be able to identify where it is that an interpreter's situatedness (i.e., horizon, presuppositions, prejudices, prejudgments, etc.) has affected his interpretation. However, the only way to identify where it is that the interpreter's situatedness has influenced his interpretation is to compare it with something outside of his horizon.

To do this there are only two possibilities. The first is to compare his interpretation to the text itself (i.e., the authorial intention). To do this would be to admit that one's horizon does not have to influence one's interpretation (for how else would one argue the charge that the interpreter was being influenced by his horizon but to compare it to the object being interpreted?). Obviously, this would not be the line of argumentation undertaken since it would be effectively undermining the assertion that all interpretations are subjective and bound to an interpretational horizon.[21] The second option is to compare the interpreter's

---

20. Rosen, "Horizontverschmelzung," 212.

21. Not only does this logic not follow, but it also demonstrates a lack of precision concerning the terms subjective and objective. The very concept of subjectivity fundamentally demands the concept of objectivity. In this case, the subject is the one who interprets and the object is the text being interpreted. The very claim that an interpretation is subjective (i.e., based in the subject and on the object) presupposes that an object exists about which the interpretation is being offered. In fact, it is a truism that all interpretations are undertaken by a subject and directed at an object (even if the subject is also the object under interpretation). However, it does not follow that all interpretations are *completely* subjective. For if an interpretation of an object were *completely* subjective, then it would be impossible to derive from the interpretation the identity of the object. Said differently, if there were no objectivity in an interpretation of an object, then it would not be discernible what the interpretation was about (i.e., the object would not be identifiable). That an interpretation has a level of subjectivity means that *elements* of the interpretation are sourced not in the object but in the subject. However, it is also possible that an interpretation of an object be accurately focused on all the attributes and details of the object and so clearly and validly communicated that the situatedness of the subject is not determinable. In other words, there is the element of the subject in the interpretation (i.e., no subjectivity). In such a case, *absolute*

interpretation to other interpretations and make an effort to leave the text (object) out of the equation. However, this also raises significant problems for the whole "fusion of horizons" argumentation. For, if the interpreter's interpretation is compared to various other interpretations (even that of the one-asserting that the original interpreter is guilty of interpreting via his horizon), then it quickly becomes apparent that all of these interpretations are interpretations of something and not interpretations of nothing! That is to say, all of these interpretations contain at least an element of the object (i.e., text) in their interpretation—and therefore a level of objectivity. So, while a reader's interpretation *often contains elements* that are subjective, it does *not* follow that his interpretation is doomed to complete subjectivity nor is it excluded from complete objectivity.

Rejection of All Authority in All Places at All Times

This study exposes the claims of current reader-oriented approaches to texts as a rejection of and in a disparate relationship with the very claims of any authoritative text (along with any other holy book for that matter) that claims to be the word of God and thus authoritative for all times and all peoples without exception. Law codes function in the same manner. However, the assertion of authority in the texts is rejected *a priori* by reader-oriented approaches. Instead, the current reader-oriented interpretive view asserts that it is the non-authoritative reader's interpretation, and not the author's/Author's text that is authoritative. Holy books, laws, royal edicts, etc. make authoritative claims over their readers. Because of their authoritative nature these works reject any notion that it is the interpreter and not the author who provides their meaning. Ironically, it is the current hermeneutical philosophical approaches that must violate their own aversion for foundationalism by authoritatively demanding that no text at any time, in any place has the authority to make authoritative claims.

Further, how can the reader ever understand such claims, much less be held accountable to them, if the reader/interpreter either gets to provide the meaning of such writings or can only understand to the extent that his own "horizon" fuses with that of the text? Pleading "fusion of horizons," or any other reader-oriented approach for that matter, as a means by which to reject the author's intent has never been an adequate defense. Instead, Vanhoozer clearly understands the point that a rejection of the author is

---

objectivity can be claimed. In addition, it can be claimed that the interpreter has arrived at the *correct* interpretation.

at its core a theological rejection.[22] The importance of this point in biblical studies cannot be overstated. Reader-oriented approaches to texts pit the reader against the author, or in the case of biblical studies, the Author, in a power struggle for sovereignty over the meaning of the text. For biblical studies, the implication of these approaches is that the reader is the authoritative god of the Bible and not God himself via the inspiration of his apostles and prophets. It is for this reason that orthodox Christianity has always held that the reader is not free to interpret the Bible according to "what is right in his own eyes."[23]

Objectivity and Subjectivity

Before we can launch headlong into an in-depth discussion on subjectivity and objectivity, we must ensure that there is clear understanding concerning these terms. According to Webster's Dictionary, *objective* means "of, relating to, or being an object, phenomenon, or condition in the realm of sensible experience independent of individual thought and perceptible by all observers: having reality independent of the mind."[24] Conversely, *subjective* means "characteristic of or belonging to reality as perceived rather than as independent of mind."[25] To say that an interpreter is a subject is self-evident since to be an interpreter, the interpreter must be interpreting an object (even if the object is himself). To say that the subject's interpretation is subjective is to say that his interpretation belongs to his perceptions and not the thing in itself (i.e., the object as independent of the mind). In other words, his interpretation has been influenced by and thus corresponds to his situatedness, perspective, presuppositions, prejudgments, prejudices, etc. instead of corresponding to the object under interpretation. To say that the subject's interpretation is objective is to say that his interpretation has not been influenced by his situatedness, perspective, presuppositions, prejudgments, prejudices, etc. but instead accurately corresponds to the object (i.e., the thing in itself independent of the subject's perceptual biases) being interpreted. It is self-evident that all interpreters are subjects. It is likewise self-evident that all things being interpreted are objects. However, it is a logical non sequitur to argue that all interpretations therefore must be subjective.

22. Vanhoozer, *Is There a Meaning in This Text?*, 70.

23. See, for example, 2 Peter 1:20–21.

24. *Merriam Webster*, s.v. "objective," accessed September 1, 2009, http://www.merriam-webster.com/dictionary/objective.

25. *Merriam Webster*, s.v. "subjective," accessed September 1, 2009, http://www.merriam-webster.com/dictionary/subjective.

Validity and Veracity

The goal of this present work is *not* to provide a means by which an interpretation can be proven correct with Cartesian certainty. Instead, the goal of this work is to set forth a means by which an interpretation of a literary allusion can be demonstrated as valid.[26] There is a difference between the validity of an interpretation and the veracity of an interpretation. If validity in interpretation can be demonstrated, then the veracity of an interpretation cannot be ruled out. However, if the validity of an interpretation is an impossibility, then the veracity of an interpretation can be ruled out. In other words, if an assertion is made, yet its supporting logical deductions cannot be demonstrated to be valid (i.e., they violate the laws of logic), then the assertion is proven false. However, if an assertion is made and its supporting logical deductions can be demonstrated to be valid (i.e., be in accord with the laws of logic) then the assertion is not proven false. However, just because an interpretation is valid does not necessarily prove that it is true. Instead, the assertion stands as valid and potentially true (i.e., a level of probability must be assigned).

GENERAL METHOD OF INQUIRY

What will be demonstrated below is that *all* literary allusions function in the same basic manner and therefore their interpretation can be validated. What follows below then is predominantly a theoretical work. For this reason, specific examples will be utilized only *after* the theoretical defense of the thesis that there can be validity in the identification and interpretation of literary allusions. Upon completion of the theoretical defense of the thesis, specific examples from the Old Testament text will be set forth. However, while only Old Testament texts will be utilized as examples, the intention of this study is that the procedures and principles spelled out below will be applicable to any texts involving literary allusions.

In light of the discussion up to this point, several issues concerning the validation of the interpretation of a literary allusion are in need of address. The exploration and explanation of these issues will provide the logical backbone for the general method of inquiry for this study. First, a brief summary of the development of the philosophical underpinnings that provide the foundation for current reader-oriented approaches will be presented. Only then can the grounds for their rejection be clearly delineated and a

---

26. For an extended explanation of validity in interpretation, see Hirsch, *Validity in Interpretation*.

logical defense of the hermeneutical approach being utilized throughout this present work be presented and defended. This endeavor will take up all of chapter 2. Next, an exact definition for "literary allusion" will be sought in chapter 3. After establishing a working definition for a literary allusion, chapter 4 will address the question of how scholars have sought to identify and classify literary allusions. This discussion will raise three additional points that have been overlooked in the discussion: the role of relevance theory in literary allusions, the role of genre in literary allusions, and the importance of understanding the working parts of literary allusions. In chapter 5, two issues will be addressed: (1) how one validates his assertion that a literary allusion is present in a text and (2) why interpreters disagree about the identification and validation of literary allusions in texts. Chapter 6 will set forth a few examples of alleged literary allusions in the Old Testament in order to demonstrate this approach in practice. Finally, chapter 7 will serve as a summary reviewing both the logical movement of this work as well as the key contributions that it has sought to make.

2

The Historical Progression of Hermeneutical Thought

THE PRECEDING INTRODUCTION POINTED out that the current philosophical belief that all interpretations are subjective and biased is guilty of violating the law of non-contradiction and is therefore self-defeating. However, to simply point out the logical inconsistency of postmodern hermeneutical philosophers' truth assertion does not go far enough. Instead, the goals of this chapter are threefold: (1) to explain the history and progression of philosophical thought that has produced the current hermeneutical conclusions, (2) to expose the power play behind the current hermeneutical conclusions, and (3) to ensure that the logical inconsistencies present in the current hermeneutical conclusions are explained and exposed.

In order to do this, three areas must be covered. First, it is important that the current state of affairs in the field of hermeneutics be clearly laid out in order to see exactly what conclusions are being rejected in this present work. Second, it is necessary to track the historical progression of philosophical thought that has led to the current state of affairs in order to see that many of the philosophers along the way have been guilty of their own subjectivity. Third, once the historical progression of philosophical thought is followed and its logical inconsistencies pointed out, an argument for how to proceed will be presented.

CURRENT PHILOSOPHICAL HERMENEUTICS AND THE POSTMODERN TURN

While the field of hermeneutics has a long and storied history, the current hermeneutical discussions have moved beyond interpretive theory and are now based on issues of metaphysics and epistemology.[1] Kevin Vanhoozer explains:

> [T]raditionally, hermeneutics—the reflection on the principles that undergird correct textual interpretation—was a matter for exegetes and philologists. More recently, however, hermeneutics has become the concern of philosophers, who wish to know not what such and such a text means, but what it means to understand. "How is understanding possible?" has become the theme of much European philosophy.[2]

Vanhoozer further explains, "[T]he very meaning of 'interpretation' has shifted; instead of being a knowledge claim concerning some discovery one has made about the meaning of the text, interpretation has become a way of referring to what the reader *makes* of the text."[3] As Friedrich Nietzsche argues, "Ultimately, man finds in things nothing but what he himself has imported into them."[4] As stated above, if this statement were true then it is not the author who alludes, but the reader.[5] It is for this reason that before one can adequately interact with today's hermeneutical discussions, one must first understand the philosophical movements that serve as the theoretical foundation upon which many current scholars in the field of hermeneutics base their work. In addition, it must be understood that what Vanhoozer here calls "European philosophy" is also widely designated as "Continental philosophy." As Vanhoozer correctly points out, today's field of hermeneutics is interacting with continental philosophy rather than Western philosophy. The reason for this shift in focus is that it is Continental philosophy

---

1. While Plato used the term ἑρμηνευτικη several times in his dialogues, Aristotle wrote at length on the subject of interpretation in his work *De interpretatione*. (For a translation in English see Aquinas and Cajetan, *Aristotle*) However, hermeneutics emerged as a full-blown discipline when the theologians needed to defend and validate their interpretations of biblical texts. Augustine was the first to make claims concerning the universality of hermeneutics that greatly influenced later scholars such as Dilthey, Heidegger, and Gadamer.

2. Vanhoozer, *Is There a Meaning in This Text?*, 19.

3. Vanhoozer, *Is There a Meaning in This Text?*, 38.

4. Nietzsche, *The Will to Power*, 327.

5. As introduced above, Ben-Porat's definition of a literary allusion should be recalled (cf. Ben-Porath, "The Poetics of Allusion," 1).

that has produced the "postmodern turn" which is the logical conclusion of Western philosophy's modern era. Vanhoozer explains:

> The celebrated turn to the subject—"that we exist"—is the discovery of human situatedness, perhaps the central insight of postmodernity. Human situatedness—in history, social class, gender, culture, religion—has become the focus of postmodern investigations. The result: every issue is ultimately about identity politics, about where, what, and who one is.[6]

By implication, reality, meaning, and truth in the postmodern mind are always historically and culturally derived as well as historically and culturally bound since there is no "true" meaning, no "true" reality, or no "absolute" truth that transcends culture. Said more clearly, there is no universal meaning, reality, or truth since *all* beliefs are *always* and *only* historically and culturally bound.[7] As a consequence of this new view of "reality," there is no ultimate meaning in history, life, language, or texts. Instead, ultimate truth is unknowable and reality is not directly accessible. There is no ultimate meaning of life (i.e., a "true" understanding of reality), whether Hegelian, biblical, or any other. Hegel was wrong: there is no meaning in the events of history.[8] They are simply the random happenings in a purely physical universe. There is no real meaning in language since there is no correlation between reality and language. Nietzsche, Derrida, and Rorty are in agreement in their rejection of Plato's endeavor to find, in Vanhoozer's words, "language and concepts that approximate or correspond to truth."[9] Instead, all languages are arbitrary and are in fact *incapable* of correlating to reality. There is no meaning in texts.[10] They are simply objects to be 'interpreted' for one's own purposes. In fact, it is currently held that assertions to the contrary are simply naïve and possess no basis in fact.[11]

If there is no absolute and timeless truth or meaning, then there can also be no absolute morality, no absolute aesthetic, and no absolute reason.[12]

---

6. Vanhoozer, "Pilgrim's Digress," 76.

7. The logical inconsistency of this assertion is easily apparent. In fact, by this point in the study, assertions such as these that violate the law of non-contradiction are becoming increasingly simple to recognize.

8. Hegel argues these points in two main works: Hegel and Baillie, *The Phenomenology of Mind*; Hegel, *The Philosophy of History*.

9. Vanhoozer, *Is There a Meaning in This Text?*, 57.

10. See for example, Barthes, "The Death of the Author"; Fish, *Is There a Text in This Class?*

11. See Vanhoozer, *Is There a Meaning in This Text?*, 48.

12. This is a point that Nietzsche is well aware of and is seen in his "Madman" (Nietzsche, *The Gay Science*, 119–20), as well as in his "Problem with Morality"

If there is no absolute source of truth, then "truth" is not something *derived from* events, language, or texts. Instead, "truth" is something *assigned to* events, languages, and texts by individuals and homogeneous groups. Good and evil are simply a matter of personal preference. Beauty is in the eye of the beholder. Reason is a shell game to be won by its best players.[13]

Ultimately then, utilitarianism and pragmatism win the day against such absolutes.[14] Not only have these two –*isms* defeated all universal truth claims, but they have also defeated even *the possibility of a universal truth*. Actions are to be taken not because they are based on some misdirected notion of "universal truth" or "universal ethic," but because they are "true" or "right" for the individual. The end justifies the means in that they produce the desired results. Vanhoozer explains this point well:

> Indeed, we may liken the postmodern condition to a third Copernican revolution, a revolution that results in a further decentering of humanity from the center of the universe. Instead of history and culture revolving around reason, reason is now seen to orbit particular cultures and particular times in different ways. If no one set of linguistic and conceptual distinctions is less arbitrary than another, then no one system is deserving of absolute belief. Such is the premise of our distinctly postmodern condition, namely, *the awareness of the deconstructibility and contingency of every text and system of meaning and truth*.[15]

If we cannot know what is real then the next logical question must be, "Can we *know* at all?" According to Vanhoozer, "postmoderns excel in specifying the 'conditions of impossibility' of truth, of universal reason, even of belief in general. They prefer to do so ironically rather than indicatively. Both Rorty and Derrida have exposed the latent irony in metaphysics: the metaphysician sets out to speak about the real but ends up saying something about himself."[16] A. C. Grayling offers a standard preliminary definition of knowledge as "justified true belief."[17] However, with the destruction, or better, deconstruction of "true" beliefs, all forms of knowledge have fallen

---

(Nietzsche, *The Gay Science*, 202–3).

13. Not only is this is Fish's basic argumentation in *Is There A Text In This Class?*, this line of reasoning is central to Nietzsche's philosophy (to be discussed below).

14. For a good, brief summary of the philosophical history of Pragmatism, see Haack, "Pragmatism," 643–61.

15. Vanhoozer, "Pilgrim's Digress," 78.

16. Vanhoozer, "Pilgrim's Digress," 75.

17. Grayling, "Epistemology," 38.

under the spell of skepticism—including knowledge of the authorial intention of a text. This then brings the discussion full circle.

Before the postmodern turn, the pursuit of hermeneutics was to determine the meaning of a text (i.e., authorial intention or 'what the author meant by what the author said'). However, when hermeneutics turned philosophical, the pursuit was no longer aimed at discovering the meaning of a text. Instead, the focus of philosophical hermeneutics was on whether meaning (i.e., the author's meaning) was discoverable in any text. The resounding philosophical conclusion has been to the negative producing a whole host of reader-response approaches to texts. In other words, the same realization of one's situatedness in history, social class, gender, culture, religion, language, etc. (i.e., the horizon of an interpreter or author) that has preoccupied the broader field of philosophy now preoccupies the discussions in hermeneutics as well—with the same predictable conclusion. The conclusion for the interpretation of texts is that the author and the reader are hopelessly separated by each one's situatedness. E. D. Hirsch, a leading advocate of authorial intention, sums up his adversaries' argumentation well when he explains:

> Since we are all different from the author, we cannot reproduce his intended meaning in ourselves, and even if by some accident we could, we still would not be certain that we had done so. Why concern ourselves, therefore, with an inherently impossible task when we can better employ our energies in useful occupations such as making the text relevant to our present concerns or judging its conformity to high standards of excellence? The goal of reproducing an inaccessible and private past is to be dismissed as a futile enterprise. Of course, it is essential to understand some of the public facts of language and history in order to not miss allusions or mistake the contemporary senses of words, but these preliminary tasks remain squarely in the public domain and do not concern a private world beyond the reach of written language.[18]

18. Hirsch, *Validity in Interpretation*, 14. Hirsch's quote accurately summarizes the current state of affairs with regard to the interpretation of texts. However, some logical inconsistencies with the second half of this statement need to be highlighted in order to begin to demonstrate the kind of self-defeating argumentation that will be found in the rest of this chapter. When Hirsch states, "it is essential to understand some of the public facts of language and history in order to not miss allusions or mistake the contemporary senses of words," two points need to be made. First, one must ask the question, why is it "essential" to understand some public facts of language and history in order to not miss allusions if it is not the author who is alluding? If the author's intended meaning cannot be found in a text, why would one be naïve enough to believe that an author's intended allusion placed in the text for the purpose of assisting him in the

It is argued then that the "naïve" interpreter, like the metaphysician, sets out to speak about a text but ends up only saying something about himself.[19] Today textual understanding (i.e., knowledge of authorial intention) is regarded as impossible. Instead, the reader's interpretive enterprise is usually regarded in one of two ways. Either the reader is swayed by his "horizon" (i.e., interpretive bias via his situatedness) with the result that his ensuing interpretation is some new "text" existing somewhere between the horizon of the author and the horizon of the reader, or the reader is simply a user of texts with the result that the author's text is simply something to be used by the pragmatic (i.e., "making the text relevant to our present concerns") or utilitarian (i.e., "judging its conformity to high standards of excellence") reader to validate his own opinion or interpretation.[20] Again, this is because,

conveyance of his intended meaning be any easier to find? This logical inconsistency cannot be overstated. Further, it serves to show the level of incoherent thought with which many of today's hermeneutical scholars operate. Second, if the goal of reading a text is to "make it relevant" or "judge its conformity to high standards of judgment" then why and how would one go about seeking to "understand some public facts of language and history" in order to not "mistake the contemporary senses of words"? Is this not an effort to discover possible word usage during the time in which the text was written? Written by whom? And how might one seek to understand "some public facts of language and history" if not by reading other contemporary texts? And what would be the aim of reading those other contemporary texts to determine word usage if not textual meaning? And if these contemporary texts were written by someone (since they do exist, it's safe to assume that they were) and they are being read in order to determine textual meaning, then are these texts not being read for the author's textual meaning? And would not textual meaning then be the same as the original author's intended meaning? In fact, this is exactly how lexicons function. They determine meaning via contextual determination of authorial usage. Therefore, if one rejects authorial meaning as the controller of textual meaning, then, to be logically consistent, there should be no effort expended to "understand some of the public facts of language and history" through contemporary texts since the reader is hopelessly separated from those authors and therefore hopelessly unable to "reproduce" their "intended meaning in himself."

19. Vanhoozer, "Pilgrim's Digress," 75–76.

20. Cf. Fish, *Is There a Text in This Class?*; Gadamer, *Truth and Method*; Ricœur, *Interpretation Theory*. Concerning the charge that interpreters are simply "users of texts" (or better, misusers of texts), it should be pointed out that the only way that this charge can stand is if it can be demonstrated that the interpreter's meaning and purposes for the text are different from someone else's meaning and purpose. Further, it must be demonstrated that these meanings and purposes are different from those of the author. Otherwise, the charge cannot stand. And, if the author's meaning and purpose can be determined then it is possible not to be simply a "user" of a text. Concerning the "fusion of horizons," it should be pointed out here in brief that the only possible way that such a charge could be levied is if both "horizons" (i.e., that of the author and that of the reader) were distinguishable. In other words, if one is charging that a "fusion" of meaning has taken place then both the meaning of the author and the meaning of the interpreter must be apparent so that the charge of a "fusion of horizons" can be sustained! The very fact that such a charge is levied is proof in and of itself that the

at least in current philosophical thinking, everyone and everything is always and only understood via each individual or group's interpretive situatedness. Vanhoozer explains Fish's view on this point:

> To say that we must read in order to recover the intention of the author is, for Fish, authoritarian. How dare you tell me what to be interested in or what to do with a text! Interpretive communities must be free to pursue their own interests. The neopragmatist is, hermeneutically speaking, pro-choice. Neither the author nor even the notion of truth has authority for the user. Truth is demoted from its prior status as timeless and absolute to "what is good for us to believe here and now" or "what works for me in this situation." Truth—in metaphysics, morals, or meaning—is a label we assign beliefs that seem good to us, beliefs that perform some useful purpose.[21]

This belief system has so infiltrated our society that today the belief that "everything is hermeneutics" is predictably commonplace.[22] Everyone has a right to their own interpretation of the facts, events, and causes. In fact, as Vanhoozer rightly explains, hermeneutics (i.e., individual or group interpretation) has now replaced epistemology and metaphysics at the top of the philosophical food chain:

> [H]ermeneutics has of late exercised a certain hegemony over other disciplines. We now look at hermeneutics not only as a discipline in its own right but especially as an aspect of all intellectual endeavors. The rise of hermeneutics parallels the fall of epistemology. Instead of making robust claims about absolute knowledge, even natural scientists now view their theories as interpretations.[23]

Everything is now a matter of one's own interpretation. There are absolutely no absolutes. This insight was most clearly foreseen and explained by

---

author's intended meaning is available to be sought. So, while it may well be that some interpreters simply "use texts" rather than interpret them, or that a "fusion of horizons" is what often occurs when many interpreters interpret texts, neither of these views must occur at all. The very fact that these views exist is proof that they only can occur, not that they always occur.

21. Vanhoozer, *Is There a Meaning in This Text?*, 57.

22. With this statement also comes the accepted conclusion that no one interpretation is correct. Thus, "everything is hermeneutics" is equivalent to "everyone is entitled to their own interpretation."

23. Vanhoozer, *Is There a Meaning in This Text?*, 19.

Nietzsche who understood the ramifications of such a rejection of Authority. For Nietzsche, the death of God was the precursor for all that was to follow:

> *The Madman.* Haven't you heard of that madman who in the bright morning lit a lantern and ran around the marketplace crying incessantly, "I'm looking for God! I'm looking for God!" Since many of those who did not believe in God were standing around together just then, he caused great laughter. Has he been lost, then? asked one. Did he lose his way like a child? asked another. Or is he hiding? Is he afraid of us? Has he gone to sea? Emigrated?—Thus they shouted and laughed, one interrupting the other. The madman jumped into their midst and pierced them with his eyes. "Where is God?" he cried; "I'll tell you! *We have killed him*—you and I! We are all his murderers. But how did we do this? How were we able to drink up the sea? Who gave us the sponge to wipe away the entire horizon? What were we doing when we unchained this earth from its sun? Where is it moving now? Where are we moving to? Away from all suns? Are we not continually falling? And backwards, sidewards, forwards, in all directions? Is there still an up and a down? Aren't we straying as though through an infinite nothing? Isn't empty space breathing at us? Hasn't it got colder? Isn't night and more night coming again and again? Don't lanterns have to be lit in the morning? Do we still hear nothing of the noise of the grave-diggers who are burying God? Do we still smell nothing of the divine decomposition?—Gods, too, decompose! God is dead! God remains dead! And we have killed him! How can we console ourselves, the murderers of all murderers! The holiest and the mightiest thing the world has ever possessed has bled to death under our knives: who will wipe this blood from us? With what water could we clean ourselves? What festivals of atonement, what holy games will we have to invent for ourselves? Is the magnitude of this deed not too great for us? Do we not ourselves have to become gods merely to appear worthy of it? There was never a greater deed—and whoever is born after us will on account of this deed belong to a higher history than all history up to now!" Here the madman fell silent and looked again at his listeners; they too were silent and looked at him disconcertedly. Finally he threw his lantern on the ground so that it broke into pieces and went out. "I come too early", he then said; "my time is not yet. This tremendous event is still on its way, wandering; it has not yet reached the ears of men. Lightning and thunder need time; the light of the stars needs time; deeds need time, even after they are done, in order to be seen and heard. This deed is still more remote to them than

the remotest stars—*and yet they have done it themselves!*" It is still recounted how on the same day the madman forced his way into several churches and there started singing his *requiem aeternam deo*.²⁴ Led out and called to account, he is said always to replied nothing but, "What then are these churches now if not the tombs and sepulchers of God?"²⁵

The sponge that wiped away the horizon also wiped away all God is. The death of God is the death of morality, the death of authority, the death of meaning, the death of truth, the death of aesthetics . . . and by implication, the death of the author. For their part, Derrida and Barthes make this last insight, which was implicit in Nietzsche's writing, explicit in their own writings. Vanhoozer explains:

> Like Derrida, Barthes holds that the belief in meaning, in something that transcends the play of signs, is inherently theological. The author is God to his text: its creator, cause, and master. The reader is obliged to be the author's servant, passively collecting the meaning that, like manna, comes from the hand of the maker. Freed from the author, however, the text becomes a playground on which readers can exercise their own creativity. The death of the author becomes a necessary step in refusing to assign a "real" meaning to the text. Non-realism demands the death of the author in order to turn the traditional "Platonism of meaning" on its head. No longer reduced to a single message with a single correct interpretation, the text is opened to a pluralism of readings; meaning is effectively destabilized, and authority withers on the textual vine.²⁶

The death of God and the death of the author are inextricably linked. Mark Taylor states, "The death of God was the disappearance of the Author who had inscribed absolute truth and univocal meaning in world history and human experience."²⁷

---

24. "Grant God eternal rest."

25. Nietzsche, *The Gay Science*, 119–20. Here Nietzsche is not suggesting that man really killed god. Instead, he is explaining by way of story the fact that god never existed in the first place. However, man has not yet realized the full implications of this truth.

26. Vanhoozer, *Is There a Meaning in This Text?*, 70. Also see Barthes, "The Death of the Author"; Foucault, "What Is an Author?" The problem here is not simply one in which the author is rejected as the determiner of meaning for his text. Both Derrida and Barthes correctly understand that the move that they are making is a theological one. Even Fish understands the significance of his stance: "To someone who believes in determinate meaning, disagreement can only be a theological error" (Fish, *Is There a Text in This Class?*, 338).

27. Taylor, *Deconstructing Theology*, 90.

Unfortunately, while this "postmodern turn" has been in the works for some time, Western philosophy has been slow to recognize the significance of the work of influential Continental philosophers. David West observes, "as recently as the 1970's a course in philosophy that failed to mention Hegel or Nietzsche, Husserl, Heidegger or Sartre, was not considered in the least deficient."[28] In contrast, today the writings of these philosophers serve as the very foundation upon which hermeneutical discussions are based. For example, consider the words of Gadamer in his introduction to *Truth and Method*:

> That conscientiousness of phenomenological description which Husserl has made a duty for us all; the breadth of the historical horizon in which Dilthey has placed all philosophical, and not least, the penetration of both these influences by the impulse received from Heidegger, indicate the standard by which the writer desires to be measured, and which, despite all imperfection in the execution, he would like to see applied without reservation.[29]

So, even Gadamer himself desires that his contribution be understood in light of Husserl, Dilthey, and Heidegger. The powerful influence of Continental Philosophy then on the field of hermeneutics cannot be overstated. In fact, without an understanding in Continental thought, one struggles to make correct sense of Gadamer, Fish, Eco, Rorty or Ricoeur. However, most scholars in the fields of literary or biblical studies are not well versed in the historical progression of the theory and philosophy of hermeneutics. Thus, a brief discussion is necessary.

ORIGIN, PROGRESSION, AND IMPACT OF CONTINENTAL PHILOSOPHY

Gadamer is certainly not alone as the only scholar in the field of hermeneutics impacted by Continental philosophy. Instead, most of the biggest names in the field of hermeneutics today have been deeply impacted by Continental thought. So, before one can fully appreciate the conclusions of the philosophical discussion in hermeneutics regarding authorial intention, one must be aware of the philosophical foundations upon which the rejection of the author and authorial intention have taken place. Once the progression of thought leading to the current hermeneutical conclusions is considered, two issues will become apparent. First, it will be seen that many

---

28. West, *An Introduction to Continental Philosophy*, 3.
29. Gadamer, *Truth and Method*, xxiv.

of these philosophers *begin* with a foundation of the rejection of God (i.e., they are not objective in their conclusions but are instead only operating according to their presuppositions). Second, it will be seen that the progression of conclusions drawn from previous "unbiased findings" are guilty of non-sequiturs.

Origin of Continental Philosophy

As is so often the case in modern philosophical discussions, our discussion of the progression of hermeneutical thought must begin with Descartes for two reasons: Cartesian Dualism and Representationalism.

Renè Descartes (1596–1650)[30]

In describing Descartes' effort to determine how one can know reality, West writes:

> Descartes soon arrives at the conclusion that the only thing that is certain is that "I am, I exist." I can doubt the evidence of my senses, the existence of an external world, even the existence of my own body. But when I doubt that I exist, it seems that I unavoidably presuppose my own existence. When I am doubting, I am thinking, and if I am thinking then I must exist. This train of reasoning delivers the famous *cogito ergo sum* or "I think, therefore I am" of Cartesian philosophy. Descartes proceeds apace the more controversial conclusion, that what I am "essentially" is a thing that thinks.[31]

For his part, Descartes was well aware of the implications of his new revelation. In his letter to Mersenne dated January 28, 1641, Descartes states, "these six meditations contain all the foundations of my physics. But please do not tell people, for that might make it harder for supporters of Aristotle to approve them. I hope that readers will gradually get used to my principles, and recognize their truth, before they notice that they destroy the principles of Aristotle."[32]

The "principles of Aristotle" that would be destroyed were far reaching. Descartes rejects Aristotle's belief that reality was accessible through one's

---

30. For helpful works on Descartes, see Williams, *Descartes*; Ree, *Descartes*; Cottingham, "Cartesian Dualism."

31. West, *Introduction to Continental Philosophy*, 13.

32. Friedman, "Descartes and Galileo," 79.

senses and thus they are unable to pass his stringent test for knowledge (*scientia*), since one's senses are capable of being doubted. This ability to doubt one's senses leads to the conclusion that the use of the five senses cannot lead to absolute certainty and therefore produces lower levels of certainty or levels of conviction (*persuasio*). As John Cottingham explains, "there is a 'real' *(realis)* distinction between the mind and body; in other words, the mind is a distinct and independent 'thing' *(res)*. The thinking thing that is 'me' is 'really distinct from the body and can exist without it.' (AT VII 78: CSM II 54)."[33] What is important to note is that in the Aristotelian model of sense cognition, man has direct access to reality via his five senses.

However, in Descartes' model a dualism is created by which the mind does not have direct access to the world. Instead, a gap is created since the five senses are deemed as untrustworthy by Descartes to provide knowledge (*scientia*). The mind must make a copy of the external world (i.e., Representationalism). The problem is that there is no way of determining whether or not the picture in the mind directly corresponds to the external world since there is no direct access to the external world available to the mind. Therefore, as West explains, "Descartes's dualism of mind and matter . . . serves to drive a wedge between the scientific explanation of bodies in space and what become strictly 'mental' categories of purpose and will. A purely mechanical model of the material world as matter extended in space is combined with a picture of mind as essentially immaterial and disembodied."[34]

The problems with Descartes' views were immediately recognized and the circularity of his argumentation pointed out. However, Descartes was so sure of his conclusions that he was unbothered by their logical circularity. Cottingham explains:

> The gap between subjective cognition and objective reality, once acknowledged, is not easily closed; and though Descartes does at least attempt to close it—most notably in the argument from divinely guaranteed clear and distinct perceptions in the Sixth Meditation—it is familiar ground, and was so even in the seventeenth century, that his argument is highly vulnerable. The most notorious pitfall is Arnauld's circle: The gap between subjective cognition and essential reality is bridged by proving God's existence; yet the proof itself depends on the reliability of just that subjective cognition which needs to be validated. But even *granting* the divinely underwritten reliability of the intellect, there is a second trap (which again Arnauld was the first to highlight): my ability clearly to perceive X apart from Y (e.g.,

33. Cottingham, "Cartesian Dualism," 236.
34. West, *Introduction to Continental Philosophy*, 12.

mind apart from body) cannot, since my intellect is limited, rule out the possibility that there is a chain of necessary connections, *unperceived* by me, which would reveal that Y is after all essential to X.

That Descartes' metaphysical manoeuvres fail to provide a plausible defence of the incorporeality thesis is hardly a new complaint. What is interesting is that Descartes' confidence in that thesis was entirely unshaken by the telling criticisms to which his arguments were repeatedly subjected, by Arnauld and many others. It is almost as if he felt that, irrespective of whether his metaphysical demonstrations could be shored up, there were still solid, and quite independent considerations for insisting on the incorporeal nature of the mind.[35]

Cartesian Dualism and the Representationalist system that it creates is the source of a recurring problem for later philosophers. Stated simply, the problem is, "How do I know that what I perceive corresponds to reality?" From this beginning point, it is easy to see how the field of hermeneutics (i.e., the interpretation of an object [text]) will be affected.

David Hume (1711–1776)

In order to situate Continental Philosophy as a distinct and distant relative of Analytic Philosophy, it is important to begin this discussion with Hume's fork.[36] "Hume's fork" simply refers to Hume's division of all truth into one of two categories: *matters of fact* or *relation of ideas*. If an issue did not fall into one of these two categories, then its truth could not be determined and therefore irrelevant to the philosophical discussion.[37] In Hume's day the humanism of the Renaissance was in full bloom and philosophers were essentially divided into two camps—the rationalists and the empiricists. The rationalists (e.g., Rene Descartes [1596–1650], Benedict de Spinoza [1632–1677], and G. W. F. von Leibniz [1646–1716]) argued that reason, rather than experience, must be the basis for certainty in knowledge. In contrast, the empiricists (e.g., John Locke [1632–1704] and David Hume [1711–1776]) believed that experience must by necessity precede reason—for one must experience through his senses before he could know

---

35. Cottingham, "Cartesian Dualism," 245.

36. For a brief summary of David Hume's life, beliefs, and works, see Jones, "Hume," 571–88. For a good summary of the history of the church leading up to this era, see Gonzalez, *The Early Church to the Dawn of the Reformation*.

37. For a discussion on Hume's fork see Norton, *The Cambridge Companion to Hume*, 96.

anything about it. However, the empiricists did not reject reason. Instead, they only argued that reason was based upon one's experience and therefore occupied a secondary and derivative function. Hume's fork served to divide philosophy into two branches. These two branches would serve to define the concerns of Analytic Philosophy as well as distinguish it from the main concerns of Continental Philosophy.[38] In Hume's view, "All the objects of human reason or enquiry may naturally be divided into two kinds, to wit, *Relations of Ideas*, and *Matters of Fact*."[39] *Relations of Ideas* include things such as the truths of mathematics and logic that are "discoverable by the mere operation of thought, without dependence on what is anywhere existent in the universe."[40] For the rationalist then, these *Relations of Ideas* are the core basis of knowledge and are available for human knowledge *a priori* human experience. Conversely, *Matters of Fact* are contingent truths about the world which "seem to be founded on the relation of *Cause and Effect*."[41] It is here that the empiricist argues that the core basis of human knowledge is available for human knowledge *a posteriori* human experience. For the empiricist, the human mind was a *tabula rasa*. Anything that did not belong in either category (e.g., metaphysics, religion, scholastic philosophy) was viewed as irrelevant to the pursuit of genuine knowledge and reason—at least as far as Analytic Philosophy is concerned. As West explains:

> Although analytic philosophers relax this principle somewhat in practice—if only to make sense of their own activity, which itself does not fall clearly into either category—they continue to work very much in this spirit. Since philosophy is neither a branch of logic or mathematics nor a natural science comparable to physics or biology, it must restrict itself austerely to the careful analysis of concepts. The only scientifically respectable philosophy is henceforth analytical.[42]

Conversely, West regards Continental philosophers as follows:

> Continental philosophers, on the other hand, can be regarded as the distant relatives of those metaphysicians, moralists, and believers so caustically dismissed by Hume, at least in the sense that they are unwilling to abandon the concerns and insights

---

38. For an excellent delineation of Hume's fork and its serving as a dividing line between Analytic Philosophy and Continental Philosophy, see West, *Introduction to Continental Philosophy*, 1–6.

39. West, *Introduction to Continental Philosophy*, 4; Hume, *Enquiries*, 25–26.

40. Hume, *Enquiries*, 25–26.

41. Hume, *Enquiries*, 25–26.

42. West, *Introduction to Continental Philosophy*, 4.

> intimated by these modes of experience. Similarly, they continue to address questions which ordinary common sense has never ceased to regard as important elements of the philosopher's task. These are, above all, existential, moral or ethical and aesthetic questions: questions about the nature of existence and the meaning of life, questions of right and wrong or of the meaning of art and beauty.[43]

Hume's views not only regarded religious and metaphysical pursuits as irrelevant to knowledge and reason, they also served as the early dividing lines between what would become known as Analytic Philosophy and Continental Philosophy. As West explains, they also bring into clarity the "full implications of the Cartesian view of nature."[44] Before Descartes, most thinkers and philosophers understood that there was a teleological purpose in everything. However, Descartes' conclusion, *cogito ergo sum* served to create a dualism between the mind and matter. Man was essentially a thinking being, or in Charles Taylor's words, a "self-defining subject."[45] West explains the implication of this: the physical world is "essentially nothing more than a mechanistic system of extended matter without religious or moral significance."[46] West also explains that Hume follows this line of thinking by rejecting the medieval view that history is a "teleological system of entities propelled by inner necessity to fulfil [sic] their essential purpose or goal."[47] In fact, as West summarizes well, Hume goes even further:

> Hume challenges all attempts to base religious belief on our experience of the world, whether in the form of the argument from design or from the alleged evidence of miracles. Overall, he directs some of his most biting irony at religion, in particular its dogmatic morality and high-flown claims of theology. But Hume's skepticism also challenges the claims of moral and aesthetic judgment more generally. His classic statement of the distinction between facts and values announces that "virtue is not founded merely on relations of objects." There can be no derivation of an "ought" from an "is"; no collection of facts, however exhaustive, implies an evaluative conclusion. Judgments of value, whether good or evil or of "beauty and deformity," simply reflect our sentiments, our inclinations or taste. Morality and

---

43. West, *Introduction to Continental Philosophy*, 4–5.
44. West, *Introduction to Continental Philosophy*, 15.
45. Taylor, *Hegel*, 8.
46. West, *Introduction to Continental Philosophy*, 14.
47. West, *Introduction to Continental Philosophy*, 15.

aesthetics are not based on reason or knowledge but on feelings of pleasure and pain.[48]

However, while Hume argues that morality and aesthetics are a matter of one's personal preference, the Bible places the source of morality, ethics, and aesthetics in the very nature and character of God. Further, since man was created in the image and likeness of God, complete with the faculties to receive revelation from God (i.e., language) concerning his nature, character, and desires for mankind, Hume's conclusions reject the Bible's claim that morality, ethics, and aesthetics are sourced in God. Instead, Hume begins to logically flesh out the philosophical argumentation that every man is a god unto himself in that each individual determines what is right and wrong, good and evil for himself.[49] As will be seen, this is a recurring theme that will repeatedly rear its head throughout this present study.

Therefore, Hume is important to the present discussion for at least three reasons. First, Hume was one of the first to regard theological and metaphysical issues as irrelevant to the philosopher's pursuit of knowledge and reason. Second, Hume's fork serves to draw a lasting distinction between what were correctly the pursuits of philosophy and what were not. Hume's categories have been largely accepted by Analytic philosophers and provide the philosophical distinction between Analytic Philosophy and Continental Philosophy. The irony with Hume's relation to Continental Philosophy then is that while Hume's views would consider the metaphysical pursuits of Continental philosophers "irrelevant," these same philosophers would flesh out with ever-increasing clarity the implications of his conclusions concerning morality, ethics, and aesthetics. Third, Hume argues that morality, ethics, and aesthetics (being based on religious and/or metaphysical grounds) are simply a matter of one's personal preference.

Immanuel Kant (1724–1804)

Immanuel Kant is prominent in both the Analytical and Continental traditions. Further, Kant's philosophy was at least partially aimed at addressing some of the issues raised in the radical skepticism of Hume's philosophy.[50] In Kant's most famous work, *Critique of Pure Reason*, he sets out to address the issues at the heart of the disagreement between the rationalists and

---

48. West, *Introduction to Continental Philosophy*, 16.

49. This issue is at the very core of the fall of mankind in Genesis 3. See Waltke, *Genesis*, 92.

50. West, *Introduction to Continental Philosophy*, 3.

empiricists. Kant calls his conclusions his "Copernican revolution." Just as Copernicus demonstrated that the belief that the sun revolved around the earth was caused by man's naïve reliance upon mere appearance when in fact the earth spun on its axis and revolved around the sun, so also Kant's "Copernican revolution" served to overcome another naïve belief concerning the relationship between perception and reality. David Bell summarizes Kant's point well by stating:

> [I]t had hitherto been assumed that there appear to be spatio-temporal objects that exist independently of us because there really are such things. Kant replaced this naïve realism with a theory according to which the apparent nature and independence of the objective world is a product of our perceptions, concepts and judgments; in the last analysis, it is because we perceive and think as we do that the world seems to be as it does.[51]

In Kant's words, "hitherto it has been assumed that all our knowledge must conform to objects. But all attempts [for instance, to account for the possibility of objective knowledge] have, on this assumption, ended in failure. We must therefore make trial whether we may not have more success in the tasks of metaphysics, if we suppose objects conform to our knowledge."[52]

Kant's goal then was a metaphysical one. As West explains, "the essential task Kant sets for his critical philosophy is to expunge the ultimately religious sources from previous metaphysical confusion. Human knowledge must be understood in purely human terms rather than according to the misleading and unattainable standard of divine intuition."[53] However, Kant's goal was not to eliminate faith in God. In fact, his goal was exactly the opposite by finding the point at which knowledge ends and faith must begin. As Kant explains in the Preface to his second edition, "I have therefore found it necessary to limit knowledge, in order to make room for faith."[54]

In the portion of his argumentation entitled "Transcendental Analytic," Kant argues that humans are endowed *a priori* with twelve "categories" (Unity, Plurality, Totality, Reality, Negation, Limitation, Substance, Causality, Community, Possibility, Existence, and Necessity) that "serve as the antecedent conditions under which alone anything can be . . . thought as object in general."[55] However, in the view of Analytic philosophy, Kant's

---

51. Bell, "Kant," 592.
52. Kant, *Critique of Pure Reason*, xvi.
53. West, *Introduction to Continental Philosophy*, 71.
54. Kant, *Critique of Pure Reason*, xxx.
55. Kant, *Critique of Pure Reason*, 125.

"transcendental idealism" fails in its metaphysical endeavor (mostly over their objection that his "Transcendental Deductions" do not amount to successful logical deductions) and most analytical philosophers revert back to Hume's fork and the regarding of religious and metaphysical issues as irrelevant to the pursuit of knowledge and reason.[56]

While the focus of Analytic philosophers was primarily of the failures of Kant's *Critique of Pure Reason*, Continental philosophers focus on different aspects of Kant's philosophical work.[57] In *Grundlegung zur Metaphysik ser Sitten* (*The Fundamental Principles of the Metaphysics of Morals*), Bell explains that Kant sets out to "seek and establish the supreme principal of morality."[58] By following the same line of reasoning that Hume had employed concerning values—namely, that no matter how exhaustive the physical evidence, there can be no moral or aesthetic judgment (i.e., "ought") based on what "is", Kant develops his concept of a moral Categorical Imperative. As Bell explains, Kant's Categorical Imperative is not a "descriptive assertion specifying what *is* the case and the ways in which we *do* in fact act, but rather a normative rule which will specify what should be the case and how we *ought* to act."[59] Bell continues:

> In the *Critique of Pure Reason* Kant had attempted to establish the limits of genuine knowledge, that is, to discover the *a priori* conditions that must obtain if knowledge is to be possible. One of his conclusions was that, for us, there can be no knowledge of any super-sensible, non-empirical reality. In other words, a necessary condition of the possibility of human knowledge is that it involve not only intellectual concepts, but also sensory intuitions. For Kant, therefore, there could be no *knowledge* of God, the immortality of the soul, or the freedom of the will. To such matters as these, he maintained, concepts like observation, discovery, evidence, truth, science, explanation and the like must remain forever inapplicable. But about such matters we can nevertheless have faith. Faith in God, commitment to the moral law, respect for other persons, appreciation of the dignity that autonomy bestows—these were for Kant amongst

---

56. For a good summary of analytic philosophy's objections to Kant's transcendental idealism, see West, *Introduction to Continental Philosophy*, 22–23.

57. As West points out, Continental philosophers agree with Kant that there are metaphysical, moral, and aesthetic questions that simply cannot be ignored. Further, they are more sympathetic to Kant's "transcendental deductions" arguing that Kant did not intend for them to be strict logical deductions anyway. West, *Introduction to Continental Philosophy*, 23.

58. Bell, "Kant," 599.

59. Bell, "Kant," 600.

the highest ideals that his philosophy, as a whole, was intended to protect. And in particular, his metaphysics of experience and his account of the limits of knowledge were intended to show that no empirical, naturalistic, or scientific treatment of these transcendent matters could possibly be intelligible.[60]

So, in order to establish some grounds upon which moral, ethical, and aesthetical standards can be based (since they cannot be based on anything "transcendental"), Kant argues for what he calls "Categorical Imperatives" derived through autonomous human reasoning that can serve as the basis for moral, ethical, and aesthetic judgments. In Kant's view, one is autonomous if he is "free, that is, capable of acts of will that are not causally determined, either by inner forces like inclinations, desires, and passions, or by external forces in the outer world."[61] To be autonomous also for Kant entails the ability to "exercise rational self-control over their decisions and their actions."[62] Finally, and most importantly to the present discussion, the sole responsibility of the autonomous agent to act with self-control must come from within the individual agent. In other words, as Bell explains, "no genuinely autonomous agent can relinquish responsibility of the principles on which he or she acts to any external authority—whether it be the church, the state, the law, society, family, teachers or friends."[63] On the contrary, all such principles must be chosen and imposed by the agent alone. And the supreme principle of rational, moral autonomy is the Categorical Imperative."[64] Unfortunately, the philosophers who would come after Kant would effectively demonstrate that all of Kant's talk of morality, good will, and autonomy equated to nothing more than what Hume would call "personal preference."

---

60. Bell, "Kant," 601.

61. Bell, "Kant," 600. This line of reasoning is reminiscent of the calls for "objectivity" of those who would come after Kant. However, as will be seen, the recognition that autonomous objectivity is not possible will lead to the conclusion that there is no truly autonomous individual. Instead, all individuals are influenced by their interpretive horizon.

62. Bell, "Kant," 600.

63. Bell, "Kant," 600. To be consistent, this list would obviously apply to any religious text (e.g., the Bible) or any god as well (e.g., the God of the Bible).

64. Bell, "Kant," 600. For Kant, a Categorical Imperative must include the following: (1) Act only on that maxim through which you can at the same time will that it should be a universal law. (2) So act as to use humanity, both in your own person and in the person of every other, always at the same time as an end, never simply as a means. (3) So act as if you were always through your maxims a law-making member of a kingdom of ends. "So an act is morally good if it is performed for the sake of a morally good maxim; and a maxim is morally good if it conforms to the Categorical Imperative." Bell, "Kant," 601.

Kant's work is relevant to the present discussion then for two primary reasons. First, while some Continental philosophers would be more sympathetic to Kant's "transcendental idealism" his new theory fails to win over many supporters in either camp. However, much of the progression in both traditions is a direct response to Kant's work. Because of the nature of the present study, the responses within the Continental tradition will be examined more closely. Second, Kant's Categorical Imperatives, simply a logical argumentation of the golden rule, are based on the notion of free humans as autonomous agents. Further, Kant assumed, as did Hume, that these autonomous agents were all endowed with the same constitutional makeup—a concept that Herder would soon reject.

Johann Gottfried Herder (1744–1803)

Important to any discussion on the history and philosophy of hermeneutics is Johan Gottfried Herder's *Discourse on the Origin of Language*.[65] Herder's philosophy had enormous impact on Hegel, Nietzsche, Dilthey, Goethe, and Schleiermacher. In fact, Herder developed much of modern hermeneutical theory. However, there is one facet of Herder's teaching that has been tremendously detrimental to the field of hermeneutics. Before Herder, philosophers by and large operated on the assumption that all of humanity had essentially the same human constitution. This meant that different languages were essentially different ways of expressing the same thoughts, feelings, and desires. However, as West explains:

> [C]entral to Herder's thought is his view of language as the essential medium for our humanity. . . . For Herder, crucially, language, as the essential medium for human thought and consciousness, is not just a vehicle for the expression of thoughts or ideas, which might have existed without it. Language is what makes thought possible and, as such, is inseparable from it. By the same token, different languages are not simply alternative instruments for the expression of the same ideas, but rather correspond to different ways of thinking and feeling, different thoughts and feelings.[66]

For this reason Hegel, being influenced by Herder, marks a radical new direction in the humanities. West continues:

---

65. Herder, *Discourse on the Origin of Language*.
66. West, *Introduction to Continental Philosophy*, 31.

> This "constitutive role" of language for human thought and culture is also incompatible with the idea of a universal human essence, whether natural, intellectual or spiritual, independent of particular societies, an implication which further undermines universalist assumptions of human nature [i.e., Kant or Hume] or historical progress favored by the Enlightenment [i.e., Hegel].[67]

While Jean-Jacques Rousseau's (a contemporary of Herder) philosophy was prescriptive,

> Herder's thought . . . tends towards relativism. His account of human society seems to imply the incommensurability of the values and "qualities of character" of different peoples and cultures. The unique way of life of a nation or people cannot be measured against any other, let alone definitively evaluated in terms of some universal human essence [i.e., Kant] or single model of the ideal society [i.e., Hegel leading to Feuerbach/Marx]. Even though Herder does suppose an underlying, shared "humanity" (*Humanitat*), it is overlaid by differences of language and culture. Other Enlightenment philosophers, such as Hume and Montesquieu, had acknowledged the diversity of human societies, but they saw the variety of laws and customs as alternative means to the satisfaction of common human wants. Herder's account of self, on the other hand, suggests that even human wants are inseparable from the concrete forms of life of particular communities.[68]

The problem that Herder's thought presents then is one of relativism. As will be seen in the ensuing progression of philosophical thought,

> [R]elativism is for some only a few steps from nihilism. If there is no universal moral standard, then there might as well be no standard at all. Any value can be defended as an essential component of a discrete cultural tradition. . . . [T]he apparently short path from the social constitution of the individual through relativism to nihilism sets a stubborn and recurrent problem for subsequent thinkers in the continental tradition.[69]

As will be seen, this line of thinking will lead to the annihilation of God, the annihilation of the author, the annihilation of the text, and by logical progression—the annihilation of races and societies.

---

67. West, *Introduction to Continental Philosophy*, 32.
68. West, *Introduction to Continental Philosophy*, 32.
69. West, *Introduction to Continental Philosophy*, 33.

Georg Wilhelm Friedrich Hegel (1770–1831)

Hegel's teleological view of history was a response to Kant's *Critique of Pure Reason*.[70] However Hegel's philosophy is of importance to this study not for what it taught, but for how it was reacted to. Two responses to Hegel's dialectical philosophy become apparent. West states:

> One outcome of the decay of Hegelianism was thus the emergence of what is called "critical philosophy of history", a tendency which also drew inspiration from Schleiermacher, Savigny, and others. Where speculative philosophy of history assigns an overall purpose to human history as a whole, critical philosophy of history investigates the nature of historical knowledge and appropriate methods of historical research. It was associated with the emergence of history as a respectable academic discipline. Many historicists drew the explicitly relativist conclusion, that the values and norms of different cultures are, in their particular social and historical context, equally valid. If moral values can only be understood in terms of the community to which they belong, and it is no longer plausible to locate different human societies within a historical dialectic, then there is no obviously rational way to decide between conflicting values. The validity of values can only be judged for a particular time rather than for all time. In this variant moral and cultural values are historicized.[71]

This line of thinking is obviously in direct contradiction to the teaching of the Bible since the Bible clearly assigns a teleological purpose to history.[72] Further, the Bible also teaches that there is one moral, ethical, and aesthetic standard by which all will be judged. Therefore, it will be seen below that many will reject Hegel's philosophy of history and with it all teleological views of history.

The second response to Hegel's philosophy was not the rejection of it, but the radicalization of it. Hegel believed that all of history was progressing upward toward freedom. For some of Hegel's followers (commonly referred to as the "Young Hegelians"), the incompleteness of the historical process

---

70. Inwood, "Hegel," 608.

71. West, *Introduction to Continental Philosophy*, 80–81.

72. It is important to note that Hegel's dialectical system was not intended to be anti-Christian. Instead, "Hegel held that his philosophical system expressed in the form of thought the essential 'content' of Trinitarian Christianity. In religious imagery, God the Father 'alienates' or externalizes himself by producing a natural world (the 'son') as the object of his 'consciousness', and becomes self-conscious in the spiritual reclamation that people make of nature and of themselves (the 'holy spirit')." Inwood, "Hegel," 613–14.

meant the need for a more intentional force on the upward dialectical spiral.[73] Feuerbach and Marx were the two most prominent Young Hegelians.

> They interpreted Hegel's writings rather differently [than the "Old Hegelians" who were conservative], asserting the incompleteness of the historical process and the need for a further turn of the dialectical spiral. Both the existing political order and the prevailing philosophy and religion must be transformed or even abolished.... Of the Young Hegelians Ludwig Feuerbach, in particular, was to exert long-lasting influence, mainly through his influence on the thought of Karl Marx and Friedrich Engels.[74]

Progression of Continental Philosophy

Now that the origin of Continental thought has been highlighted in brief fashion, our study is ready to track the progression of Continental thought along the lines of the two responses to Hegel's philosophy of history. What will be seen below is that both responses to Hegelian philosophy logically lead to the annihilation of Christianity.

Ludwig Feuerbach (1804–1872)

At the center of Feuerbach's philosophy is his view of religion in general and Christianity in particular.[75] Feuerbach's progression of thought is quite straightforward. He first posits that to be human (as opposed to the "brute"—i.e., animals) is to have religion. The reason for this is that humans, unlike animals, are self-conscious in that they think about and converse with themselves.[76] Feuerbach states:

> Religion being identical with the distinctive characteristic of man, is then identical with self-consciousness—with the consciousness which man has of his nature. But religion, expressed generally, is consciousness of the infinite; thus it is and can be nothing else than the consciousness which man has of his own—not finite and limited, but infinite nature. A really finite being has not even the faintest adumbration, still less consciousness,

---

73. West, *Introduction to Continental Philosophy*, 42.
74. West, *Introduction to Continental Philosophy*, 42–43.
75. For his view of Christianity, see Feuerbach, *The Essence of Christianity*.
76. Feuerbach, *The Essence of Christianity*, 2.

of an infinite being, for the limit of the nature is also the limit of consciousness. . . . The consciousness of the infinite is nothing else than the consciousness of the infinity of the consciousness; or, in the consciousness of the infinite, the conscious subject has for his object the infinity of his own nature.[77]

What then is the nature of man for Feuerbach? Reason, Will, and Affection.[78] "Reason, Will, Love, are not powers which man possesses, for he is nothing without them, he is what he is only by them; they are the constituent elements of his nature, which he neither has nor makes the animating, determining, governing powers—divine, absolute powers—to which he can oppose no resistance."[79] Therefore, Feuerbach argues, "every limitation of the reason, or in general of the nature of man, rests on a delusion, an error. . . . If he makes his own limitations the limitations of the species, this arises from the mistake which is intimately connected with the individual's love of ease, sloth, vanity, and egoism."[80] For Feuerbach then, "the divine being is nothing else than the human being, or, rather, the human nature purified, freed from the limits of the individual man, made objective—i.e., contemplated and revered as another, a distinct being. All of the attributes of the divine nature are, therefore, attributes of the human nature."[81]

West summarizes Feuerbach's conclusions well:

> [A]lthough religion is literally false, it is nevertheless deeply rooted in human needs. If religion is not the product of divine revelation but of humanity itself, then it must also reflect human needs and aspirations. Adapting Hegel's understanding of the process of human self-realization through history, Feuerbach understands the divine as an externalization of "objectification" of human nature.[82]

For Feuerbach then, the concept of 'God' limits man's potentiality. "To enrich God, man must become poor; that God may be all, man must be nothing."[83]

As for the progression of religion, Feuerbach describes

> historical progression from primitive polytheism to more advanced monotheistic religions such as Judaism and Christianity.

---

77. Feuerbach, *The Essence of Christianity*, 2.
78. Feuerbach, *The Essence of Christianity*, 3.
79. Feuerbach, *The Essence of Christianity*, 3.
80. Feuerbach, *The Essence of Christianity*, 7.
81. Feuerbach, *The Essence of Christianity*, 14.
82. West, *Introduction to Continental Philosophy*, 43–44.
83. Feuerbach, *The Essence of Christianity*, 26.

> Protestantism, with its emphasis on the inward experience of faith and the direct relationship between the individual and God, comes closest to recognizing as human what less advanced religions idolatrously worship as divine. Still, Feuerbach believes that it is only by means of a thoroughgoing demystification of all religion, that humanity can fully reappropriate its alienated capacities and concentrate on a real rather than merely illusory satisfaction of its needs.[84]

So for Feuerbach, Protestantism is simply a good and necessary step in the "demystification" of religion. However, Karl Marx has a much harsher view of Christianity and the Protestant movement.

Karl Marx (1818–1883)

While Feuerbach believes that religion must go through the process of demystification, Marx believes that religion must be eradicated. Marx explains:

> Feuerbach starts out from the fact of religious self-alienation, of the duplication of the world into a religious world and a secular one. His work consists in revolving the religious world into its secular basis. But that the secular basis detaches itself from itself and establishes itself as an independent realm in the clouds can only be explained by the cleavages and self-contradictions within this secular basis. The latter must, therefore, in itself be both understood in its contraction and revolutionized in practice. Thus, for instance, after the earth family is discovered to be the secret holy family, the former must then itself be destroyed in theory and in practice.[85]

While Feuerbach sees the Protestant movement as a step in the right direction toward the demystification of religion, Marx views it quite differently:

> Luther certainly conquered servitude based on *devotion*, but only by replacing it with servitude based on *conviction*. He destroyed faith in authority, but only by restoring the authority of faith. He transformed the priests into laymen, but only by transforming laymen into priests. He freed mankind from external religiosity,

---

84. West, *Introduction to Continental Philosophy*, 44.
85. Raines, *Marx on Religion*, 183.

but only by making religiosity the inner man. He freed the body from its chains, but only by putting the heart in chains.[86]

In effect then, the proletariat was just as much in bondage after the Protestant movement as it was before it. For Marx then, all religion in general, and Christianity in particular, was the problem:

> The social principles of Christianity declare all vile acts of the oppressors against the oppressed to be either just punishment for original sin and other sins, or suffering that the Lord in his infinite wisdom has destined for those redeemed. The social principles of Christianity preach cowardice, self-contempt, abasement, submission, humility—in brief, all the qualities of the canaille; and the proletariat, not wishing to be treated as canaille, needs its courage, its self-respect, its pride, and its sense of independence even more than its bread. The social principles of Christianity are hypocritical, but the proletariat is revolutionary. So much for the social principles of Christianity.[87]

In many ways, Marx's views represent one of the two logical responses to Hegel's dialectical philosophy. For the Marxist, all religion is simply an unnecessary "externalization" of mankind's potential. For mankind to reach its full potential (i.e., a utopian state), all religion, especially Christianity, must be annihilated. The reason that this is relevant to the present discussion is that the Marxist views concerning the annihilation of Christianity are still alive and well in philosophical thought. In the mind of the Marxist, no religious claim is authoritative and no religious book is authoritative since the "revelation" contained therein is not from a divine being, but from man himself. Today many of the leading philosophers are self-proclaimed Marxists. This explains why many of their literary approaches are revolutionary in nature and either reject out of hand or read against the clear and plain meaning of a religious text, especially the Bible.

Finally, it should be noted that Feuerbach and Marx follow Hegel. This means that they ascribe to a teleological view of history. As for all followers of Hegel, history has a purpose and is heading toward a utopian state. As will be seen below, the death of God and the eradication of Christianity will be declared by Nietzsche, most philosophers will reject Hegelian thought, and Marxist ideology will lead to Nazi Germany and World War II. As Lyotard will explain, these events will lead to the postmodern age and the rejection of *all* meta-narratives (i.e., all-inclusive explanations of history).

---

86. Raines, *Marx on Religion*, 176–77.
87. Raines, *Marx on Religion*, 185–86.

Wilhelm Dilthey (1833–1911)

It is important to point out from the onset that Dilthey, like Johann Gottfried Herder before him, believed that authorial intention was recoverable, at least at some level, but, as West observes, only "through knowledge of the broader cultural and linguistic context. The practice of hermeneutics promises an always improving, though in some versions never perfect, interpretation of meaning—an always improving degree of mutual understanding between subjects."[88] Therefore, the knowledge of the "broader cultural and linguistic context" becomes of first importance for Dilthey. In addition, "Dilthey's faith in the possibility of objectively true or valid interpretations depends on the assumption of a common humanity, underlying the variety of human language, culture and personality."[89]

Herder's hermeneutical approach greatly influenced Schleiermacher. Herder was the first to point out what was to become known as the hermeneutical circle or spiral. Words, sentences, even paragraphs taken in isolation can be misinterpreted. However, once these are considered in light of the whole work then their meaning becomes clearer. In addition to Herder's hermeneutical principal that the parts make up the whole and the parts are understood better by the whole, Schleiermacher also followed Herder in his 'divination' in interpretation.

While Schleiermacher's hermeneutical approach was greatly influenced by Herder, Dilthey's hermeneutical approach to history was greatly influenced by Schleiermacher. It comes as no surprise then that what Schleiermacher applies to the principles of interpretation of texts, Dilthey applies to the interpretation of history—namely the hermeneutical circle. For Dilthey then, a people in history can be understood only in light of the whole of history and the whole of history can be only understood in light of its parts. Palmer summarizes Dilthey's view, "there is really no true starting point for understanding, since every part presupposes the others. This means that there can be no 'presuppositionless' understanding. Every act of understanding is in a given context or horizon; even in the sciences one explains only 'in terms of' a frame of reference."[90] Dilthey states:

> In this sense one can speak of the spirit of a time, whether of the Middle Ages or of the Enlightenment. This entails that each such epoch finds a delimitation in a *life-horizon*. I understand by this a mode of delimitation through which the people of a time

---

88. West, *Introduction to Continental Philosophy*, 160.
89. West, *Introduction to Continental Philosophy*, 86.
90. Palmer, *Hermeneutics*, 120–21.

orient their life by their thinking, feeling, and willing. Such a horizon places life, life-concerns, life-experience, and thought-formation in a certain proportion that restricts and binds the sphere within which individuals can modify their cognitive, evaluative, and volitional outlooks. Shades of the inevitable are cast over the single individual.[91]

In effect, there is no beginning point. As Palmer explains, "since we understand always from within our own horizon, which is part of the hermeneutical circle, there can be no nonpositional understanding of anything."[92]

As will be seen below, the concept of the hermeneutical circle that Herder and Schleiermacher apply to the interpretation of texts (i.e., the whole is understood in light of its parts, and vice versa), Dilthey applies to history, and Heidegger applies to being (*Dasein*). From there, Gadamer will reapply the hermeneutical circle back to the interpretation of text but adds the insights of Dilthey and Heidegger to it.

Finally, it should be pointed that out that the common view today that "everything is hermeneutics" began most directly with Dilthey's essay "The Rise of Hermeneutics," which makes hermeneutics the connecting link between philosophy and history.[93] The ramifications of Dilthey's undertaking are far-reaching, as Gadamer explains: "In Dilthey's eyes, then, hermeneutics comes into its own only when it ceases serving a dogmatic purpose—which, for the Christian theologian, is the right proclamation of the gospel—and begins functioning as a historical organon."[94]

Friedrich Nietzsche (1844–1900)

Friedrich Nietzsche's philosophy not only had a significant impact on many who followed him, but his beliefs also serve to show the trajectory of the conclusions up to this point. Additionally, he may not have been the first to see the effects of the rejection of any concept of god, but he certainly was the first to spell it out in detail.

---

91. Dilthey, *The Formation of the Historical World*, 198.

92. Palmer, *Hermeneutics*, 121.

93. It should be pointed out at this juncture that subjectivity had gained a stronghold in both the philosophical and religious beliefs of this period. Consider Edmund Husserl's intersubjective constitution of objectivity or Søren Kierkegaard's rejection of church dogma for individual subjective passion. Although very different in both their content and focus, both were impacted by the Cartesian philosophy of the day.

94. Gadamer, *Truth and Method*, 178.

For Nietzsche, the Madman's cry in the streets announcing the death of god has had and will continue to have significant and lasting ramifications. Man could now be free from the oppressive confines of religion, especially Christianity. However, modernity was not yet ready to acknowledge its newfound freedom. Nietzsche explains, "*New battles.*—After Buddha was dead, they still showed his shadow in a cave for centuries—a tremendous, gruesome shadow. God is dead; but given the way people are, there may still for millennia be caves in which they show his shadow.—And we—we must still defeat his shadow as well!"[95] For Nietzsche then, "What decides against Christianity now is our taste, not our reasons."[96]

To say that Nietzsche turned hostile toward Christianity in his last years is hardly an understatement. Among his many criticisms of Christianity, Jesus, and the Jewish people, Nietzsche writes, "Christianity also stands in opposition to all intellectual well-constitutedness—it can use only the morbid mind as the Christian mind, it takes the side of everything idiotic."[97] In the final words of his work *The Anti-Christ* Nietzsche writes:

> Wherever there are walls I shall inscribe this eternal accusation against Christianity upon them—I can write in letters which make even the blind see. . . . I call Christianity the one great curse, the one great intrinsic depravity, the one great instinct for revenge for which no expedient is sufficiently poisonous, secret, subterranean, petty—I call it the one immortal blemish of mankind. . . . And one calculates time from the *dies nefastus* [unlucky day] on which this fatality arose—from the first day of Christianity!—Why not rather from its last?—From today?—Revalution of all values![98]

As West correctly assesses then, Nietzsche "was suspicious of religion and is notorious for his announcement of the 'death of God', his absolute conviction that religious faith is no longer tenable and that this has fateful implications for western culture and civilization. At times his suspicion turns into outright hostility."[99]

Nietzsche not only rejects any formal religion, but also any teleological view of history. West explains, "Hegel's ambitious dialectical system is seen as little more than the pursuit of religion by other means, the substitution of

---

95. Nietzsche, *The Gay Science*, 109.
96. Nietzsche, *The Gay Science*, 123.
97. Nietzsche, *Twilight of the Idols*, 169.
98. Nietzsche, *The Anti-Christ*, 499.
99. West, *Introduction to Continental Philosophy*, 126.

history for divine providence."[100] Instead, Nietzsche holds to the concept of the "supra-historical man" "who does not envisage salvation in the process but for whom the world is finished in every single moment and its end attained" (i.e., his doctrine of "eternal recurrence").[101]

Nietzsche's influence on many who came after him is enormous. Among them are Heidegger, Derrida, and Foucault. If one announces the "death of God" and rejects the notion that history has any ultimate meaning, as Nietzsche does, then it is easy to see how one arrives at the conclusion that there is no "correct" interpretation of anything—of history, of truth, of reality, of beauty, of morality. Instead, truth, reality, beauty and morality are all in the eye of the beholder—conclusions that intentionally and emphatically stand in direct contradiction to the Christian faith.

Edmund Husserl (1859–1938)

Not only is Edmund Husserl widely considered the founder of phenomenology, but his impact on Martin Heidegger is unmistakable.[102] However, his brand of phenomenology and that of his colleague and one-time assistant Heidegger are very different. In fact, Husserl was critical of both the work of Heidegger and Max Scheler, calling them his "antipodes."[103]

Hirsch states:

> In his chief work, *Logische Untersuchungen*,[104] Husserl sought, among other things, to avoid an identification of verbal meaning with the psychic acts [as had Schleiermacher before him] of speaker or listener, author or reader, but to do this he did not adopt a strict, Platonic idealism by which meanings have an actual existence apart from meanings experienced. Instead, he affirmed the objectivity of meaning by analyzing the observable relationship between it and those very mental processes in which it is actualized, for in meaning experiences themselves, the objectivity and constancy of meaning are confirmed.[105]

---

100. West, *Introduction to Continental Philosophy*, 134.

101. West, *Introduction to Continental Philosophy*, 135.

102. Phenomenology has been variously defined and explained. As a starting point however, it is best to define phenomenology as the study of phenomena, or the study of things as they appear. One of the outcomes of Cartesian dualism is that a gap is created between objects in the world "in themselves" and the way that they appear to the subject (i.e., phenomena).

103. Husserl, *Psychological and Transcendental Phenomenology*.

104. Husserl, *Logische Untersuchungen*.

105. Hirsch, *Validity in Interpretation*, 217.

In order to arrive at the objective meaning (i.e., the author's intent), Husserl employs his eidetic phenomenology by which subjective personal bias is supposedly eliminated.

Martin Heidegger (1889–1976)

By the time of Heidegger, the problems with Cartesian dualism (with its object/subject dichotomy) were apparent. West explains, "like Hegel, he is committed to a view of life and philosophy as essentially historical. For him the practice of philosophy is inseparable from the interpretation of previous philosophical texts."[106] For Heidegger, according to West:

> [W]estern metaphysics is governed by the underlying conviction that there must be some being or beings, which are fundamental or "truly real" in both an explanatory and a justificatory or normative sense. In other words, all other levels or kinds of being are causally dependent on them and all norms and values have their ground or justification in them. The history of western metaphysics consists of a number of attempts to identify such a fundamental being or beings, from Plato's "Forms" and Aristotle's "unmoved mover" to the God of the medieval theology and Hegelian "spirit."[107]

West explains well the point being made by Heidegger:

> [S]ubjectivism and objectivism are contrasting symptoms of the same underlying disorder of western thinking, what Gadamer has called the "objectivistic" subjectivism of the modern age. It is not enough to reassert the "subjective" pole of life or existence as a distinct order of being opposed to the "objective" pole of being of physical things in space. It is necessary to address the primordial question of Being in general.[108]

Heidegger thus rejects Husserl's claim that he can somehow eliminate his subjective viewpoint. Instead, Heidegger believes that the core of the problem is that the pursuit of knowledge must not begin with the subject, but with the fact of being. So, Descartes' statement, "I think therefore I am" is exactly backwards. For Heidegger, thinking is predicated on being. Therefore, Descartes statement should have read more like, "I am (exist—Dasein), therefore I think."

---

106. West, *Introduction to Continental Philosophy*, 97.
107. West, *Introduction to Continental Philosophy*, 97.
108. West, *Introduction to Continental Philosophy*, 99–100.

West adds:

> Crucially, it is impossible to think of the situated Dasein of Heidegger's ontology as a detached observer of the world like the Cartesian ego: "Being-in-the-world is a structure which is primordially and constantly whole." Dasein, as "being-there", is inseparable from the world, and so it is essentially Being-in-the-world. It is equally important to realize that, by implication, the world is just as inseparable from the idea of conscious existence as Dasein is inseparable from the world. Heidegger's radical challenge to the objectivism of western metaphysics could not be more apparent.[109]

For Heidegger then, the world of objects is inseparable from the subject because they are all part of Dasein. The part (i.e., individual consciousness) can only be understood in light of its situatedness in the whole (i.e., Being), and vice versa—there is no view from outside one's situatedness in the world. The Cartesian Dualism, with its "subjects" and "objects," is a false dichotomy.

Before Heidegger, Dilthey had applied Schleiermacher's (or Herder's) hermeneutical circle to historical situatedness to the effect that one cannot understand the whole of history without an understanding of its parts, and vice versa. In like fashion, Heidegger applies the hermeneutical circle to being (*Dasein*) itself. In doing so, Howe explains, "Heidegger expands the traditional view of the hermeneutical circle to encompass the very being of Dasein. Traditionally, the hermeneutical circle assumed a distinction between the subject and the object in which the knowing subject stood over against the known object."[110] However, according to David Hoy, "Heidegger conceives of Dasein and the world as forming a circle, and he thus extends the traditional hermeneutic circle between a text and its reading down to the most primordial level of human existence."[111] Heidegger argues that the hermeneutical circle "belongs to the structure of meaning, and the latter phenomenon is rooted in the existential constitution of Dasein."[112]

While these explanations are helpful, Gadamer's description of the distinction between Heidegger's philosophy and those who had come before him spells out exactly what is at issue here:

---

109. West, *Introduction to Continental Philosophy*, 101–2.
110. Howe, *Objectivity in Biblical Interpretation*, 209.
111. Hoy, "Heidegger and the Hermeneutic Turn," 172.
112. Heidegger, *Sein und Zeit*, 153.

> The tendency which Dilthey and Yorck formulated as common to them, of "understanding in terms of life," and which was expressed in Husserl's going back behind the objectivity of science to the life-world, was characteristic of Heidegger's own first approach. But he was no longer dependent on the epistemological requirement that the return to life (Dilthey) and the transcendental reduction (Husserl's way of absolutely radical self-reflection) be based methodologically on the self-givenness of experience. On the contrary, all this became the object of Heidegger's critique. Under the rubric of a "hermeneutics of facticity," Heidegger confronted Husserl's eidetic phenomenology, as well as the distinction between the fact and essence on which it depended, with a paradoxical demand. Phenomenology should be ontologically based on the facticity of Dasein, existence, which cannot be based on or derived from anything else, and not on pure cogito as the essential constitution of typical universality—a bold idea, but difficult to carry through.[113]

Beginning with Descartes and ending with Nietzsche's proclamation of the "death of God," any possibility of an appeal to God or his Word as the authority on reality and truth was removed. However, Cartesian philosophy placed reality and truth in the mind of the subject. Here, Heidegger effectively removes all appeals to reality or truth other than that of Dasein. Heidegger's philosophical thought then was a driving force behind the antifoundationalism movement that includes the likes of Stanley Fish, Richard Rorty, and Michel Foucault as well as Gadamer's philosophical hermeneutics and Derrida's deconstruction.

Jean-François Lyotard (1924–1998)

In 1979, Lyotard coined the term "postmodern" with his publication of *The Postmodern Condition*.[114] According to West, Jean-Francois Lyotard

> defines modernity in terms of the role played in western societies since the Enlightenment by "metanarratives" for the legitimation of both science and the state. A metanarrative in Lyotard's sense is equivalent to a philosophy of history. The contingent events of history are understood in terms of an all-inclusive narrative, which is supposed to encapsulate "the" meaning of history.[115]

---

113. Gadamer, *Truth and Method*, 245.
114. Lyotard, *The Postmodern Condition*.
115. West, *Introduction to Continental Philosophy*, 197–98.

In other words, "The onset of a postmodern mood or condition, then, is marked by a gradual erosion of faith in meta-narratives, provoked by far-reaching developments in both society and culture."[116] West adds:

> There is skepticism about all philosophies of history, all claims to foresee the inevitable goal of history and all political ideologies which promise to lead us to that goal. There is even skepticism about the universal validity of the values that define a particular historical future as good or bad. The "death of God" announced by Nietzsche is closely followed by the death of history and progress. There is even a loss of faith in anything other than the instrumental effectiveness of western rationality. Paradoxically, this loss of faith is the ultimate outcome of the Enlightenment's own historically novel demand for the rational justification of every claim to truth, rightness and authority. In other words, the Enlightenment project has fallen victim to its own skeptical onslaught against religious dogma, tradition and authority.[117]

The Impact of Continental Philosophy on Hermeneutics

The preceding discussion concerning Continental Philosophy was necessary to set the stage for the hermeneutical discussions of our day. Beginning with Herder and continuing through Lyotard, the interpretation of texts had become increasingly philosophical in nature with dramatic results. Nietzsche summarizes the philosophical progress of his day by declaring the death of God. With the failure of Hegelianism and Marxism, Lyotard declares the death of the metanarrative. Finally, with Dilthey and Heidegger, the assault on objective determinate meaning was well under way.

Our attention will now turn to discussions that have taken place more recently. While there have been several significant works in the field of hermeneutics in the last few decades, a few are in need of emphasis because they continue with the nihilistic trajectory of the Continental tradition. As a result, determinate meaning (i.e., authorial intention), the author, and the text will be unable to escape their assault.

---

116. West, *Introduction to Continental Philosophy*, 198.
117. West, *Introduction to Continental Philosophy*, 199.

Georg Hans Gadamer (1900–2002)

In 1964, James Robinson observed that Gadamer's influence and significance was growing: "in the present situation Dilthey and increasingly Heidegger are being superseded by the Heidelberg philosopher Hans-Georg Gadamer, a former pupil of Heidegger and Bultmann, whose magnum opus grounds the humanities in a hermeneutic oriented not to psychologism or existentialism, but to language and its subject matter."[118] The result of Gadamer's work (most specifically *Truth and Method*) has had an enormous and lasting impact as Schreiner explains:

> No one has done more to shake the confidence of historians in the old ideal of objectivity than Gadamer. As Gadamer explained, the goal of Romantic hermeneutics to find authorial intention presupposed the Enlightenment ideal of a mind free from prejudices. Historians were to enter the mind of the author and transpose themselves into the culture of an earlier age. To this presupposed ideal of objectivity and historical empathy, Gadamer opposed the historicity of understanding. Rejecting the "prejudice against prejudice" inherited from the Enlightenment, Gadamer argued that readers cannot free themselves from their prejudices and thereby recover the mind of the author. Such shedding of presuppositions is neither possible nor desirable. Presuppositions or prejudgments are the necessary preconditions for understanding.[119]

West observes that according to Jean-Paul Sartre (1905–1980), "an object which is perceived has an infinity of potential aspects or 'profiles' (*Abschattungen*), corresponding to the infinity of possible perspectives we can adopt in relation to it. Perception is, in that sense, inexhaustible."[120] Gadamer's words sound very much like Sartre's. However, what Sartre observes of the perception of objects, Gadamer applies to texts: "Not just occasionally, but always, the meaning of a text goes beyond its author. That is why understanding is not merely a reproductive but always a productive activity as well."[121] He adds, "every interpretation has to adapt itself to the hermeneutical situation to which it belongs."[122] In other words, the possible perspectives that can be adopted in relation to a text are inexhaustible.

---

118. Robinson, "Hermeneutic since Barth," 69.
119. Schreiner, *Where Shall Wisdom Be Found?*, 10–11.
120. West, *Introduction to Continental Philosophy*, 139–40.
121. Gadamer, *Truth and Method*, 296.
122. Gadamer, *Truth and Method*, 398.

With this line of thinking, it is not difficult to see how those who follow Gadamer end up rejecting the notion that a text has any determinate meaning. Hirsch's objection to Gadamer is most appropriate: "Quite clearly, to view the texts as an autonomous piece of language and interpretation as an infinite process is really to deny that the text has any determinate meaning, for a determinate entity is what it is and not another thing [Aristotle's Law of Identity], but an inexhaustible array of possibilities is an hypostatization that is nothing in particular at all."[123]

The reason for Gadamer's argumentation is that he is wholly committed to Heidegger's view of Being and Dilthey's radical historicism. Hirsch states, "but while the position of radical historicism is very probably false, one must acknowledge that its adherents, particularly those of a Heideggerian cast, hold to its tenets as to a religion—and the claims of a religion are absolute."[124] It is understandable then that Gadamer religiously and fanatically argues that a phenomenon *can only be* understood via one's historical horizon. In other words, an interpreter *is not capable of* an "a-historical, transcendent claim about historical knowledge." However, would not such a sweeping assertion include Gadamer's assertion as well? For, is not Gadamer guilty of making an a-historical, transcendent claim himself? Gadamer rejects the notion that this self-contradiction is a problem:

> However clearly one demonstrates the inner contradictions of all relativist views, it is as Heidegger has said: all these victorious arguments have something of the attempt to bowl one over. However, cogent they may seem, they still miss the point. In making use of them one is proved right, and yet they do not express any superior insight of value. That the thesis of skepticism or relativism refutes itself to the extent that it claims to be true is an irrefutable argument. But what does it achieve? The reflective argument that proves successful here rebounds against the arguer, for it renders the truth value of reflection suspect. It is not the reality of skepticism or of truth-dissolving relativism but the truth claim of all formal argument that is affected.[125]

It is as Howe points out, "Gadamer appears to have access to an a-historical, transcendent perspective on historicism that he disallows for everyone else."[126] The problems with Gadamer's statement here are numerous and quite telling. First, Gadamer appeals to Heidegger as an authority.

---

123. Hirsch, *Validity in Interpretation*, 249.
124. Hirsch, *Validity in Interpretation*, 44.
125. Gadamer, *Truth and Method*, 339–40.
126. Howe, *Objectivity in Biblical Interpretation*, 281.

For Gadamer then, Heidegger is not one who was historically situated and therefore bound by his subjective horizon, but one who somehow overcame such situatedness to arrive at a-historical, transcendent truths. Second, while Gadamer's claim is that his opponents are attempting to "bowl one over" is this not *exactly* what he is doing here? Is he not the one claiming victory, even in the face of rejecting all that is in keeping with basic logic? Third, he appears to dismiss as trivial the *indisputable* fact that he is violating one of the most basic laws of logic: the law of non-contradiction. One can almost hear Avicenna's response to such a line of reasoning: Could someone please get a club and a match? Gadamer's argumentation is so adamant that he is absolutely and irrefutably right, that he is willing to reject the law of non-contradiction to retain his claim! It appears then that only Gadamer himself is allowed to engage in the blind faith of a truth claim that is invalidated (and therefore must by necessity be deemed as errant) on its very surface. Would not such a commitment to illogical argumentation functionally serve to obliterate *all* of the argumentation upon which he, and others who had preceded him, had built their conclusions?

Finally, a word must be said about Gadamer's "fusion of horizons."[127] The only way for one to argue that a "fusion of horizons" had occurred between the author and the reader of a text would be to locate the points at which a "fusion" had occurred. The logical problem with such an undertaking is that for one to validate a claim that a "fusion" had in fact occurred, one must be able to distinguish between the horizon of the author and that of the reader. However, if these are somehow distinguishable, then the "fusion of horizons" was not prescriptive (in that it must happen), but descriptive (in that it did happen). In other words, to claim a "fusion of horizons" has occurred, one must be able to evaluate an interpretation of a reader (another subject) with the text of the author (object). Only upon such an evaluation can such a claim be made. Of course, the problem here is that such a claim would by necessity be an objective claim, since it was the text (object) that was utilized in the evaluation. Therefore, while it may very well be the case that a "fusion of horizons" is often what *does* happen, it does not follow that a "fusion of horizons" is what *must* happen. For, if a "fusion of horizons" is recognizable to any interpreter, then it *cannot* be prescriptively mandated.

---

127. Gadamer, *Truth and Method*, 305–82. The same line of argumentation that will be pursued here in brief is identical with that on pp. 13–14 above (particularly footnote 21) concerning the issue of subjectivity in interpretation.

Stanley Fish (1938–present)

According to Stanley Fish, "the text as an entity independent of interpretation . . . drops out and is replaced by the text that emerges as the consequence of our interpretive activities."[128] It is for this reason that Fish argues concerning settling interpretive disputes, "one cannot appeal to the text, because the text has become an extension of the interpretive disagreement that divides them; and, in fact, the text as it is variously characterized is a consequence of the interpretation for which it is supposedly evidence."[129]

As Vanhoozer correctly explains, "the significance of Fish's position must not be underestimated: on his view, it is not the author that is the historical cause of the text and creator of meaning, but the reader. In a real sense, for Fish, the commentary (viz., the work of interpretation) *precedes* the text."[130] As Vanhoozer explains this view, "if interpreters would only come clean about the impossibility of literary knowledge, they would see that the only honorable course would be to admit that the truth is not out there, to be discovered eventually by reason, but is rather in the eye of the beholding community."[131]

The consequence for Fish's line of thinking then is simple. Fish argues, "there is no such thing as literal meaning if by literal meaning one means a meaning that is perspicuous no matter what the context and no matter what is in the speaker's or hearer's mind, a meaning that because it is prior to interpretation can act as a constraint on interpretation."[132] However, one cannot help but wonder if Fish applies this sentiment (i.e., meaning) to this statement. If so, then he has in fact made no assertion at all.[133]

Further, if there is no such thing as literal meaning *then one is left absolutely bewildered* with Fish's essay entitled, "A Reply to John Reichert."[134] Fish begins this essay with the words, "Reading John Reichert's objections to 'Normal Circumstances . . . and Other Cases' [a previous essay written by Fish] is a curious experience because he is often on the verge of embracing the position that distresses him. Consider for example . . ."[135] What is so bewildering is that Fish is "reading John Reichert's objections" as if he

---

128. Fish, *Is There a Text in This Class?*, 13.
129. Fish, *Is There a Text in This Class?*, 340.
130. Vanhoozer, *Is There a Meaning in This Text?*, 56.
131. Vanhoozer, *Is There a Meaning in This Text?*, 56–57.
132. Fish, *Doing What Comes Naturally*, 4.
133. This is still another example of the "there are absolutely no absolutes" statements that seem so commonplace in this line of reasoning.
134. Fish, *Is There a Text in This Class?*, 293.
135. Fish, *Is There a Text in This Class?*, 293.

[Reichert] really means something by them. Further, by reading Reichert's objections, Fish concludes that "he [Reichert] is often on the verge of embracing the position that distresses him." Fish even goes so far as to offer examples and quotes from Reichert—as if Reichert's words serve as proof of his [Reichert's] intended meaning. In fact, the very fact that Fish responds to Reichert's words *can only mean* that Fish intended to convey a meaning in his previous essay—meaning that was taken issue with by Reichert. Further, Fish shows no signs of consulting his "interpretive community" for validation of his interpretation of Reichert's words.

The hypocrisy of Fish's approach is both staggering and telling. The apparent truth of the matter is that Fish, like Gadamer before him, desires to have his words, meaning, and philosophy regarded as authoritatively true while denying his detractors the same privilege. Therefore, I believe that Fish's previous quote concerning coming "clean" be turned back around on him to read: If Stanley Fish would only come clean about the possibility of literary knowledge, he would see that the only honorable course would be to admit that the truth of the meaning is right there in the text, to be discovered by reading the author's words. It is not found in the eye of the beholder, nor is it in the eye of the beholding community. That is to say, words mean things. Therefore, textual meaning is both determinable and able to be validated.

Jacques Derrida (1930–2004)

Nietzsche pronounces the death of God, Gadamer declares the death of determinate meaning, and Fish declares the death of the text. It is only fitting that the death of the author be declared as well. If this line of reasoning is followed then Jacques Derrida, Roland Barthes, and Michel Foucault take the next logical step. Of these, Derrida has been the most influential. However, when the author is declared dead, the ramifications, as Vanhoozer correctly point out, are enormous:

> Behind the innocuous figure of the author as the determiner of textual meaning, according to Derrida, lies the whole edifice of Western philosophy, together with its metaphysical scaffolding. In challenging the traditional picture of what an author is and does, Derrida attempts nothing less than an undoing of the central ideas of philosophy and theology alike. This is not surprising, for the crisis in contemporary philosophy and literary theory is fundamentally a theological crisis.[136]

136. Vanhoozer, *Is There a Meaning in This Text?*, 48.

Derrida's attack then is not simply on the author, but on the grave of God as well. Hence, Ingraffia argues that Derrida "excludes God and anything that would take his place."[137]

Derrida argues that since there is no transcendent authority who is the creator and originator of truth and who, because of his authority, the world will be held accountable, then all truth claims as well as all authority claims are ultimately subjective, relative, and baseless—even those of the author. Michel Foucault agrees with Derrida in this belief. In other words, as Vanhoozer explains, "the author saves us from the hermeneutic relativism and from the indeterminacy of meaning. Interpreters want to believe in a rational presence who controls textual meaning, but such a belief, according to Foucault, is dishonest if not adulterous."[138] For Foucault then, "the author is a principle of thrift in the proliferation of meaning. . . . The author is therefore the ideological figure by which one masks the manner in which we fear the proliferation of meaning."[139]

Foucault also agrees with Derrida that claims to the control of textual meaning are a form of oppression. Vanhoozer explains:

> For Derrida, proper meaning (*le sens propre*) connotes both propriety and property. Disputes about literal meaning are disputes over who "owns" meaning. Interpretive disputes are really power struggles. To ask a reader to conform to the "proper" meaning of a text is, in Derrida's opinion, a form of oppression, the same kind of oppression that pretends there is a "proper" way to dress or a "proper" way to paint. It is the oppression that inevitably follows the claim that one possesses truth. Derrida states that this oppression of "the proper interpretation" is actually the source of all oppression in the world.[140]

For not even the author, or the feeble attempt at preserving the author's ownership of the meaning of a text via attaching his signature, can keep control of the meaning of a text, as Derrida explains: "Signatures do nothing to endure the passage of an author's 'true' intentions to those who read and set themselves up as authorized heirs and interpreters." In Derrida's view then, no one "owns" meaning—except, of course, Derrida, who authoritatively asserts that no one owns meaning . . . ironically, in books that bear his name on the spine. It is not difficult to see then why Jacques Derrida is called the "father of deconstruction."

---

137. Ingraffia, *Postmodern Theory and Biblical Theology*, 224.
138. Vanhoozer, *Is There a Meaning in This Text?*, 119–20.
139. Foucault, "What Is an Author?," 159.
140. Vanhoozer, *Is There a Meaning in This Text?*, 119–20.

A RESPONSE TO CONTINENTAL PHILOSOPHY

In response to Gadamer, Hirsch writes, "If we cannot enunciate a principle for distinguishing between an interpretation that is valid and one that is not, there is little point in writing books about texts or about hermeneutic theory."[141] Yet the hermeneutical philosophers who follow Gadamer have taken his illogical argumentation to new heights of contradiction. Therefore, while Hirsch's statement makes the point, it is severely understated. Instead, the implication of this trajectory of warped and illogical thinking is much more far reaching. For, *if we cannot enunciate a principle for distinguishing between an interpretation that is valid and one that is not, then there is little point in speaking or listening, writing or reading, or for that matter, interacting with any other human being, the world, or even one's own thoughts.* Yet most interestingly, they continue to write. The only logical question is, "*why*?" Could it be anything other than to fulfill their quest to establish grounds upon which to justify themselves in their desire to do what is right in their own eyes, to be their own god, and in doing so grant everyone else the right to be their own god as well?

The only thing that they have managed to do is deconstruct a foundation that is not in keeping with their likings in order to re-construct one that is. And what is the core belief of this new foundation? Simply stated, *there is absolutely no absolute truth*. There is no meaning—every man is now free to do what is right in his own eyes. However, for all of their extended treatises, technical jargon, abstract considerations, and philosophical gyrations, one persistent problem remains: this brand of philosophy is self-defeating illogical nihilism. Yet its adherents continue to ascribe to it blindly, intolerantly, religiously, and absolutely.[142]

That there is an intended meaning in the use of words, both spoken and written, is not only evident, but hardly in need of defense. The problem that these philosophers ultimately have is that they are unable to deconstruct this one stubborn and unchanging truth: words mean things. Since words

---

141. Hirsch, *Validity in Interpretation*, 251.

142. While Derrida argues that all language is interdependent, descriptive, and subjective, the Bible's creation account tells of language that is independent, prescriptive, and objective (i.e., God's prescriptive naming in Genesis 1:4 and Adam's prescriptive naming of the animals in Genesis 2:19). While these philosophers have tried in vain to liberate themselves in order to do what is "right in their own eyes," the Bible's account of the fall tells that this was precisely the Serpent's enticement. What was rejected at the fall was God's view of good and evil, right and wrong. What was substituted was Adam and Eve's view of good and evil, right and wrong. Since the fall, mankind has been conflicted with the desire to do what is "right in his own eyes," yet all the while knowing that he will be held to account for it.

mean things, and since words, both spoken and written, are the means by which meaning is conveyed, then it is important that the pursuit of the correct interpretation of an author's or speaker's words not be abandoned.

In summary then, since the philosophical infrastructure of current reader-oriented hermeneutical approaches has been exposed as illogical and nonsensical, our commitment to authorial intention must now be reaffirmed and our focus return to the topic at hand: validity in the identification and interpretation of literary allusions. Chapter 3 will begin this task by arriving at a workable definition for "literary allusion" that fully takes into account all that is required of it. Once a definition for literary allusion is set forth, the task of explaining how one identifies an allusion and validates his interpretation can begin.

3

What Is a Literary Allusion?

NEED FOR A DEFINITION

BEFORE ONE CAN BEGIN a theoretical work concerning how to identify a literary allusion and then validate the claim that a literary allusion is present in a text, he must first precisely define exactly what it is that he is looking for.[1] In addition, the definition must be distinguished from other similar terms. In the general field of literary study there has been not only a shortage of theoretical works dealing with allusions, but there has also been a lack of attention given to the presentation of an adequately detailed definition of literary allusion. This acknowledgment is the beginning point for William Irwin's article, "What is an Allusion?"[2] In fact, Irwin could find only one theoretical book (Gian Biagio Conte's Italian work entitled, *Memoria die poeti e sistema letterario: Catullo, Virgilio, Ovidio, Lucano*) dealing with the topic of allusion.[3] Therefore, Irwin is correct as he explains:

---

1. This issue of the need for clarity in use of terms is raised by Garrick Allen when he states, "The cacophony of competing terms and definitions currently in use in Biblical Studies increases the chances for misunderstanding and imprecision." Allen, *The Book of Revelation and Early Jewish Textual Culture*, 7.

2. Irwin, "What Is an Allusion?," 287.

3. Irwin, "What Is an Allusion?," 296. This work has now been translated into English (Conte, *The Rhetoric of Imitation*.) In this work, Conte begins by separating himself from Giorgio Pasquali's historicism (Pasquali, "Arte Allusiva," 11–20, which also appeared as part of a later book, Pasquali, *Pagine stravananti*, 275–83).

There is, to be sure, no shortage of studies detailing the use of allusion. Witness, for example, the vast quantity of work devoted to T. S. Eliot's use of allusion in *The Waste Land* and Alexander Pope's use of allusion in *The Rape of the Lock*. Still, what nearly all such studies neglect is the basic question: What is an allusion? And the result is confusion. Whereas there is no shortage of theoretical work on such subjects as irony and metaphor, there is a scarcity of theoretical work on allusion.[4]

Marko Jauhiainen makes the same point when he states:

> One would expect adequate definitions to exist and to be in use already, especially given the fact that the quest for developing objective criteria for discerning and labeling allusions has been going on for more than a decade now and has been taken up by many scholars. However . . . this is not the case, yet suitable definitions are indeed required, especially for the term "allusion" which is at the centre of a study such as this.[5]

In her discussion on providing a definition of allusion, Ziva Ben-Porath states:

> The problem is not one of a plethora of contradictory theories. On the contrary, there are in fact scarcely any theories dealing with allusion, and there is a lack of studies on allusion qua allusion. Allusion has either been treated as a very vague term, covering so many structures that it could not be discussed phenomenologically, or it has been taken for granted as a very common feature of the language.[6]

Therefore, the fact that there is both a lack of an adequate definition and a need for a comprehensive theoretical work on the topic of literary allusion has been well recognized. The complicating factor is that any discussion on the definition of literary allusion must also serve to distinguish it from other related terms.

---

4. Irwin, "What Is an Allusion?," 287.
5. Jauhiainen, *The Use of Zechariah in Revelation*, 3.
6. Ben-Porath, "Poetics of Allusion," 19–20.

BRIEF SURVEY OF CURRENT PROPOSALS AND PROBLEMS

One of the first problems one becomes aware of when interacting with the issue of allusion is that there is no consensus or consistency in the use of terms. The result is that many terms are used interchangeably and inconsistently. Not only is this true from scholar to scholar, but some scholars refer to the same phenomenon under consideration in this study (i.e., literary allusion) in many different ways within one text. Consider for example Richard B. Hays' work *Echoes of Scripture in the Letters of Paul*. While the book is titled "Echoes," Hays addresses these "echoes" in the same manner that allusions are usually addressed. Further, he not only calls the literary phenomenon under his consideration "echoes," but also "allusion," "allusive echo," "literary echo," "intertextual allusions," and "intertextual echo"—and this is over the course of only two pages![7] In fact, Hays admits that he makes "no systematic distinction between" echo and allusion.[8] Instead he states, "Allusion is used of obvious intertextual references, echo of subtler ones."[9] Therefore, while Hays' entire work is on this literary phenomenon, he offers no definition of it or how it differs from other similar literary phenomena in Paul's letters.

Several definitions of allusion have been set forth in literary studies. However, each of these definitions suffers from at least one of three main problems. The first problem that is common among them is that the definitions offered thus far are too brief, and therefore incomplete. Definitions with this problem omit many of the key points that serve to both define allusion and set it apart from other like terms.

The second problem is that some of the definitions are too general. While it is helpful in a discussion about allusions to discuss *common* features of allusions, or how allusions *commonly* function, it is imperative that a definition of literary allusion spells out the features and functions that are *always* present in allusions. What is being sought then is not a general description of allusion, but a precise definition of allusion.

The third problem is that some of these definitions are simply incorrect. As will be seen below, several definitions have been proven errant with no adequate definition to take their place.

In an effort to clarify and define literary allusion, the most commonly cited and utilized definitions will now be surveyed and examined in order

---

7. Hays, *Echoes of Scripture in the Letters of Paul*, 20–21.
8. Hays, *Echoes of Scripture in the Letters of Paul*, 29.
9. Hays, *Echoes of Scripture in the Letters of Paul*, 29.

to spell out both the strengths and deficiencies in each. As will be seen, most of these definitions contain central points that must be preserved in our definition of literary allusion. However, they also contain weaknesses that need to be corrected.

Earl Miner

Earl Miner defines *allusion* as a "tacit reference to another literary work, to another art, to history, to contemporary figures, or the like" and requires "an echo of sufficiently familiar yet distinctive and meaningful elements."[10] However, as Irwin asks:

> Why could it not be that an entire epic poem alludes to the Odyssey? In a sense, does not Paradise Lost do just that? While certainly this is not typical, it is also not impossible. More commonly, an entire stanza in one poem may allude to an entire stanza in another poem. Clearly, it is possible to imitate the style or form of a work without necessarily alluding to that work: Not every Petrarchan sonnet need be an allusion to Petrarch. Still it is possible for a work to allude to another work by imitating its style or form; it would be possible, for example, to compose a sonnet that as a whole alludes to Shakespeare's Sonnet 55.[11]

Irwin's point is that allusions need not be tacit. In addition, it should be noted that Miner's is not only errant (as pointed out by Irwin's quote above), but it is also incomplete and too general. First, Miner's definition is incomplete in that no mention is made of the purpose of an allusion. Allusions are *literary devices* utilized by an *author* in order to assist him in the *conveyance of meaning*. Second, Miner's definition is too general. Phrases such as "and the like" are too open-ended and ultimately unhelpful in a definition.

In a later work, Miner defines allusion as "a poet's deliberate incorporation of identifiable elements from other sources, preceding or contemporaneous, textual or extratextual."[12] This is an improvement for two reasons. First, authorial intention is explicitly included in this definition. Authors allude, not readers. This point will become important below. Second, this definition makes explicit the fact that allusions allude to something already in existence. One cannot allude to a text that has not yet been written.[13]

10. Miner, "Allusion," 18.
11. Irwin, "What Is an Allusion?," 288–89.
12. Miner, "Allusion," 38–39.
13. For example, one can allude to one of the future apocalyptic events, but only because they have been previously revealed in the pages of Scripture.

This point will be helpful later in this study concerning the dating of texts.[14] However, this definition is still deficient in that no mention is made of the rhetorical function that allusions play in the conveyance of the author's intended meaning.

M. H. Abrams

M. H. Abrams defines allusion as "a brief reference, explicit or indirect, to a person, place or event, or to another literary work or passage."[15] As was noted above, an allusion is not necessarily "brief." Therefore, this definition suffers from being errant. Second, there is no mention of the rhetorical function that allusions play in the conveyance of the author's (or speaker's) intended meaning. Third, Abrams' definition probably assumes some things that at that time did not need to be stated, but today need to be made explicit (e.g., the fact that it is the author or speaker who makes the allusion, or that the person, place or event, or other literary work or passage being alluded to must by necessity precede the allusion). Fourth, Abrams' definition does not explain how the reference is made (i.e., verbal or textual markers).

H. Morier

Morier defines allusion as "*une figure consistant à dire une chose avec l'intention d'en faire entendre une autre.*"[16] However, Ben-Porath criticizes Morier's definition on two fronts. First, this definition places allusion wholly in the realm of linguistics. While allusions can be linguistic in nature (i.e., utilized in speech, they can also be literary in nature. Second, Ben-Porath accuses Morier of "a basic inconsistency in the introduction of a formal allusion as a category in a classification of functions. As he describes it, the formal allusion is based on formal likeness—the parodistic principle of imitation—which is clearly developing a mode and not a function."[17] Ben-Porat's point is well taken: any good definition of allusion must make explicit the fact that allusions serve a rhetorical function.

---

14. If one can persuasively argue that one text alludes to another, then the alluding text (i.e., the text making the allusion) *must* precede the text being alluded to. Otherwise, the allusion is not possible.

15. Abrams, *A Glossary of Literary Terms*, 8.

16. Morier, "Allusion," 4. (A figure consisting in saying one thing with the intention of meaning something else.)

17. Ben-Porath, "Poetics of Allusion," 21.

Michael Leddy

Michael Leddy states that "allusion-words typically describe a reference that invokes one or more associations of appropriate cultural material and brings them to bear upon a present context."[18] Irwin disagrees and argues that additional associations are not just *typical* but are *necessary* for "correct and complete understanding."[19] In addition, Irwin states, "we are not just to substitute one thing for another. We are supposed to make unstated associations, and in this sense the reference is indirect... unless I make further indirect connections I have failed to understand the allusion."[20] This discussion is helpful in that it brings to the surface the purpose for alluding (i.e., the importation of meaning).

Michael Leddy states that one of the "limits of allusion" is that an allusion is a "small-scale device."[21] Again, Irwin's quote above points out that allusion need not be brief or "small-scale" in nature. However, one notable item in Leddy's words is that he has correctly identified the fact that allusion is a "device." That is to say, it is important to recognize that literary allusions are literary devices utilized by an author.

Oxford English Dictionary

In another example, Irwin's article, "What Is an Allusion?" begins with the Oxford English Dictionary's definition of an allusion as "a covert, implied, or indirect reference."[22] However, Irwin uses the argumentation of Carmela Perri in her article "On Alluding" to make the point that allusions need not be covert but instead can be overt.[23] The effect of this on the definition of allusion is that the word "covert" should be eliminated from the definition of allusion leaving only *allusion as an implied, indirect reference*. The problems with this definition are, in many ways, the same as those offered above. First, there is no mention that it is the author or speaker who makes the allusion. Second, there is no mention of the verbal or literary markers by which the allusion is made. Third, there is no mention of the rhetorical function of a literary allusion.

18. Irwin, "What Is an Allusion?," 288. Also see Leddy, "The Limits of Allusion."
19. Irwin, "What Is an Allusion?," 288.
20. Irwin, "What Is an Allusion?," 288.
21. Leddy, "The Limits of Allusion," 111.
22. Irwin, "What Is an Allusion?" 287.
23. Irwin, "What Is an Allusion?" 287; Perri, "On Alluding," 290.

Ziva Ben-Porath

Ziva Ben-Porath defines literary allusion as "a device by which the reader links one or more elements in a given text with other independent and not identical elements in an evoked text."[24] The problems with this definition are several. First, Ben-Porath's definition puts allusion as something that the reader "links." However, is an allusion really a device whereby the *reader* is doing the connecting of texts, or is it the author who alludes? Ben-Porath later explains how it is that the reader actualizes an allusion. However, her work assumes that an allusion is already there to be actualized. This makes her definition very misleading as well as categorically incorrect. Literary allusions are literary devices utilized by an author whereby literary signals or markers are placed into a developing textual meaning in order to activate meaning in the evoked text. While it is true that a reader may link "one or more elements in a given text with other independent and not identical elements in an evoked text," it is not the reader who alludes. Instead, authors allude. That the reader is able to recognize an allusion is another issue altogether.

Second, Ben-Porath rejects the notion of authorial intention, her definition does not account for the fact that the purpose of allusion is to convey meaning from the author to the reader.[25] In fact, none of the above definitions make this crucial point. Authors allude to convey meaning to the reader. Therefore, allusions have a rhetorical function. That the reader "links" (what Ben-Porath calls "actualizes" throughout her dissertation) one text to another could mean two things: that the reader has correctly identified and correctly interpreted the author's intended allusion or that the reader has falsely concluded that the author has intended an allusion.[26] If the second of these two is the case then the reader has not correctly understood the meaning that the author desired to convey but has in fact created meaning that the author did not intend to convey.

A few years later, Ben-Porat (now spelling her last name without the final h) defines *literary allusion* as follows:

> [A] device for the simultaneous activation of two texts. The activation is achieved through the manipulation of a special signal: a sign (simple or complex) in a given text characterized by an additional larger "referent." This referent is always an independent text. The simultaneous activation of the two texts

---

24. Ben-Porath, "Poetics of Allusion," iii.
25. Ben-Porath, "Poetics of Allusion," 29.
26. How one determines which of these is the case is the focus of Chapter 4.

thus connected results in the formation of intertextual patterns whose nature cannot be predetermined.[27]

Ben-Porat's definition is helpful for several reasons. First, she correctly defines literary allusion as a *device*. Second, she correctly notes that there are two texts involved: the alluding text (i.e., the text doing the alluding) and the alluded text (i.e., the text being alluded to). Third, she has correctly noted that there is a "special signal: a sign (simple or complex)." This study will call this "special signal" a "marker." Fourth, she correctly notes that the referent is an independent text. Fifth, her explanation of four stages of actualization that the reader experiences when recognizing an allusion is extremely helpful.

While this definition is a marked improvement over her previous one, it is still not without its problems. First, it must be clearly stated that a literary allusion is something that is the creation of the author, not the reader. Authors make allusions, readers "actualize" allusions (to use Ben-Porat's terminology). Second, the portion of her definition that reads, "thus connected results in the formation of intertextual patterns whose nature cannot be predetermined" needs to be clarified. There is a predetermined function for literary allusions. Specifically, literary allusions are made so that the textual meaning from the independent text being alluded to is imported into the alluding text. For this to occur, the textual meaning of the independent text must be stable. In addition, the manner in which this importation occurs is not as limitless as her definition would seem to indicate.[28]

William Irwin

At the end of his article "What Is an Allusion?," William Irwin provides the following definition:

> A reference that is indirect in the sense that it calls for associations that go beyond mere substitution of a referent. An author must intend this indirect reference, and it must be in principle possible that the intended audience could detect it. Allusions often draw on information not readily available to every member of a cultural and linguistic community, are typically but not necessarily brief, and may or may not be literary in nature. The indirect nature of the reference is a necessary but not a sufficient condition. In the same way, authorial intention and

27. Ben-Porat, "The Poetics of Literary Allusion," 107–8.

28. All of the points being made in this section will be clarified in detailed discussion below.

the possibility of detection in principle are necessary but not sufficient. Taken together as a whole, the indirect nature of the reference, the authorial intent, and the possibility of detection in principle amount to a sufficient condition for allusion.[29]

Several points need to be made in response to Irwin's definition. First, Irwin's point that the associations between the two texts call for more than mere substitution of a referent is important in that there is a contextual meaning in the alluded text that the author of the alluding text intends for the reader to both recognize and utilize for the importation of that meaning into the developing context of the alluding text. Second, Irwin correctly points out that an allusion is a device intended by the author. Third, for an allusion to fulfill its intended function, it must be detectable by the intended audience.

Merrill Tenney

Merrill Tenney offers the following definition of allusion: "An allusion consists of one or more words which by their peculiar character, and general content are traceable to a known body of text, but which do not constitute a complete reproduction of any part of it."[30] While some of the previous definitions make mention of some literary marker (i.e., signal, sign, marker, etc.), Tenney's definition is the first to state that the allusion is made up of unique words (i.e., they are of "peculiar character" with a "general content" that is "traceable to a known body of text"). Others will argue that these markers can also be thematic or structural in character. However, Tenney's definition lacks some of the necessary components mentioned above: authorial intention and rhetorical function being the two most prominent.

Michael B. Thompson

Michael B. Thompson explains that allusions contain three parts: "Allusion involves (1) the use of a sign or marker that (2) calls to the reader's mind another known text (3) for a specific purpose."[31] This explanation is succinct and covers several of the key issues in an allusion. However, this explanation is not without its problems. While Thompson's words make mention of the reader, they do not mention the author. That the reader's mind is called to

---

29. Irwin, "What Is an Allusion?," 293–94.
30. Tenney, *Interpreting Revelation*, 102.
31. Thompson, *Clothed in Christ*, 29.

another text is quite irrelevant if such a connection was not intended by the author. In this case, the author's intended meaning has been missed. Conversely, if the author intends an allusion yet the reader does not recognize it, the result is the same in that the author's intended meaning has been missed. Second, Thompson's words are quite general. The fact that authors allude for a specific purpose is a truism that will be explained in detail below. Additionally, the specific purpose for which authors allude is always the same. Authors allude to convey meaning.

Carmela Perri

Carmela Perri explains that an allusion "refers at least doubly: the sign of the allusion-marker refers within its text's world as well as allusively, to some referent outside this text."[32] While this is a true statement, it hardly serves as a definition for allusion. Therefore, while there have been several definitions of "allusion" offered, these definitions have been either incomplete, errant, or too generalized to provide a clear and detailed definition of allusion. In addition, any definition of allusion must also distinguish it from other forms of intertextuality such as citation, reference, quotation, influence, or echo.[33]

DEVELOPING A DEFINITION: THE NECESSARY CATEGORIES AND COMPONENTS

The preceding survey of definitions of allusion has been helpful in that it has successfully served two purposes. First, while each of these definitions was found lacking in some way, they were also useful in pointing out many of the necessary components of a good definition of allusion. Second, the

---

32. Perri, "On Alluding," 295.

33. It should be noted from the outset that there are two ways in which "intertextuality" is understood in today's scholarly communities. "Intertextuality" as it is used by Clayton and Rothstein (cf. Clayton and Rothstein, "Figures in the Corpus") is a synchronic approach which "encompasses manifold connections between a text being studied and other texts, or between a text being studied and commonplace phrases or figures from the linguistic or cultural systems in which the text exists.... The intertextual approach relies heavily on structural linguistics and its postmodern heirs in seeing all signs, including those in literary text, as signs" (Sommer, *A Prophet Reads Scripture*, 6). This understanding of intertextuality comes from the work of Derrida and is currently utilized by several contemporary scholars, most prominently Roland Barthes and Mikhail Bakhtin. The second way in which "intertextuality" is understood is as a diachronic study of how one text utilizes another text. It is this second understanding that will be in view when the term "intertextuality" is used throughout this work.

above definitions were predominately of allusion. However, the matter currently under consideration is not one of providing a definition for *allusion* in general, but *literary allusion* in particular. Therefore, the development of a definition for literary allusion must convey the point that literary allusions specifically relate to allusions made in literature to literature. Specifically, this reality raises the issue of intertextuality.

Developing a Category for Literary Allusion

Once one sets out to develop a definition for literary allusion, it quickly becomes apparent that there is a need for several other terms that are either related to or used synonymously with literary allusion to be defined as well. Moreover, a system of categorization needs to be spelled out so that the relationship of these terms (both similarities and differences) can be more clearly understood. In order to do this, a brief word needs to be said about the broad term "intertextuality."

Intertextuality

Intertextuality is a term that has been used very broadly to refer to many different phenomena that occur in and between texts. In the broadest sense, *intertextuality* refers to the various ways in which texts are interrelated. Unfortunately, this is where much of the confusion concerning the topic of intertextuality begins.

There are two very different approaches to the study of texts that have claimed the title "intertextuality," and rightly so, since both approaches study ways in which different texts relate to each other. However, this is where their similarities end. It is for this reason that more specific labels need to be given to each so that the two separate categories are no longer confused within the broader discussion of intertextuality. Therefore, for the purposes of this study, we will divide the topic of intertextuality into two subcategories, designating them *Intertextual Dependence* and *Intertextual Relation* (see Table 3.1 below).[34]

---

34. Sommer summarizes these two approaches clearly but titles them differently; cf. Sommer, *A Prophet Reads Scripture*, 6. Sommer names these two competing claimants to the title *intertextuality* as "intertextuality" and "influence and allusion." The problem with Sommer's designations is that both of these approaches rightly fall into the broad category of *intertextuality*. Therefore, in an effort to bring clarity to the current state of affairs, what will be argued below is that these two approaches should be understood and presented as subcategories of the broad topic of *intertextuality*.

Figure 3.1

Intertextuality

Intertextual Dependence
- Diachronically focused
- Concerned with dependence

Textual Dependence
- Concerned with the rhetorical appeal of a text to something contained in a previous text
- Contributes to meaning of developing text via appeal to previous text

Literary Reference
- Relates to providing the identity of a person, place, or thing in a previous text or that text itself.

Literary Citation
- Relates to the location of meaning in a previous text

Literary Quotation
- Relates to the word for word validation of meaning via a previous text

Literary Paraphrase
- Relates to the paraphrastic validation of meaning via a previous text

Literary Allusion
- Relates to the importation of meaning from a previous text

Text Dependence
- Concerned with logical dependence of the whole of one text upon the whole of a previous text
- Based on or builds upon a previous text

Intertextual Relation
- Synchronically and semiotically focused
- Concerned with interrelation, not dependence

Echo
- Terms or phrases originating in a text that have become colloquial in meaning and used in other texts.

Intertextual Relation

As explained above, the term "intertextuality" has been used to describe two distinctly different literary approaches to the study of texts.[35] The first to be considered here is designated in this study as *Intertextual Relation*. Sommer explains the intertextual literary approach well:

> Intertextuality (as Clayton and Rothstein use the word) encompasses manifold connections between a text being studied and other texts, or between a text being studied and commonplace phrases or figures from the linguistic or cultural systems in which the text exists. As Ziva Ben-Porat explains, these connections do not arise exclusively from an intentional signaled use of an earlier text, such as citation (which might be studied under the rubrics of influence or allusion). The connections may result from the way that expressions in a given text reflect linguistic, esthetic, cultural, or ideological contexts of the text at hand; other texts may share those contexts, and hence links among many texts may be noticed, whether the authors of the texts know each other or not.[36]

---

35. Sommer, *A Prophet Reads Scripture*, 6–10.
36. Sommer, *A Prophet Reads Scripture*, 7.

According to Jonathan Culler, the term *intertextuality* (or what is designated here as *Intertextual Relation*)

> becomes less a name for a work's relation to particular prior texts than a designation of its participation in the discursive space of a culture. . . . The study of intertextuality is thus not the investigation of sources and influences as traditionally conceived; it casts its net wider to include anonymous discursive practices, codes whose origins are lost, that make possible the signifying practices of later texts.[37]

In other words, as Sommer states, "intertextuality [i.e., *Intertextual Relation*], then, concerns itself with the relations among many texts; it is synchronic, reader-oriented, semiotic method."[38]

The need for the establishment of this category of consideration is relevant to the present study because the word most often used interchangeably with allusion is *echo*. However, it is in the category of intertextual relation that the discussion concerning literary *echo* needs to take place.

Jon Paulien distinguishes the difference between an *echo* and an allusion as follows:

> An "outright allusion" assumes the author's intention to point the reader to a previous work as a means of expanding the reader's horizons. The portion of the text alluded to can only be fully understood in light of its context within the original work. . . . An echo indicates that the author picked up an idea that can be found in previous literature, but was probably unaware of the original source. The idea was "in the air" of the environment in which the author lived. It was part of "the freely circulated legal tender of a period's mind," it was the "common domain."[39]

Note the consistency between Paulien's words here concerning *echo* ("the idea was 'in the air' of the environment in which the author lived. It was part of 'the freely circulated legal tender of a period's mind,' it was the 'common domain.'") and those of Sommer above discussing the type of intertextuality as defined by Clayton and Rothstein, what we have named *Intertextual Relation* ("Intertextuality . . . encompasses manifold connections between a text being studied and other texts, or between a text being studied and commonplace phrases or figures from the linguistic or cultural systems in which the text exists").

37. Culler, *The Pursuit of Signs*, 22.
38. Sommer, *A Prophet Reads Scripture*, 7.
39. Paulien, "Elusive Allusions," 39–40.

In *echo*, the term or phrase has become part of the common speech of the day. It has become idiomatic or colloquial—with a meaning that is able to stand for itself. In the same way for Ben-Porath, an *echo* "is an element that can be recognized as coming from another context, but whose interpretation does not require that it be traced back and linked with its original context so as to activate the latter."[40]

Much of the confusion concerning the definition of allusion comes from the mixing of these two terms. Take for example William Irwin's statements concerning whether or not an author can unintentionally allude to another text. Irwin argues, "clearly authors are not always conscious of their motivations for alluding or even that they are alluding. . . . What we really have is a situation in which the author intended an allusion but was nonetheless unaware that he or she was alluding. That is, we have an allusion unconsciously intended."[41] However, as will be seen below, conscious intention is a prerequisite of intention. Irwin tries to make his argument by citing E. D. Hirsch Jr. who "gives the example of an author who uses parallel sentence structure to emphasize similarity in thought, yet is unaware that he has done this. Upon having this pointed out to him, the author can legitimately claim to have intended it."[42]

Two things need to be said in response to Irwin's argumentation here. First, Irwin apparently misses the point that Hirsch is making as he distinguishes between subject matter and meaning.[43] Second, Irwin also seems to confuse allusion and echo. Irwin states, "in the same way, an author could, for example, allude to Milton by speaking of pandemonium, be unaware of this allusion, and yet, if it is drawn to his or her attention, legitimately claim to have intended it." However, the phenomenon to which Irwin is referring here is not *allusion*, but *echo* since in this case the author is not trying to summon the various connections between his work and Milton's capital of hell in *Paradise Lost* for the purpose of importing some meaning into his text. Instead, the word pandemonium (not capitalized) has become part of common day language meaning a *tumult, mayhem, chaos, bedlam* or *uproar*. Thus, this is a perfect example of an *echo*, not an *allusion*. Paulien explains this point well:

> To summarize, allusive references to previous literature can enter a work two ways. The author may use a source directly and consciously with its original context in mind. Such an allusion

---

40. Ben-Porath, "Poetics of Allusion," 84.
41. Irwin, "What Is an Allusion?," 291.
42. Irwin, "What Is an Allusion?," 291.
43. Hirsch, *Validity in Interpretation*, 20–21, 51–57, 221–23.

is "willed into being." The author is fully conscious of the source as well as of its relevance to his composition. He/she is assuming the reader's knowledge of the source and of his/her intention to refer to that source. On the other hand, an author may "echo" ideas, the origin of which he/she is unaware. In an echo, the author does not point the reader to a particular background source, but merely utilizes a "live symbol" that would be generally understood in his original situation.[44]

Therefore, *echo* is best defined as a term or phrase that has its source in a literary text that has over time become a colloquialism or figure of speech with a meaning that stands on its own with the effect that its mentioning is no longer intended to summon the literary context of the source text in order for contextual connections to be made. It is for this reason that *echo*, as well as all other figures of speech, rightly falls within the category of *Intertextual Relation*.

Intertextual Dependence

Sommer describes what we call *Intertextual Dependence* in a helpful way:

> Literary critics have long focused on the former approach [what is being designated in this study as *Intertextual Dependence*], asking how one composition evokes its antecedents, how one author is affected by another, and what sources a text utilizes. That approach is diachronic, because it distinguishes between the earlier text (the source or the influence) and the later one (the alluding text or the influenced). It focuses the attention on the author as well as on the text itself.[45]

Intertextual Dependence is different from *Intertextual Relation* in that *Intertextual Dependence* studies how a specific pre-existing text impacts a specific later text. Further, this relationship can take place in one of two ways. A text can presuppose the conclusions of a previous text. In this instance, a whole text is predicated on a preexisting text. This phenomenon will be titled *Text Dependence* in this study. However, a text can refer to (i.e., quote, cite, allude to, paraphrase the wording of, etc.) portions of a previous text in order to assist in some rhetorical function (i.e., validate an argument, illustrate a point, contribute meaning, etc.). This phenomenon will be titled

---

44. Paulien, "Elusive Allusions," 40.
45. Sommer, *A Prophet Reads Scripture*, 6–7.

Textual Dependence in this study. Therefore, *Intertextual Dependence* can occur in one of two ways: *Text Dependence* or *Textual Dependence*.

Text Dependence is when one text is logically dependent upon another pre-existing text for its conclusions and/or argumentation as they relate to theology, philosophy, conclusions, worldview, etc. In *Text Dependence*, the previous text functionally serves as the latter text's prerequisite. For example, the New Testament Epistles presume the death, burial, and resurrection of Jesus Christ as portrayed in the four Gospels. If there were no death, burial, and resurrection of Christ as spelled out in the Gospels, there would be no church age and no letters from the apostles to the various New Testament churches and believers. In this way then, the Epistles are dependent (i.e., have *Text Dependence*) upon the gospels. However, this does not *necessarily* mean that the epistles refer to something specifically contained in one of the four Gospels (i.e., contain *Textual Dependence* from the four Gospels).

Textual Dependence, on the other hand, is when the author of a literary work intentionally refers to a portion of a previous text. It is on this category of classification that the remainder of this present work will concentrate. Authors refer to previous works for several reasons. For example, authors quote an authoritative voice to lend credence to their argumentation. They cite other sources to provide additional documentation to their argumentation. In doing so, authors refer to a previous work to fulfill a specific rhetorical function in their text. What will be argued below is that literary allusions are no different. Authors allude for a rhetorical purpose. It is at this point in the study that a detailed definition of literary allusion needs to be provided and the components of its definition defended.

A Definition of Literary Allusion

While it would be reasonable to save the stating of the proposed definition of literary allusion until the end of this section, it seems better to state it at the beginning so that the reader can understand the logical progression of thought that was followed in the definition's construction throughout this section. The definition of literary allusion that will be defended below is as follows: *A literary allusion is a literary device utilized by an author whereby allusive textual markers are placed into the alluding text (i.e., developing textual meaning) in order to activate meaning in a prior alluded text (i.e., the stable textual meaning of a previous text) so that the rhetorical relationship between the two contexts can be determined and the meaning created by the allusion can then be imported into the author's developing textual meaning.* In order to substantiate this definition, each of the components of it will now be defended and explained.

Literary Allusions are Literary

All allusions, whether literary or not, are identical in their parts and function.[46] For this reason, M. H. Abrams is correct in stating that all allusions (whether literary or not) can refer to a "person, place or event, or to another literary work or passage,"[47] However, the focus of this study is on *literary* allusions and therefore our definition must be narrower than that of M. H. Abrams. Specifically, since our concentration is on literary allusions, our definition must make explicit the fact that literary allusions are bound at both ends of an allusion. That is to say, literary allusions are allusions made in one literary text (i.e., the alluding text) to another literary text (i.e., the alluded text). Therefore, since literary allusions are made in literary texts, several relevant issues need to be made explicit. The implication for our definition is that both texts must be explicitly mentioned. The definition being presented in this study does just that.

Literary Allusions Are Literary Devices

In addition to the fact that literary allusions are literary, the second point to be noted is that literary allusions are literary devices. As cited above, Ben-Porat states that a literary allusion is a "device for the simultaneous activation of two texts."[48] This statement raises an important point, namely, a literary allusion is a literary device.

Jay Braiman defines a literary device as follows:

> [A literary device] refers to specific aspects of literature, in the sense of its universal function as an art form which expresses ideas through language, which we can recognize, identify, interpret and/or analyze. Literary devices collectively comprise the art form's components; the means by which authors create meaning through language, and by which readers gain understanding of and appreciation for their works. They also provide a

---

46. The parts of a literary allusion will be the focus of Chapter 5 that deals with validity in the interpretation of a literary allusion. If one is going to argue that a literary allusion exists in a text, then one must also be able to explain each working part of the proposed allusion in order to validate one's claim.

47. Abrams, *A Glossary of Literary Terms*, 8.

48. Ben Porat, "The Poetics of Literary Allusion," 107–8.

conceptual framework for comparing individual literary works to others, both within and across genres. Both literary elements *and* literary techniques can rightly be called literary devices.[49]

In addition to a superb definition of literary device, Braiman also provides excellent definitions of literary elements and literary techniques. Literary elements are defined as follows:

> [P]articular identifiable characteristics of a *whole text*. They are not "used," per se, by authors; they represent the elements of storytelling which are common to all literary and narrative forms. For example, every story has a theme, every story has a setting, every story has a conflict, every story is written from a particular point-of-view, etc. In order to be discussed legitimately as part of a textual analysis, literary elements must be *specifically identified* for that particular text.[50]

Finally, Braiman offers the following definition of literary techniques:

> [A]ny specific, deliberate constructions or choices of language which an author uses to convey meaning in a particular way. An author's use of a literary technique usually occurs with a single word or phrase, or a particular group of words or phrases, at one single point in a text. Unlike literary elements, literary techniques are *not* necessarily present in *every* text; they represent deliberate, conscious choices by individual authors.[51]

If these definitions are followed, literary allusion is a literary device in the sense that it is a literary technique on par with any other literary techniques such as irony, metaphor, characterization, etc. utilized to convey meaning.

Literary Allusions Are Literary Devices Utilized by an Author

Thirdly, not only is a literary allusion a literary device, it is a literary device utilized *by the author*, not the reader. While this may on its surface sound obvious, in the current reader-response hermeneutical environment this point needs to be emphasized. Because literary allusions are made in literary texts, Irwin is correct in his assessment that "allusion is bound up with a vital and perennial topic in literary theory, the place of authorial intention

---

49. Braiman, "Literary Devices."
50. Braiman, "Literary Devices."
51. Braiman, "Literary Devices."

in interpretation, and in literature itself allusion has become an increasingly pivotal device."[52] Paul Noble states, "allusion entails authorship; and wide-ranging allusion entails wide-ranging authorship.[53]

Ever since the publication of W. K. Wimsatt and Monroe Beardsley's essay, "The Intentional Fallacy," in 1946, the notions of the author and authorial intention have been under direct assault.[54] As explained in the previous chapter, Stanley Fish has been among the most vocal in his rejection of the author as the determiner and controller of meaning. It is not surprising then that Ben-Porath, a student of Fish, follows in his footsteps in her definitions of allusion. Ben-Porath's definition of literary allusion specifically places the reader in the essential role of making (i.e., actualizing) an allusion:

> My insistence on including the reader in the definition may seem trivial at this point in view of the fact that I have already described his role and since everyone is ready to acknowledge that there must be a reader to detect an allusion. Yet, although the reader's role is implied in all the discussions of the "shared tradition," "recognition," and the "close poet-audience relationship," the reader is curiously absent from all the definitions. This exclusion of the reader betrays a belief in the notion of the independent existence of a literary text. Inclusion of the reader aims at emphasizing the approach which sees the text as a reservoir of potentialities and the reader as an active participant in the creation of the work, whose role is far more complex than a simple process of linguistic decoding of ordinary discourse.[55]

However, Ben-Porath's application of such argumentation is not only illogical (as argued in chapter 2), but contradictory to her own words as well.[56] Later in the same work Ben-Porath argues as follows:

> Yeats leads the reader to establish a very specific connection between Christ and Dionysus, and between Athena and Mary. Regardless of the typological tradition concerning Christ and Dionysus, and regardless of Yeats' more esoteric mystical beliefs

---

52. Irwin, "What Is an Allusion?," 287.
53. Noble, "Esau, Tamar, and Joseph," 247.
54. Wimsatt and Beardsley, "The Intentional Fallacy," 468–88.
55. Ben-Porath, "Poetics of Allusion," 29.
56. To hold that the text is a reservoir of meaning waiting to be created by the reader on the one hand, and yet to insist that something be included in her definition on the other, is contradictory. Her insistence here on a specific definition betrays her own words. Clearly she is desirous that *her* definition be utilized rather than have the reader create one from a reservoir of potential meanings.

and his cyclical concept of history, every reader can establish the exact pattern through an actualization of this allusion.[57]

Here Ben-Porath is not arguing that the reader gets to act as an "active participant in the creation of the work" out of a text that is a "reservoir of potentialities." Instead, Ben-Porath states "Yeats leads the reader to establish a very specific connection." In addition, she states, "allusion is obviously a way of directing the reader's attention, and the marked elements can represent 'an area of experience' which cannot for various reasons be directly described."[58] In fact, other than her repeated assertion that allusion is not something that an author does, her words repeatedly betray her:

> The fact that the pattern formed by linking the marker and the marked components in the evoked texts is an undetermined pattern does not mean that when marker and marked are linked the resulting pattern will differ significantly from reader to reader. On the contrary, once the link has been established, it will be possible for the reader to establish a recognizable pattern, and the types of patterns which may result from the linking could provide the means for the classification of allusions into different categories. However a definition which claims that the nature of the pattern cannot be predetermined rules out a list of closely related devices whose major *diferentia specifica* with regard to allusion is the fixed and predetermined nature of the pattern created between an element in the text and an element outside it.[59]

While Ben-Porath does not say this, the reason that different informed or ideal readers can and do identify undetermined patterns of allusion resulting in the same conclusions is because they are able to recognize and understand the author's intention via his use of literary elements and techniques (i.e., literary devices).

Again Ben-Porath states, "the decisive factor is not the mode of referring, but the fact that undesignated elements have to be activated by the reader and related to the given elements."[60] The main problem in Ben-Porath's thinking is her failure to acknowledge that the "undesignated elements" that she claims "have to be activated by the reader and related to the given elements" are the same elements that were first activated by the author

---

57. Ben-Porath, "Poetics of Allusion," 109.
58. Ben-Porath, "Poetics of Allusion," 116.
59. Ben-Porath, "Poetics of Allusion," 73.
60. Ben-Porath, "Poetics of Allusion," 30.

and then placed in the text via allusion so that they could be activated by the reader. Authors utilize literary devices—readers recognize them.

Note the underlined emphasis in our definition that highlight the author's role in literary allusions: *A literary allusion is a literary device <u>utilized by an author</u> whereby allusive textual markers are placed into the alluding text (i.e., developing textual meaning) in order to activate meaning in a prior alluded text (i.e., the stable textual meaning of a previous text) so that the rhetorical relationship between the two contexts can be determined and the meaning created by the allusion can then be imported into the author's developing textual meaning.*

Literary Allusions Utilize Textual Markers

The fourth component of our definition of literary allusion that must be explained is that literary allusions utilize allusive textual markers that serve to activate (i.e., make the connection to) the alluded text. This is the area within which most of the efforts concerning literary allusions have been focused. In fact, if there is any one aspect of literary allusion that has received at least some of the attention that it is due, it is the question of determining how one identifies the textual markers of an allusion. Invariably, the presence of textual markers in the alluding text is the focus of the topic. Chapter 4 will address this issue in more detail. Therefore, this brief section will serve only to introduce two points.

The first point is that textual markers are an integral part of how allusions function and therefore must be included in any adequate definition of literary allusion. Although most of the discussions in this area have focused around like terms, like themes, or like structures, there continues to be wide disagreement about the conclusions reached using these criteria and their helpfulness in identifying the presence of an allusion.

The fact that *something* in the alluding text points the reader to the alluded text is readily acknowledged. The problem is in identifying exactly what that *something* is. It is most commonly argued that these allusive textual markers come in the form of like terms, like themes, or like structures. However, like terms, like themes, or like structures without like contexts that are being connected for an identifiable rhetorical purpose are insufficient grounds for claiming the presence of an allusion. Ben-Porath explains this point well:

> The independent existence of the marked component and the activation of related elements prove once again to be the major features of allusion as a literary device and the essential criteria

for defining it. The role of the marker can be played by a single word, even by a single morpheme, but the marked component must be more than a single word since it must be independent not only as a linguistic unit, but must also be part of a specific context of its own, independent of the context of the marker.[61]

Further, Ben-Porath's statement is helpful because it correctly points out that the allusive textual markers occur in a "specific context." Therefore, any discussion concerning the identification of allusive textual markers must not only include a discussion on like terms, like themes, and like structures, but also like contexts.

The second point to be introduced here is that genre plays a key role in how literary allusions function. Narrative literature will allude differently than poetic literature, prophetic literature, or epistolary literature. In addition, narrative literature will allude differently to another narrative work than it will to a prophetic work. Therefore, one would expect allusions contained in a narrative which allude to a narrative to behave differently than allusions made from within epistolary literary to a poetic passage. Failure to recognize the complicating factors that genre plays for both the alluding text and the alluded text render the investigator of literary allusions incapable of accounting for the many nuanced variables at work within them.

In light of this discussion, another component of a good definition of literary allusion can be highlighted. *A literary allusion is a literary device utilized by an author whereby allusive textual markers are placed into the alluding text (i.e., developing textual meaning) in order to activate meaning in a prior alluded text (i.e., the stable textual meaning of a previous text) so that the rhetorical relationship between the two contexts can be determined and the meaning created by the allusion can then be imported into the author's developing textual meaning.*

The Alluding Context

The fifth component of a good definition of literary allusion is that literary allusions are based in a textual literary context. Unfortunately, this is a key component of literary allusions that has not been emphasized. It must always be remembered that the goal of the author of any text is to achieve an end, to convey something. In order to achieve his desired end, an author has available to him a plethora of literary genres, conventions, and devices. He implements these into his literary work in order to assist himself in the

---

61. Ben-Porath, "Poetics of Allusion," 47.

conveyance of his desired meaning. It is for this reason then that authors utilize literary allusions.

Literary allusions are placed in the author's developing context so that meaning made explicit in the text being alluded to can be implicitly imported into the author's developing text. Therefore, since allusions serve to add meaning to the text, it only stands to reason that the meaning being added would be contextually warranted. It should be noted that this is the first place in which interpreters can disagree, for a disagreement concerning the developing context of the alluding text could lead to a disagreement about the presence, absence, or nature of a literary allusion. Therefore, the validation of one's interpretation of the "alluding" text necessarily precedes the claim for the presence of an allusion.

A literary allusion is a literary device utilized by an author whereby allusive textual markers are placed into the alluding text (i.e., developing textual meaning) in order to activate meaning in a prior alluded text (i.e., the stable textual meaning of a previous text) so that the rhetorical relationship between the two contexts can be determined and the meaning created by the allusion can then be imported into the author's developing textual meaning.

Activation of a Prior Alluded Text

The sixth item that must be understood is that literary allusions allude to a prior stable meaning in context. Literary allusions "work" (i.e., fulfill their rhetorical function) when both the developing alluding textual meaning and the stable prior alluded textual meaning are understood so that the exact rhetorical relationship between them can be determined. Therefore, the interpreter must not only demonstrate his understanding of the alluding text, but he must understand the textual meaning of the prior text being alluded to as well. Therefore, not only can interpreters disagree about the developing textual meaning of the alluding text, they can also disagree about the stable literary textual meaning of the prior alluded text. Either of these disagreements will ultimately lead to a disagreement about the presence, absence, or nature of a literary allusion. Consequently, the validation of one's interpretations of both the alluding text and the text allegedly being alluded to necessarily precede the claim for the presence of an allusion.

THE TIME SIGNIFICANCE OF THE ALLUDED TEXT

One significant point concerning the alluded text that should be emphasized is that the text being alluded to must by necessity *precede in date of authorship* the text doing the alluding. As Irwin states, "we should . . . note that allusion moves in only one direction. If A alludes to B, then B does not allude to A. The Bible does not allude to Shakespeare, although Shakespeare may allude to the Bible."[62] The reason that this is true is that the prior text is unaware of the latter text. Therefore, the latter text is unavailable for the author of a prior text to allude to.

In this way the validation in the identification and interpretation of literary allusions can also be used as internal evidence for the dating of literary texts. For example, there is no rhetorical function for Genesis 19:1–29 (the story of the judgment of Sodom and Gomorrah) to allude to Judges 19:10–30 (the story of the wickedness of the men in Gibeah). Instead, there is a significant rhetorical function for Judges 19:10–30 to allude to Genesis 19:1–29 (this example will be illustrated in Chapter 6). Therefore, if one can adequately validate that a literary allusion is present, then an argument has also been made for the relative dating of the two texts involved in the literary allusion.

Stable Textual Meaning of the Alluded Text

Literary allusions do not operate by *changing*, *reinterpreting*, or *adding to* the textual meaning of the alluded text. Instead, literary allusions function by *importing* meaning from the stable literary meaning of the alluded text. To add to the words of Irwin, not only is it true that "if A alludes to B, then B does not allude to A," it is also true that if A alludes to B, A does not change B. Instead, A uses the stable meaning of B to make its point. Allusions only "work" if the meaning that is to be imported into the alluding text is stable and unchanging. If it is argued that the meaning of the alluded text is variable, indiscernible, or shifting, then the allusion fails to have any import in the development of the meaning of the alluding text. Ben-Porath makes this point well:

> [T]he independence of the marked component, an essential feature of the allusion as I define it, is a *contextual* independence. That is, in a literary allusion what is alluded to is not simply a word, but *a word in a context of its own*. Some elements of that context remain unmentioned in the alluding text, but various of these unmentioned elements will be activated in the process of actualizing the allusion.[63]

---

62. Irwin, "What Is an Allusion?," 289.
63. Ben-Porath, "Poetics of Allusion," 43.

Again she argues:

> [T]he independent existence of the marked component and the activation of related elements prove once again to be the major features of allusion as a literary device and the essential criteria for defining it. The role of the marker can be played by a single word, even by a single morpheme, but the marked component must be more than a single word since it must be independent not only as a linguistic unit, but must also be part of a specific context of its own, independent of the context of the marker.[64]

Utilization as a Type

Ben-Porath argues that the marked (i.e., the thing being alluded to) is often overlooked in favor of too much concentration on the marker:

> Definitions and descriptions of allusion which depart from the commonest aspect of the linguistic notion dwell at some length on the marker but tend to ignore the marked. This neglect may be the result of concentration on a limited number of rhetorical functions of allusion, the heightening and embellishment of style or the appealing to the reader's vanity by flattering his sense of being familiar with a cultural or literary tradition.[65]

This is particularly true in one aspect that must now be highlighted.

One issue of importance that may be implicit in this discussion but now must be made explicit is that the situatedness of the thing being alluded to in its own literary contextual meaning is what allows it *to function as a type* in that the thing being alluded to typifies all those that fit within a certain class, genre, or category (i.e., to carry a rhetorical function).[66] It is only after the allusion to the type and its context are recognized that its relation to the alluding context can be understood and evaluated.

A literary allusion is a literary device utilized by an author whereby allusive textual markers are placed into the alluding text (i.e., developing textual meaning) in order to activate meaning in a prior alluded text (i.e., the stable

---

64. Ben-Porath, "Poetics of Allusion," 47.
65. Ben-Porath, "Poetics of Allusion," 30.
66. For example, the Bible often alludes to "Babylon" or "Sodom and Gomorrah" as typological or representative of evil and rebellion against God. If one of these is alluded to, it always represents a certain "type" that has been contextually developed in the alluded text. At no time do Babylon or Sodom and Gomorrah become representative of anything other than what it is contextually in the alluded text.

textual meaning of a previous text) so that the rhetorical relationship between the two contexts can be determined and the meaning created by the allusion can then be imported into the author's developing textual meaning.

Rhetorical Relationship and Function

Now that it has been pointed out that the thing being alluded to is situated in a literary context expressing a stable meaning and is therefore able to function as a type, a seventh point for building a good definition of literary allusion can be stated.

Like all other forms of *Literary Reference* (e.g., citation, quotation, and paraphrase), literary allusions serve a rhetorical function. Concerning quotation, Stanley argues:

> [W]ith all the recent interest in hermeneutical questions, relatively little attention has been paid to the rhetorical significance of these appeals to Scripture. Certainly there are places in the literature where a Jewish or Christian author shows a concern to understand the biblical text for its own sake. In most cases, however, the ancient author quotes a passage from Scripture as part of a broader argument designed to convince others to believe or act in a certain way. This is a rhetorical act, and it should be investigated as such.[67]

Therefore, not only do authors quote for a reason—often to validate their view or argumentation, but authors allude for a reason as well. One of the first to make the point that allusions produce a desired effect was Giorgio Pasquali when he argues, "*Le reminiscenze possono essere inconsapevoli; le imitazioni, il poeta può desiderare che sfugano al pubblico; le allusioni non producono l'effecto voluto se no su un lettore che si ricordi chiaramente del testo cui si riferiscono.*"[68] When they do, two issues of importance need to be recognized: rhetorical relationship and rhetorical function.

---

67. Stanley, "The Rhetoric of Quotations," 44.

68. Pasquali, *Pagine stravananti*, 275. ("The poet may be unconscious of reminiscences [i.e., echoes], and he may wish that his imitations escape his public's notice; but allusions do not produce the desired effect if the reader does not clearly remember the text to which they refer.")

Rhetorical Relationship

Rhetorical Relationship refers to the interplay or relation between the two texts of a literary allusion. As the developing alluding textual meaning is being understood, alluding textual markers identified, the stable alluded meaning summoned, and the alluded type recognized, the relationship between the alluding context and the alluded context can then be determined.[69] However, according to Ben-Porath, these relationships cannot be *predetermined*. Instead, "whether it is complementary, constructive or ironic, the allusive pattern must be linked with other similar elements in the alluding text. The nature of the allusive pattern is accordingly then the function of the interaction of the two texts and can be determined only in retrospect."[70]

That the relationship between the alluding text and the alluded text can be determined only in retrospect does not mean, however, that the relationship between the two texts cannot be anticipated. In fact, once all the relational possibilities are considered, it becomes clear that they can be placed into one of five basic categories. These basic categories serve to describe the rhetorical relationship between the two contextual meanings: greater than, less than, equal to, not equal to, and like.[71]

Greater Than

One way that literary allusions function is to say that $A > B$.[72] For example, several Johannine passages allude to the Passover Lamb of the Old Testament for the rhetorical function of demonstrating Jesus' superiority to the Old Testament figure. For example, John 19 alludes to Exodus 12, presenting Jesus as being greater than the Passover Lamb of the Exodus.

Less Than

A second way that literary allusions function is to say that $A < B$. For example, Joshua is presented as taking Moses' place, but being a lesser Moses.

---

69. This process will be discussed in Chapter 4.
70. Ben-Porath, "Poetics of Allusion," 8.
71. It should be pointed out that while the individual examples provided in these categories may be rejected by an individual interpreter, the point here is only to establish these categories as representing the possible relationship between an alluding text and the text being alluded to.
72. In the following categorical examples, A = the allusion in the alluding text and B = the thing being alluded to in the alluded text.

For example, while Moses' sends out twelve spies, crosses the sea, and leads Israel in the institution of the Passover, Joshua sends out two spies, crosses the Jordan, and leads Israel in the observance of the Passover instituted by Moses. In this way, the text may be presenting Joshua as a "less than" replacement for Moses.

Equal To

A third way that literary allusions function is to say that A = B. Several passages in the Gospels present Jesus as the Greater Prophet of Deuteronomy 18 via literary allusion.[73] In addition, this type of relationship can take several forms. Sommer argues that allusions can function as a positive repredication, negative repredication, or fulfillment of earlier prophecies.[74]

Not Equal To

A fourth way that literary allusions function is to say that A ≠ B. Concerning this point, Ben-Porat states, "In allusion the basic meaning of the marker or of the marked can be independent of the interaction and can even be contradictory."[75] Sommer also explains this point and provides an example when he states, "words and images earlier prophets used in rebuking the people or predicting their doom often reappear in passages where Deutero-Isaiah comforts the exiled Judeans or announces their restoration. Thus Deutero-Isaiah consoles the people with language resembling that with which Isaiah or Jeremiah castigated them."[76]

Like

A fifth way that literary allusions function is to say that A ≈ B. Sommer identifies two different ways that literary allusion functions that would logically fit here: historical recontextualization and typological linkages.[77] In addition, Ben-Porat argues that literary allusions can function metaphorically: "A metaphorical allusion is then one in which the relationship between the marker and the marked or between the alluding text and the

---

73. For example, see Matt 5–7; John 6:1–14; 7:1–52.
74. Sommer, *A Prophet Reads Scripture*, 46–57, 78–92.
75. Ben-Porat, "Poetics of Literary Allusion," 99.
76. Sommer, *A Prophet Reads Scripture*, 36–37.
77. Sommer, *A Prophet Reads Scripture*, 52–54, 60–65.

text to which allusion is made approaches that of tenor and vehicle."[78] She further states, "allusion is similar to metaphor or simile insofar as two fields of reference are brought together and some interaction takes place. It is particularly close to metaphor in that 'a word may be simultaneously both literal and metaphorical, . . . support several metaphors (and) may serve to focus into one meaning different meanings.'"[79] An example of a literary allusion functioning in this manner is the allusion in Judges 19 to Genesis 19. In this literary allusion, the wickedness of Jebus is similar to that of Sodom and Gomorrah.

Conclusion

These five relationships explain the different possible rhetorical relationships that literary allusions create between the alluding text and the alluded text.[80] This point serves to highlight another part of our definition. *A literary allusion is a literary device utilized by an author whereby allusive textual markers are placed into the alluding text (i.e., developing textual meaning) in order to activate meaning in a prior alluded text (i.e., the stable textual meaning of a previous text) so that the rhetorical relationship between the two contexts can be determined and the meaning created by the allusion can then be imported into the author's developing textual meaning.*

Rhetorical Function

While Rhetorical Relation refers to the interplay or relation between the two texts of a literary allusion, Rhetorical Function refers to the meaning that is to be imported into the alluding text via the literary allusion. This entails recognizing that literary markers are placed in the developing meaning of alluding text for the purpose of summoning the related meaning of the alluded text (i.e., relevance theory) so that a rhetorical relationship can be realized. Therefore, these literary markers form a relevance bridge back from the alluding text to the alluded text. At this point, the rhetorical relationship between the two contexts must be evaluated (i.e., $A > B$, $A < B$, $A = B$, $A \neq B$, or $A \approx B$). Once this relationship is discerned, the rhetorical function of the connection (i.e., the meaning of the allusion) can be imported

---

78. Ben-Porat, "Poetics of Literary Allusion," 101.

79. Ben-Porat, "Poetics of Literary Allusion," 95.

80. Also see, Kao and Mei, "Meaning, Metaphor, and Allusion in T'ang Poetry," 328–30. While they do not provide any categories, they do suggest that allusions function in relation to equivalence.

into the alluding text with the result that the author's textual meaning is further developed, magnified and intensified via the literary allusion in an economic, but powerful way. As Ben-Porat explains, "allusion is always a means of obtaining economy of expression and condensation of the texture. Sometimes the allusion defines, explains, or enhances a statement made in the alluding text. Sometimes it may be used to counteract, call into doubt, or provide an ironic perspective. Some allusions clarify the alluding text, others add to its evocative power."[81] Ross echoes Ben-Porat's point concerning the enhancement of meaning that allusions produce when she says, "a work which alludes to another establishes a richer context with which to be viewed. It benefits from a new and enlarged web of associations, and our appreciation and understanding of the work are enhanced."[82]

Finally, it should be repeated that a literary allusion functions only one way. The alluding text does not say something about the alluded text. Instead, the alluding text points to the alluded text for the purpose of saying something about itself. Ross makes this point by explaining, "Lord Chesterfield ... did not allude to the Book of Joshua in order to say something about Joshua, but to say something about the three European kings."[83]

At this point the final phrase in the definition of a literary allusion can now be understood and the process of developing a definition for literary allusion can be finalized. *A literary allusion is a literary device utilized by an author whereby allusive textual markers are placed into the alluding text (i.e., developing textual meaning) in order to activate meaning in a prior alluded text (i.e., the stable textual meaning of a previous text) so that the rhetorical relationship between the two contexts can be determined and the meaning created by the allusion can then be imported into the author's developing textual meaning.*

DEFINING THE TERMS OF LITERARY REFERENCE

Now that a working definition of literary allusion has been provided, the terms most often associated with allusion can be defined and differentiated as well. Ben-Porat is correct in her analysis:

> Allusion has been associated with a variety of words and terms. The verbs "allude," "hint," "echo," and "refer" are often used interchangeably by literary critics, as are the adjectives "suggestive,"

---

81. Ben-Porat, "Poetics of Literary Allusion," 142.
82. Ross, "Art and Allusion," 59.
83. Ross, "Art and Allusion," 66.

> "evocative," and "allusive." The practice of using these words synonymously is usually motivated by an effort to avoid the excessive and monotonous repetition of the same term, rather than by a desire to direct the reader's attention to a particular phenomenon, allusion in this case.[84]

Therefore, it is often the case that many terms are used synonymously in an effort to avoid repetition. However, there is also an element of confusion that persists in the use of these terms. Ben-Porat explains:

> The literary forms most commonly associated with allusion are those which are in some way derivative or imitative, as well as those in which one element stands for another one outside the text, either because of a conventionalized relationship or because of a concept or immanent identity. However, the relationship of allusion to those other forms remains in most cases undefined, unclear, or simply misunderstood.[85]

The result in both of these cases is an imprecise use of terms that has led to a lack of clarity and a general state of confusion. However, now that precise categorization and definition of literary allusion has been provided, literary allusions can now be distinguished from other forms of *Textual Dependence* such as literary reference, literary citation, literary quotation, and literary paraphrase as well as from other forms of *Intertextual Relation* that may be misunderstood as literary allusion, such as echo.

Literary Reference

Within the broad category that has been designated in this study as *Textual Dependence* there needs to be a definition provided for a *Literary Reference*. A *Literary Reference* is simply when an author of a text points to or mentions a person, place, thing, or event that exists in another text.

In her doctoral dissertation, Ziva Ben-Porat explains the five steps that a reader goes through in the actualization of a literary allusion.[86] She explains that the key difference between a literary allusion and a literary

---

84. Ben-Porat, "Poetics of Literary Allusion," 78.
85. Ben-Porat, "Poetics of Literary Allusion," 104.
86. Ben-Porat, "Poetics of Literary Allusion," 10. There are five stages of the actualization of a literary allusion by a reader for Ben-Porat: (1) recognition of the marker; (2) identification of the source; (3) realization of the marked component: activation of its relevant contextual elements; (4) linking of the marker and the marked components, followed by the linking of relevant elements from their respective contexts; (5) fitting the new pattern or patterns into the alluding text.

reference is "if the process of actualizing the allusion yields no significant additional components, it can be treated as a reference."[87] This is the third step in her actualization process. Further, her excellent example serves to make the point:

> [A] poet may mention the Mona Lisa, her mysterious smile and her deep gaze. If nothing more is needed for the full interpretation of the poem, it is a reference which draws on the reader's cultural heritage, one which delights him with the sense of recognition, and which evokes memories of Italy, the Renaissance, Paris, beautiful women, and which may symbolize the epitome of a culture to be worshipped or destroyed. But such a mention is not an allusion in the sense in which we are using the term. It does not activate unstated elements of the painting. The Mona Lisa of our hypothetical poem and the Mona Lisa of the painting are identical.[88]

In explaining her example, Ben-Porat adds clarity to her statement and illustration by stating:

> If the process of actualization ends with identification, then the author is merely making a reference. If the actualization carries the reader beyond mere identification to a consideration of related but unmentioned material, the reference is in fact an allusion. The nature of the directional marker is different in allusion and in reference. In a reference it seems to say straightforwardly or obliquely, "This is me," or "This is where I come from." In an allusion the marker is telling the reader, "This is where you have to go to look for more material about me, material which will make my appearance in this new context more meaningful."[89]

Literary Reference is when an author makes a straightforward identifying mention of a person, place, or thing existing in another text with no intent for further connections to be drawn between the text doing the referring and the thing being referred to.

Literary Citation

In Jon Paulien's view, "citations occur when an author reproduces the words of an original text and identifies the source from which he drew those

---

87. Ben-Porat, "Poetics of Literary Allusion," 81.
88. Ben-Porat, "Poetics of Literary Allusion," 81.
89. Ben-Porat, "Poetics of Literary Allusion," 82.

words."[90] However, it appears that two distinct issues are present in his definition: (1) word for word reproduction and (2) the identification of the source from which the word for word reproduction came. The first point in Paulien's definition is best regarded as a literary quotation while the second point is best regarded as a literary citation. Therefore, a *Literary Citation* is a direct literary marker by which the author directly points the reader to the referenced text.

Literary Quotation

According to Paulien, "Quotations involve the selection of significant amounts of wording from a previous passage, sufficient to make it certain that the author had the previous work in mind."[91] However, a "selection of significant amounts of wording" is too vague for two reasons. First, "significant amounts of wording" leaves open the question, how many words constitute "significant?" Second, a quotation is word for word, *ipsissima verba*, and can consist of one word or many. The point is not the number of words being quoted, but the exactness of them. Therefore, Literary Quotation is when an author of one text intentionally reproduces the exact words of another text. Often a *Literary Quotation* is introduced by a *Literary Citation*.

Literary Paraphrase

The difference between a Literary Quotation and a Literary Paraphrase is the same as the difference between *ipsissima verba* (i.e., the very words) and *ipsissima vox* (i.e., the very voice). Therefore, a Literary Paraphrase is when an author of one text intentionally reproduces the same meaning of the words of another text. As with *Literary Quotation*, *Literary Paraphrase* is often introduced by *Literary Citation*.

Literary Allusion

A literary allusion is a literary device utilized by an author whereby allusive textual markers are placed into the alluding text (i.e., developing literary context) in order to activate meaning in a prior alluded text (i.e., the stable meaning of a previous text) for the rhetorical function of importing that

---

90. Paulien, "Elusive Allusions," 39.
91. Paulien, "Elusive Allusions," 39.

meaning into the alluding text in order to assist in the development of the author of the alluding text's intended meaning.

CONCLUSION

Jon Paulien correctly points out, "Commentators need to demonstrate more awareness of the distinction between allusions and echoes. Much misinterpretation occurs when echoes are treated as allusions and vice versa."[92] However, the problem is that no adequate categories and definitions have been developed for these terms. The goal of this chapter was to do just that.

---

92. Paulien, "Criteria and Assessment of Allusions," 128.

4

How Do We Identify an Allusion?

IN THE PREVIOUS CHAPTER adequate categories and definitions were sought for *Literary Allusion* as well as related terms. In this chapter the all-important question of how one identifies a literary allusion will be evaluated.

Up to this point, efforts to identify literary allusions in a text have centered on the identification of the textual markers of literary allusions. However, these efforts have been unsuccessful in producing consistent results. The first issue to be addressed in this chapter will be to summarize the many criteria that scholars have suggested for identifying the textual markers of literary allusions.

The second issue to be addressed in this chapter is directly related to the first. Since little success has been achieved developing criteria by which the textual markers of literary allusions can be identified, an environment has been created wherein scholars have been unable to validate their claims that a literary allusion is in fact present in a text. In response to this situation, several have created a scale of probability within which they can communicate their level of certainty concerning the presence of the allusion (e.g., "certain allusion," "possible allusion," "doubtful allusion," etc.). Unfortunately, this has not helped the situation. Instead, it has only served to give scholars more grounds for disagreement. What one scholar sees as a "probable allusion," another often classifies as "doubtful." In order to help clarify this situation, a brief summarization and evaluation of the several systems of categorization that have been derived is necessary.

The presence of these first two issues by necessity raises a third: obviously something, or some things, have been missed. In the final section of this chapter, two missing ingredients in the discussion of literary allusion will be added. The first is the potential impact of Sperber and Wilson's relevance theory in the identification of a literary allusion. This will begin to explain why the criteria set forth by scholars have failed to produce the desired objective results. The second missing ingredient that will be added into the discussion of literary allusion is that of genre.

CURRENT PROPOSALS AND PROBLEMS

With all of the attention on how later biblical texts utilize earlier ones (particularly with regard to the use of the Old Testament in the New Testament), the question of how one identifies a literary allusion has become an issue of recent attention and importance.[1] The history of trying to develop criteria by which intertextual influence can be identified is relatively short. In biblical studies, Paulien explains that this endeavor began with the study of the Book of Revelation:

> Although scholars had previously addressed the issue of OT use in Revelation, the earliest attempts to address the issue of criteria for selection appear to be the works of Haugg and Tenney. But these attempts were quite rudimentary. Beginning with Trudinger's 1963 dissertation, a number of researchers began to turn more seriously to the issue of method and criteria. While Trudinger's dissertation was actually on the OT text behind the allusions in Revelation, he needed to establish effective criteria in order to select the OT passages that would be the basis for his textual research. . . . He also mentions parallel criteria such as comparing the contexts of passages being examined, seeing how many words they have in common and exploring how often the OT book or chapter is used elsewhere in Revelation.[2]

---

1. There are several more recent works that have focused on intertextuality and allusion. However, their approaches are diverse and almost never explicitly stated. Instead, most seem to assume that some sort of intertextuality or allusion is present in the texts that they are considering. Some of the more helpful recent works are Oropeza and Moyise, *Exploring Intertextuality*; Zevit, *Subtle Citation, Allusion, and Translation*; Dell and Kynes, *Reading Job Intertextually*; Boda, *The Book of Zechariah*; Allen and Smith, *Methodology in the Use of the Old Testament in the New*.

2. Paulien, "Criteria and Assessment of Allusions," 116. Also see Haugg, *Die zwei Zeugen*; Tenney, *Interpreting Revelation*; Trudinger, "The Text of the Old Testament in the Book of Revelation."

Since these initial efforts, several scholars have undertaken the task of enumerating criteria by which literary allusions can be identified. Unfortunately, these efforts have produced less than impressive results. Jon Paulien gives an example of the continuing disagreement and confusion as he explains the findings of his study:

> [I]n the course of my dissertation research in the mid-1980s I examined ten major commentaries and critical margins produced over the last 100 years to determine what OT passages they felt were being alluded to in the seven trumpets of Revelation (Rev. 8:7–9:21; 11:15–18). I then placed the results in a matrix, which revealed serious irregularities in judgment among the ten sources.
>
> Among the ten scholars a total of 244 different potential allusions to the Old Testament in the seven trumpets are offered. Yet a count of individual scholars yielded a range of 29 to 121. That means that even the researcher with the most extensive list of allusions, Eugene Huhn, mentioned only 50% of the total . . . Meanwhile, in spite of the 244 allusions listed by all ten, they agree completely on only one![3]

Paulien concludes his study by stating, "There needs to be a greater consensus on the criteria for assessing potential allusions and a more consistent use of such criteria."[4] While there has not yet been any agreement among scholars on which criteria should be used, several have indeed proposed specific criteria by which they believe literary allusions can be identified. The most prominent of these will now be summarized and evaluated.

Jon Paulien

Jon Paulien has been one of the most influential scholars in developing criteria by which literary allusions can be identified. He proposes three basic criteria for identifying *Literary Allusions*: verbal parallels, thematic parallels, and structural parallels.[5]

---

3. Paulien, "Criteria and Assessment," 117–18.
4. Paulien, "Criteria and Assessment," 128.
5. Paulien, "Elusive Allusions," 40–43. Also see Paulien, *Decoding Revelation's Trumpets*, 179–90.

Verbal Parallels

Paulien's first criterion for identifying a *Literary Allusion* is verbal parallels:

> We define verbal parallel as occurring whenever at least two words of more than minor significance (articles and minor conjunctions are excluded) are parallel between a passage in Revelation and a passage in the Septuagint or other first-century Greek version. These two major words may be coupled together in a phrase or may even be separated, provided they are in clear relationship to each other in both passages of the suggested parallel. Verbal parallels are discovered by placing the text of Revelation side-by-side with the potential source text. Wording that is exact or similar is underscored, and the potential relationship between the passages is assessed on a preliminary basis.[6]

However, several issues come to mind in response to Paulien's explanation. First, how does one determine *when* one has encountered "at least two words of more than minor significance"? Can this be done preemptively? Or, can this determination only be made in retrospect?

Second, who determines whether or not words are of "more than minor significance"? Are we to understand that "words of more than minor significance" are the same as "major words"? In other words, exactly how unique (i.e., surpassing minor significance) must a word be? On one end of the uniqueness spectrum there are words that are only used a handful of times in the Bible. However, just because two passages may contain two of these words in no way guarantees that a literary allusion is intended. Conversely, at the other end of the spectrum (if *only* articles and minor conjunctions are excluded), there are "words of more than minor significance" found throughout the Bible and common to almost every passage. If several of these words are present in two texts, it is also no guarantee that an allusion is intended. In both of these hypothetical cases then, other factors could account for the presence of "two or more words of more than minor significance." For example, both of the texts under consideration could be echoing wording from another text. Or, the occurrence of these same words may simply be coincidence.

Third, is there an unstated rule that the definite article or minor conjunctions should always be considered of minor significance? After all, many have defended their interpretation of Scripture by arguing that *kai* in Gal 6:16 should be translated "even" rather than "and." Additionally, there has been much debate over the function of the definite article preceding

---

6. Paulien, *Decoding Revelation's Trumpets*, 179–80.

הָעַלְמָה in Isa 7:14. Certainly it would be unwise then to prescriptively assign all definite articles and conjunctions to the category of "minor significance." In other words, is it not *possible* that the definite article and minor conjunctions could be utilized to contribute to a literary allusion? Certainly in such a case the interpreter must give an explanation as to why he believes that the definite article or minor conjunctions are helping to signify a literary allusion. Even so, it seems conceivable that these could be used by an author to assist in the signaling of a literary allusion.

Fourth, how does one go about determining whether or not the two or more words are in "clear relationship" to one another? In fact, why is this even a necessity? Authors commonly link more than one aspect of an alluding text to the alluded text. This is particularly true when one narrative alludes to another narrative via the reoccurrence of the same events.[7] That does not mean however, that the words being connected are in "clear relationship" with one another. Instead, they can be spread throughout the alluding text. When this occurs, the cumulative effect of the textual markers may serve to signify the literary allusion being made. Further, just because two texts may have two or more of the same "major words" that appear in some related form does not demand that a literary allusion is present.

Fifth, are literary allusions really discovered by placing two texts "side-by-side" so that exact or similar wording can be underscored, and the potential relationship between the passages assessed on a preliminary basis? If this were what was necessary to find an allusion, then how would one ever complete such an endeavor? Must a New Testament passage be compared in a side-by-side manner with every Old Testament book as well as every other pre-existing New Testament book? What about the practically infinite number of extra-biblical literary works? Certainly this seems to be overstated.

Sixth, what exactly is the procedure for assessing potential relationships between the passages on a preliminary basis? This needs to be spelled out. In addition, is there something that comes after such a preliminary evaluation? If so, what?

All would agree that literary allusions often utilize verbal parallels to signify their presence in a text. However, it must also be acknowledged that verbal parallels *alone* are insufficient grounds for arguing for the presence of a literary allusion.

---

7. In fact, this is exactly the case when Judges 19 alludes to Genesis 19. This example will be illustrated in detail in chapter 6.

Thematic Parallels

Paulien's second basic criterion for identifying a *Literary Allusion* is thematic parallels:

> Many times the Revelator clearly has an Old Testament passage in mind, but uses different Greek words than the LXX, or uses only a single word to make the connection. This should not be surprising. By their very nature, allusions are not bound to reproduce the precise wording of the original. Allusions to the Old Testament may be characterized by similarity of thought and theme as well as wording. Such single-word parallels are to be distinguished from "stock apocalyptic" in that they have "direct contextual moorings in particular texts" of previous literature. The "contextual mooring" of a thematic parallel between Revelation and previous literature may express itself through deliberate contrast as well as similarity of theme. Such thematic parallels can be found not only in the LXX, but also by comparing the intent of the Greek of Revelation with the Hebrew and Aramaic Old Testament.[8]

Again, Paulien's explanation brings to mind several questions. First, how does one know that an author "clearly has an Old Testament passage in mind"? It seems that this is the source of much of the disagreement among scholars. In Paulien's own study this was demonstrated to be the case.

Second, while thematic parallels can be criteria for identifying the textual markers that signify an allusion, Stephanie Ross rightly argues, "shared sadness cannot establish to which of countless literary works a given canvas alludes."[9] While Ross' words are directed toward a painting's allusion to a literary work, her point applies for literary texts as well. In other words, thematic parallels alone are not grounds enough to claim that an allusion is present. Think of all the different themes that are present in the Bible: sin, deliverance, atonement, holiness, judgment, etc. It is not simply enough to demonstrate that two texts have the same themes. Therefore, just because two passages contain the same theme does not necessarily mean that one is alluding to the other. Ross makes this point explicit when she states: "Beardsley was right to insist that attributions of allusion must appeal to intrinsic features of the poem, painting, sonata in question. Yet reliance on intrinsic features alone will result in the following situation: any

---

8. Paulien, *Decoding Revelation's Trumpets*, 182–83.
9. Ross, "Art and Allusion," 68.

two works which share a subject matter, or structure, or tone, etc., will be said to be linked by allusion."[10]

Third, more needs to be said about "direct contextual moorings in particular texts." As will be explained below, the contextual relation between two texts is paramount in identifying a literary allusion. Admittedly, thematic parallels are *often* present with a *Literary Allusion*. However, contextual relation is one of the necessary prerequisites for a *Literary Allusion* to be present. That is to say, there is a difference between thematic parallel and contextual relation. Thematic parallel conveys the notion that the themes are the same. However, is it not possible to allude to a context with the opposite theme in order to make some ironic point?

Structural Parallels

Paulien's third basic criterion for identifying a *Literary Allusion* is structural parallels:

> Many times the Seer of Revelation uses the Old Testament by lifting whole sections and following them in general, even though exact wording may not be followed. This sort of parallel is characterized either by a similarity in the ordering of material or by an overall similarity in content. Such structural dependence could perhaps be called "apocalyptic midrash," in that an author builds at length on a previous apocalyptic passage. By the very feature of multiple parallels, these are the most certain to have been in the mind of the writer when he wrote down his visions.[11]

The main problem with this criterion for identifying a literary allusion is that just because two passages have the same content does not mean that an allusion is taking place. For example, Robert Alter has said a lot about "type scenes" in the Bible.[12] However, must we conclude that *every* text that contains a man, a well, and a woman must be an allusion to the "type scene" that Alter describes? In addition, how does one apply this criterion when a common structural convention is followed (i.e., lament psalm)? In such a case, one psalm would appear to allude to another since it follows the same structural order. However, this would be an incorrect conclusion since both may simply be following a certain common form. Ross explains why

---

10. Ross, "Art and Allusion," 62.
11. Paulien, *Decoding Revelation's Trumpets*, 184–85.
12. Alter, *The Art of Biblical Narrative*, 47–62.

this would be problematic for the identification of a literary allusion since "when one art work alludes to another . . . it is not a case of some predicate or concept referring to the two of them. Rather, one of the works refers to the other. Thus allusion involves reference *between* two works of art."[13]

As with verbal parallels and thematic parallels, structural parallels can be a way that an author signals a literary allusion. However, as with verbal parallels and thematic parallels, just because a structural parallel is present does not mean that an allusion is taking place.

Richard B. Hays

Richard B. Hays proposes seven tests for hearing echoes (i.e., what this study has defined as literary allusions): availability, volume, recurrence, thematic coherence, historical plausibility, history of interpretation, and satisfaction.[14]

Availability

The first of Hays' tests for hearing literary allusions concerns the dating of the two texts under consideration: "Was the proposed source of the echo available to the author and/or original readers?"[15] In other words, did the text that is supposedly being alluded to exist at the time of the writing of the alluding text? Certainly this test has some place in the discussion. However, because of all the disagreement concerning the dating of texts in Old Testament scholarship, such an approach is obviously limited in its value as a test.[16] However, if one were to reasonably demonstrate that one text alluded to another, then the case for the pre-existence of the alluded text would be dramatically strengthened.

Volume

Hays' second test is the volume of the echo (i.e., literary allusion):

13. Ross, "Art and Allusion," 63.

14. Hays, *Echoes of Scripture in the Letters of Paul*, 29–32. Hays continues and applies his approach to the gospels in Hays, *Echoes of Scripture in the Gospels*.

15. Hays, *Echoes of Scripture in the Letters of Paul*, 29.

16. If one has already concluded that the date of authorship of a text is late (e.g., the conclusions for the dating of the Pentateuch by those who hold to some form of the Documentary Hypothesis), then that text could not have been alluded to by a text that predated it.

> The volume of an echo is determined primarily by the degree of explicit repetition of words or syntactical patterns, but other factors may also be relevant: how distinctive or prominent is the precursor text within Scripture, and how much rhetorical stress does the echo receive in Paul's discourse? For example, 2 Cor. 4:6 should be understood as an allusion to Gen. 1:3–5, even though it echoes explicitly only the two words light and darkness. Here the source is the distinctive and memorable Genesis creation account, and Paul has placed the echo at the rhetorical climax of a unit in his letter.[17]

The first question that must be asked is why the "degree of explicit repetition of words or syntactical patterns" determines the "volume of an echo"? Must something be said repeatedly to be heard? In fact, it is often the case that key words or syntactical patterns are not explicitly repeated in literary allusions.

Second, who determines the level of distinctiveness or prominence of the precursor text in Scripture? Is there an unspoken rule that only those passages that have been referred to before are fair game to be alluded to? If this were the case, then no biblical author could allude to a passage for the first time.[18]

Third, the rhetorical stress of a potential literary allusion is directly related to one's contextual understanding of the two texts involved in the literary allusion. The extent to which two interpreters agree on the interpretation of the two contexts will go a long way toward determining whether they agree on the volume of the rhetorical stress.

Finally, must a literary allusion be loud to be heard? In other words, literary allusions either are or they are not! The author either alluded to a previous text to make a rhetorical point or he did not. The degree of volume that an interpreter claims is there does not prove that the literary allusion exists. Moreover, just because an interpreter does not hear the volume of an allusion hardly means that the literary allusion does not exist. Not all literary allusions are of the same "volume." Further, all interpreters do not hear all literary allusions. To borrow from an age-old hypothetical, if a literary allusion is in a text and no one hears it, is it still a literary allusion?

---

17. Hays, *Echoes of Scripture in the Letters of Paul*, 30.

18. Hays himself (*Echoes of Scripture in the Letters of Paul*, 21–24) violates this test in seeing (correctly) that Paul is alluding to Job 13:16 (LXX) in Phil 1:19. This Job passage hardly meets Hays' "volume" test as stated.

Recurrence

Hays' third test is that of recurrence: "How often does Paul elsewhere cite or allude to the same scriptural passage? This applies not only to specific words that are cited more than once, such as Hab 2:4, but also larger portions of Scripture to which Paul repeatedly refers, such as Deuteronomy 30–32 or Isaiah 50–54."[19]

Again, the same objection that is raised to the test of volume is raised here. Just because a text has been alluded to in another biblical passage does not necessarily raise the probability that it will be alluded to again. Conversely, just because a biblical passage has not been alluded to does not mean that it cannot be alluded to.

Thematic Coherence

Hays' fourth test is that of thematic coherence: "How well does the alleged echo fit into the line of argumentation that Paul is developing? Is its meaning effect consonant with other quotations in the same letter or elsewhere in the Pauline corpus? Do the images and ideas of the proposed precursor text illuminate Paul's argument?"[20]

It seems that several of Hays' seven tests are very similar. For example, "availability" and "historical plausibility" seem to be closely related; "volume" and "recurrence" seem to be closely related; and "thematic coherence" and "satisfaction" seem to be closely related. Of all Hays' tests, this one seems to be the best in validating the view that a literary allusion is present in a text. However, this point needs to be explained in greater detail than Hays provides. Therefore, this issue will be taken up in more detail in Chapter 5.

Historical Plausibility

Hays' fifth test is historical plausibility:

> Could Paul have intended the alleged meaning effect? Could his readers have understood it? (We should always bear in mind, of course, that Paul might have written things that were not readily intelligible to his actual readers.) This test, historical in character, necessarily requires hypothetical constructs of what might have been intended and grasped by particular first-century

---

19. Hays, *Echoes of Scripture in the Letters of Paul*, 30.
20. Hays, *Echoes of Scripture in the Letters of Paul*, 30.

> figures. . . . One implication of this criterion is to give serious preference to interpretive proposals that allow Paul to remain a Jew. However odd and controversial a reader of Scripture he may have been, he was a Jewish reader determined to show that his readings could hold a respectable place within the discourse of Israel's faith.[21]

The obvious first question in response to Hays' argumentation is who gets to determine whether or not Paul could "have intended the alleged meaning effect?" If one argues that an author could not have intended a meaning then it seems likely that one is engaging in circular reasoning (i.e., the author could not have said X, therefore he did not say X).

The second obvious objection Hays' answers himself: is it not clear that even Peter found some of Paul's writings difficult to understand?[22] Obviously the original readers' alleged ability to understand a literary allusion is hardly an argument that one is not present.

The third objection to Hays' argumentation also involves a certain circularity of reasoning. If the interpreter must construct hypothetical scenarios by which the author's intention and the first-century readers ability to understand are imposed on the text, then the present-day interpreter is not deriving contextual meaning from the text but is instead imposing textual limitations on it. (i.e., author A could not have intended X and audience B could not have understood Y, therefore X and Y cannot be present in the text).[23]

History of Interpretation

Hays' sixth test is the history of interpretation:

> Have other readers, both critical and pre-critical, heard the same echoes? The readings of our predecessors can both check and stimulate our perception of scriptural echoes in Paul. While this test is a possible restraint against arbitrariness, it is also one of the least reliable guides for interpretation, because Gentile Christian readers at a very early date lost Paul's sense of urgency about relating the gospel to God's dealings with Israel and,

---

21. Hays, *Echoes of Scripture in the Letters of Paul*, 30–31.

22. See 2 Pet 3:15–16.

23. This approach is commonly practiced. However, it can hardly be called a hermeneutical approach. In fact, if a certain meaning is ruled out as a possibility before the reading of a text, then no reading of the text is necessary to rule out said possibility. Instead, the possibility of its existence is destroyed by preemptive strike.

slightly later, began reading Paul's letters within the interpretive matrix of the New Testament Canon.[24]

What is most interesting here is that it seems that after Hays states this category, he immediately marginalizes it. While Hays' objections to his own test are certainly warranted, another point can be added to the discussion. The history of interpretation can also reveal shifts and changes in the critical approaches to biblical texts. Certain reading strategies can produce or eliminate the possibility of literary allusions. This point will be expanded upon on in the next chapter.

Satisfaction

Hays' seventh text is that of satisfaction:

> With or without clear confirmation from the other criteria listed here, does the proposed reading make sense? Does it illuminate the surrounding discourse? Does it produce for the reader a satisfying account of the effect of the intertextual relation? This criterion is difficult to articulate precisely without falling into the affective fallacy, but it is finally the most important test: it is in fact another way of asking whether the proposed reading offers a good account of the experience of a contemporary community of competent readers.[25]

It is difficult to see how the test of "satisfaction" differs dramatically from that of "thematic coherence." Certainly it is a must that the proposed allusion contributes to the developing contextual meaning of the alluding text. And, as will be argued in the next chapter, the validity of the interpretation of a literary allusion rests on its ability to satisfactorily account for all of the working parts of an allusion. However, one objection to Hays' words here must be raised, namely, "the experience of a contemporary community of competent readers" is wholly irrelevant in determining whether or not a proposed literary allusion can be validated. After all, who gets to make the final determination as to whether or not a contemporary community is made up of competent readers? Is an interpretation of a literary allusion to be accepted simply on the grounds that it satisfies a contemporary community of feminist readers, Calvinist readers, or Greek Orthodox readers? Instead, the question must be asked, does the rhetorical function of the

---

24. Hays, *Echoes of Scripture in the Letters of Paul*, 31.
25. Hays, *Echoes of Scripture in the Letters of Paul*, 31–32.

proposed literary allusion satisfactorily assist in developing the meaning of the alluding text.

Gregory K. Beale

Gregory Beale suggests that there are four determining factors or criteria upon which the identification of an allusion can be made:

> [T]he mere tracing of common themes or even of supposed isolated "allusions" cannot be sufficient to show probable dependence. But a definite and demonstrable connection between two documents can be shown when the following elements are found together: similarities of (1) theme, (2) content, (3) specific construction of words, and (4) structure. In addition, (5) a reasonable or persuasive explanation of the authorial motive should be given.[26]

In a later article, Beale argues that solecisms can also be used in the Book of Revelation as a criterion by which Old Testament allusions can be identified.[27]

As argued above, Beale agrees that none of the individual criteria provides any guarantees that a literary allusion is present in a text. However, what Beale argues instead is that the "cumulative force" of these criteria acts as a "safeguard against the danger of entering into 'parallelomania.'"[28] Unfortunately, after Paulien evaluated Beale's work on literary allusions in the Book of Revelation, he reports that Beale found more allusions than almost any other commentator that Paulien evaluated.[29] Paulien's evaluation of Beale's work at least serves to raise the question as to whether the "cumulative force" of these criteria actually can deliver one from "parallelomania."

While Beale's "cumulative force" for now must remain unresolved, he adds to this present discussion that a "persuasive explanation of the authorial motive should be given." In other words, an interpreter must validate his claim that a literary allusion is present in the text. What Beale does not provide is any guidance as to what such an explanation should include. Chapter 5 will directly address this specific issue.

---

26. Beale, *The Use of Daniel*, 308.

27. Beale, "Solecisms in the Apocalypse as Signals for the Presence of Old Testament Allusions," 421–46.

28. Beale, *The Use of Daniel*, 309.

29. Paulien, "Criteria and Assessment," 123–25.

Benjamin Sommer

For his part, Benjamin Sommer does not begin his discussion of literary allusions by setting out criteria by which he will operate in his study. For this reason, his approach must be pieced together by his comments throughout his work. One indication of Sommer's approach is found when he states:

> I shall argue that in certain passages Deutero-Isaiah draws words, images, and ideas from Jeremiah. At the beginning, such an argument must be tentative. The analysis of more and more examples will allow me to note typical thematic transformations and stylistic adaptations that will help isolate genuine allusions in Deutero-Isaiah, as opposed to texts where Deutero-Isaiah and Jeremiah resemble each other for some other reason.[30]

Vocabulary

In his discussion concerning how words can indicate a literary allusion, Sommer states:

> Several texts may use the same vocabulary not because a later author depends on an earlier one but because they utilize a common tradition, or because they are discussing a topic that naturally suggests certain vocabulary. This problem becomes acute in a highly traditional literature such as the Bible. Stock prophetic, legal, or poetic vocabulary or common use of some familiar trope or type-scene may lead two texts to look similar whether or not one author knew the other.[31]

In addition, Sommer explains that biblical texts can appear to be dependent upon non-biblical texts when in fact they are both drawing "on common ancient Near Eastern traditions."[32] In this case, what is at work is not allusion, but a form of *Intertextual Relation* that we have designated as *echo*.[33] Sommer continues by explaining that when this occurs, "we cannot regard these words and motifs as markers of allusion unless more definite markers are present."[34]

---

30. Sommer, *A Prophet Reads Scripture*, 35.
31. Sommer, *A Prophet Reads Scripture*, 32.
32. Sommer, *A Prophet Reads Scripture*, 33.
33. *Intertextual Relation* was explained in Chapter 3, pp. 71–74.
34. Sommer, *A Prophet Reads Scripture*, 33–34.

Stylistic Features

Sommer goes on to explain that stylistic features can signify the presence of a literary allusion:

> Sound play, word play, and especially the split-up pattern are common enough and distinctive enough to serve as a sort of stylistic signature of Deutero-Isaiah, a flag that points to the presence of an allusion or echo. (These features, which are so common in Isaiah 35 and 40–66, are at best rare in cases of inner-biblical allusion and exegesis culled from other books or even from other parts of the Book of Isaiah, such as chapters 24–27, which often refer to earlier biblical material.) Furthermore, the presence of these techniques makes it less likely that a similarity between Deutero-Isaiah and an older text results from their common use of a literary topos. It is true that two authors may use the same words because both are relying on stock vocabulary or discussing a particular topic, but a cluster or topic does not require a particular order for those words. Thus identical order almost certainly results from borrowing. Indeed, the later author's decision to mimic the order of the marked items may constitute an attempt to signal the borrowing in a particularly clear fashion.[35]

Later, Sommer explains each of these stylistic features. For Sommer, "the split-up pattern" is when an author "splits up a phrase from his source into two parts which are separated by several words or even verses."[36] Additionally, "sound play" occurs when an author "delights in alluding to words from his source not only by repeating them but by hinting at them through the use of similar-sounding words. In these cases, the markers and the marked are not identical vocabulary, but the link between them remains palpable."[37] Further, "word play" is when an author "employs a word borrowed from his source in a sense different from that found in the source."[38] Finally, "word order" is when an author "repeats vocabulary in the order of its appearance in the source."[39]

---

35. Sommer, *A Prophet Reads Scripture*, 71.
36. Sommer, *A Prophet Reads Scripture*, 68.
37. Sommer, *A Prophet Reads Scripture*, 69.
38. Sommer, *A Prophet Reads Scripture*, 70.
39. Sommer, *A Prophet Reads Scripture*, 70–71.

M. B. Thompson

It seemed reasonable to save Michael B. Thompson for the last since he is apparently the most eclectic. In *Clothed with Christ: The Example and Teaching of Jesus in Romans 12.1–15.13*, Thompson enumerates eleven criteria for identifying a literary allusion as follows:

Verbal Agreement

For Thompson:

> Aside from the presence of an explicit formula, the clearest sign of possible allusion is shared vocabulary. Obviously the greater number of significant shared words in G (Gospel) and E (Epistle), and the greater their rarity in E and other Epistles by the same author, the higher the probability that there exists some kind of shared tradition. On the other hand, if the saying is a commonplace or the author has chosen the only appropriate way to express the idea, the significance of the parallel diminishes.[40]

Thompson continues with the following directives: (1) How many words are shared in common? Are they identical or cognates? (2) How significant are the shared words? (3) Is there a unique combination of significant words? (4) Are possible translation variants present? (5) How can significant differences in vocabulary be explained, if dependence on a common source is accepted?[41]

Conceptual Agreement

The second criterion that Thompson explains is conceptual agreement: "Sayings in G and E can exhibit extensive verbal agreement and yet not have different meanings and origins; conceptual agreement is also a prerequisite, although it would be possible for an author deliberately to use the same language in a different sense (i.e., an antithetical or contrastive allusion)."[42]

---

40. Thompson, *Clothed in Christ*, 31.
41. Thompson, *Clothed in Christ*, 31–32.
42. Thompson, *Clothed in Christ*, 31–32.

Formal Agreement

Thirdly, Thompson asks, "to what extent are G and E parallel in form (i.e., structure, number of elements)?"[43] In other words, is there any formal agreement?

Place of the Gospel Saying in the Tradition

The fourth criterion that Thompson presents is similar to Hays' "Historical Plausibility." For this criterion Thompson asks the question, "was the logion available?"[44] For Thompson this question can be answered by asking further questions like: "Is its authenticity likely?," "Is there multiple attestation?," and "Is it relevant to the community?"[45]

Common Motivation, Rationale

Thompson's fifth criterion relates the literary allusion to ethical passages: "In the case of ethical material is there a similar rationale given or implied for correct behaviour?"[46]

Dissimilarity to Graeco-Roman and Jewish Traditions

Sixth, Thompson asks if something other than a pre-existing biblical text is being alluded to. In other words, "to what extent are sayings in G and E unparalleled outside Christian texts? Is there a more immediate and relevant parallel from another source? Is Paul more likely to know and use this source than the Jesus tradition?"[47]

Presence of Dominical Indicators

Thompson's seventh criterion is framed with regard to New Testament studies: "Is there some sign in the context that the author of E is thinking about Jesus and would therefore be inclined consciously to allude to, or

---

43. Thompson, *Clothed in Christ*, 31–32.
44. Thompson, *Clothed in Christ*, 33.
45. Thompson, *Clothed in Christ*, 33.
46. Thompson, *Clothed in Christ*, 33.
47. Thompson, *Clothed in Christ*, 33.

unconsciously to echo, his teaching?"[48] However, this same principle could be adapted to apply to other passages. For example, "is there some sign in the context that the author of (an Old Testament passage) is thinking about (the Law of Moses) and would therefore be inclined consciously to allude to, or unconsciously to echo, his teaching?" This line of argumentation is similar to that of Hays' "Thematic Coherence."

Presence of Tradition Indicators

Thompson's eighth criterion is that of the presence of traditional indicators: "There are a variety of different types of signs that an author may be using traditional material, although again no one sign in itself proves the case; it may simply reflect the author's own compositional style."[49] Among these potential indicators Thompson lists "grammar," "style," "traditional formulation," "use of tradition words in context," and "interruption of flow of context."[50]

Presence of Other Dominical Echoes or Word/Concept Clusters in the Immediate Context

Thompson's ninth criterion asks, "Are significant words from other dominical logia echoed in the context? Is there evidence of conflation of material from two or more dominical sayings? Is there evidence of serial quotation of dominical sayings?"[51] In other words, there seems to be a belief that the probability of a literary allusion is higher if other literary allusions appear alongside the potential allusion. However, that a potential allusion is surrounded by other literary allusions proves little. Instead, each potential literary allusion must be identified and evaluated on its own merits.

Likelihood the Author Knew the Saying

The tenth criterion that Thompson presents is highly questionable and guilty of circular reasoning as he readily admits. Thompson asks, "Does the author of E exhibit interest in/knowledge of Jesus tradition elsewhere? Obviously in the absence of clear citations this criterion is circular, presupposing for

48. Thompson, *Clothed in Christ*, 34.
49. Thompson, *Clothed in Christ*, 34.
50. Thompson, *Clothed in Christ*, 34–35.
51. Thompson, *Clothed in Christ*, 35.

some texts that which it seeks to prove in others. Does the author of E exhibit knowledge of a block material (found in G) of which the logion is a part?"[52]

Exegetical Value

Finally, Thompson's eleventh criterion is similar to Hays' "Thematic Coherence" and "Satisfaction." Thompson asks, "How does the saying function in the argument of E? How is the understanding of the thought of the passage and the historical situation enhanced by identifying the saying as dominical?"[53]

Summary of Criteria by Which to Identify a Literary Allusion

As was just explained, a plethora of criteria has been suggested as ways to identify literary allusions. From this discussion several points can now be made. First, there is a significant overlap among these scholars concerning the criteria by which literary allusions can be identified. In fact, it seems doubtful that few if any of the criteria raised by any one of these scholars would be rejected by the others. Their only likely responses would be to point out that (1) many of them are redundant and therefore the categories could be refined, or (2) some of the above are not criteria for identifying literary allusions as much as they are qualifications for the possibility of a literary allusion existing in a text.[54] Is the correct response to this situation to follow Hays or Thompson by becoming eclectic? Is not the outcome of such a response the production of a never-ending list of potential criteria for identifying allusions?

Unfortunately, for all of the general agreement concerning the criteria by which literary allusions can be identified, none of these criteria, either individually or utilized in tandem, has been able to produce agreement among scholars. Is the correct response then to follow Jauhiainen in rejecting the whole pursuit of objective criteria by which literary allusions can be

---

52. Thompson, *Clothed in Christ*, 35.

53. Thompson, *Clothed in Christ*, 35–36. Certainly this is not an exhaustive list. For example, Jeffrey Leonard also provides a list of criteria (see Leonard, "Identifying Inner-Biblical Allusions"). However, his work largely rehearses the criteria of those before him. Therefore, those chosen above are the scholars most often cited in regard to criteria by which literary allusion can be identified.

54. Hays' categories of "availability" and "historical plausibility" would be examples of this.

identified?[55] Should we not simply stop believing the myth that objective interpretation is possible and accept the inevitable slide into abject subjectivity that is dependent only upon the whimsical intuition of the individual interpreter?

The fact that those reading the previous two paragraphs have understood that a line in the proverbial sand has been drawn and a choice must be made effectively serves to eliminate the second option. For, if the previous two paragraphs can be understood, then objective interpretation is possible. Meaning can be conveyed in a text. And, if meaning can be conveyed in a text, then that meaning is conveyed through the conventions of language and literature. And, if allusions are a convention of language and literature, then they too can be used in the conveyance of meaning. Further, experience and intuition are persuasive factors in our belief that literary allusions exist, are understandable, and are recognizable.

Unfortunately, for all of the hermeneutical optimism of the last paragraph, the reality remains that there are currently no effective criteria by which literary allusions can be identified. In response to this dilemma, scholars have been individually developing systems of categorization whereby they can communicate their personal opinions concerning the probability that a literary allusion is present in a text.

CURRENT APPROACHES TO CLASSIFICATION

Because there have been no objective results concerning the presence of literary allusions in texts, literary scholars have created what is the effective equivalent of the Jesus Seminar's bead system of probability.

G. K. Beale

Beale classifies allusions into three categories: clear allusions, probable allusions, and possible allusions:

> Degrees of dependence will be designated according to the following three categories: (1) *clear allusion*—word order which is almost in the same form as the O.T. text and usually has the same general meaning, although this latter element may be absent; (2) *probable allusion* (with more varied wording)—(a) wording which is not as close to that of the O.T. text but still having links with it, and (b) the presence of an idea uniquely

---

55. Jauhiainen, *The Use of Zechariah in Revelation*, 33–34, especially n103.

> traceable to that text (sometimes only (b) may be present). (3) *possible allusion or echo*—parallel in wording or thought, but of a more general nature than in the other categories. The validity of the reference in each of the categories is enhanced if they can be seen to be part of the thought structure of the particular O.T. *context* from which they have been derived.[56]

The problems with these three categories as explained are myriad and can only be discussed here in brief. For example, how is it possible that a text can contain "word order that is almost the same" as another text with meaning that is different, yet still be considered a "clear allusion"? Second, if a "clear allusion" to a text does not have to have the same general meaning as the text being alluded to, is any relation required? If so what is it? Further, what "links" are required for an allusion to be considered "probable"? Further, if only an idea (i.e., theme) is traceable from an alleged alluding text to the text supposedly being alluded to then no "probable allusion" could be ruled out so long as there is a thematic similarity. Such a relation seems to fail to attain a level of "probable." Finally, it seems that if any relation at all can be surmised, then the potential allusion should be categorized as a "possible allusion." Unfortunately, such a categorization scheme seems useless.

In addition to these three criteria, Beale later adds addendums:

> First, when a suggested reference to a particular O.T. text is perceived in isolation from its own context in an apocalyptic work, its association with that of the O.T. text must be held in question. But when its own context is considered, its degree of probability as an O.T. reference increases *if* that context in which it appears has a structure which is found in that of the broader O.T. context from which it is suggested that it comes. Second, along similar lines, if the same kind of reference appears among a cluster of other *clearer* allusions to the O.T. context in question, then the degree of probability also increases. In this regard, even a cluster of only *subtle* O.T. references or echoes assumes more probability if the majority are traceable to the same O.T. context, although this is dependent on the number of references involved and the uniqueness of their conceptual association with the particular O.T. context.[57]

These two additional statements by Beale are much more helpful that his three levels of probability. However, Beale is not the only one who has developed a scheme of categorization containing levels of probability.

---

56. Beale, *The Use of Daniel*, 43n62.
57. Beale, *The Use of Daniel*, 306–7.

Jan Fekkes

Like Beale, Fekkes classifies allusions into three categories: "certain/virtually certain," "probable/possible," or "unlikely, doubtful."[58]

Jon Paulien

Paulien classifies allusions into five categories: "certain allusions," "probable allusions," "possible allusions," "uncertain allusions," and "nonallusions."[59]

M. B. Thompson

Thompson classifies allusions into six categories: "virtually certain," "highly probable," "probable," "possible," "doubtful," and "incredible."[60]

Marko Jauhiainen

For his part, Jauhiainen decides against any hierarchical system of categorization of the probability of an allusion. Instead, he settles for a simpler approach. "Thus, in essence, something either is or is not an allusion, or else it is difficult to decide. Attempts to chart the shades of grey in the 'undecided' zone are admirable, but would ultimately seem to increase subjectivity rather than objectivity."[61]

Evaluation of the Levels of Certainty

The result of this newly created approach to the probability of a literary allusion in a text is easily foreseen. Paulien argues that "much confusion could be avoided by the consistent adoption of terminology such as 'probable allusion', 'possible allusion' and 'echo'. This would provide readers with a clear and consistent picture of the commentator's judgments on this issue."[62] However, Paulien's own work reveals a much larger problem, for even if everyone were to agree on these three categories, it is clear that they would

---

58. Fekkes, *Isaiah and Prophetic Traditions*, 14–15.
59. Paulien, *Decoding Revelation's Trumpets*, 193.
60. Thompson, *Clothed in Christ*, 36.
61. Jauhiainen, *The Use of Zechariah in Revelation*, 35.
62. Paulien, "Criteria and Assessment," 127.

not agree on where potential allusions should be categorized. As stated above then is that the equivalent of the Jesus Seminar's bead system has been created. While one scholar may drop a red bead into the box signifying a "clear allusion," the next may drop a black bead into the box signifying a "nonallusion" or "echo." The problem with this however is that authors do not *potentially* allude. *Authors either allude or they do not allude.* Instead, the term *potentially* refers only to the interpreter's certainty that an allusion is present in a text.

In summary then, for all of the discussion concerning criteria for identifying the markers of a literary allusion and categories for describing the level of certainty of the interpreter, there is still little if any agreement on the identification and validation of a literary allusion. Therefore, it seems clear that something, or better, some things are missing from the discussion concerning the identification and validation of literary allusions.

UNADDRESSED ISSUES

To summarize the discussion up to this point, it has been argued that the author alone determines the meaning of a text. The reader's part then is not one of creating meaning, but recreating or discovering the intended meaning of the author. Further, it has been argued that literary allusions are a common and important literary device utilized by authors to convey their intended meaning. It was then explained that, while interpreters readily acknowledge the frequent presence of literary allusions in texts, little progress has been made in the development of objective criteria by which literary allusions can be identified. The main focus of these efforts up to this point has been on identifying the textual markers of literary allusions. Unfortunately, these efforts have failed.

What will be argued below is that three significant topics have gone unrecognized in the discussion over literary allusions. Two of them deal directly with the question of how one identifies a literary allusion and will therefore take up the remainder of this chapter. The third topic helps to address the question of how one validates a claim that a literary allusion is present in a text and will therefore be the focal point of Chapter 5.

The Impact of Relevance Theory on Literary Allusion

The first issue that has seemingly been overlooked in the discussion of literary allusions is the question of how an interpreter's intuitive senses are heightened so as to suspect the presence of a literary allusion. In part, the failure in the development of criteria whereby literary allusions can be identified is due to a lack of adequate attention to the process whereby a text being alluded to is activated in the mind of an author. Dan Sperber and Deidre Wilson's Relevance Theory may provide some helpful insights into this issue.

Explaining Relevance Theory

For Sperber and Wilson there are two extent conditions to relevance: "*Extent condition 1*: an assumption is relevant in a context to the extent that its contextual effects in this context are large. *Extent condition 2*: an assumption is relevant in a context to the extent that the effort required to process it in this context is small."[63]

For the present discussion *Extent condition 1* can be restated as follows: *a distant text is relevant in an author's context to the extent that the distant text's contextual effects are large.* The point here is that when an author is trying to make a certain point, he has at his disposal all of the shared knowledge between him and his audience at his disposal. If the same or related point (i.e., equal to, greater than, less than, similar to, or not equal to) is made in another context of shared knowledge, then the author can utilize it in the conveyance of his intended meaning. In other words, the greater the contextual impact that another text can have on the developing context of an author's text, the greater the benefit the author can receive by utilizing it.

In addition, *Extent condition 2* can be restated as follows: *a distant text is relevant in an author's context to the extent that the effort required to process the distant text is small.* Sperber and Wilson's second point stands in a directly converse relationship to their first. In short, if the effort required to process the potential impact of a distant text is great then relevance of it becomes lessened.

To summarize these two points with regard to the present discussion then, if the contextual effect of a literary allusion is great and the effort necessary to access the contextual effect are small, then an author is more likely to utilize an allusion. This assumes of course that it is the desire of the author to convey his intended meaning as efficiently and effectively as possible given the contextual confines of the genre within which he is writing. Sperber and Wilson explain this point in their discussion dealing with the topic of metaphor:

---

63. Sperber and Wilson, *Relevance*, 125.

> [S]uppose I have a complex thought P which makes manifest to me a set of assumptions I, and I want to communicate I to you. Now suppose that the following conditions are met: P is too complex to be represented literally, but the assumptions in I are all straightforwardly derivable as logical or contextual implications of an easily expressed assumption Q. The problem is that Q is not a thought of mine; it has some logical and contextual implications which I do not accept as true and which I do not want to communicate. What should I do? Given the principle of relevance, as long as you have some way of sorting the implications of Q into those I do and those I do not want to endorse, the best way of communicating I may well be to express the single assumption Q and leave the sorting to you.
>
> In these circumstances, the utterance which expresses Q is an interpretative expression of my complex thought P: they share logical properties, more specifically logical and contextual implications. Moreover, the criterion of consistency with the principle of relevance provides a means of distinguishing those contextual implications which are shared from those which are not; that is, it gives you a way of constructing the right interpretive assumption about my informative intention.
>
> We are assuming that all the hearer can take for granted is that an utterance is intended as an interpretation of one of the speaker's thoughts. This does not mean that whenever an assumption is expressed, the hearer has to compute all its logical and contextual implications and sort through them one by one to find out which subset of them are implications of the speaker's thought. In the framework we are proposing, this wasteful manoeuvre is quite unnecessary. If the speaker has done her job correctly, all the hearer has to do is start computing, in order of accessibility, those implications which might be relevant to him, and continue to add them to the overall interpretation of the utterance until it is relevant enough to be consistent with the principle of relevance. At this point, the sorting will have been accomplished as a by-product of the search for relevance, and will require no specific effort of its own.[64]

In other words, when trying to convey a thought P within an author's context, he will allude to another passage if it helps him "make his point," not because it uses the same words, has the same themes, or shares the same structure. Our focus then on identifying literary allusions cannot be, in fact

---

64. Sperber and Wilson, *Relevance*, 233–34.

must not be, on the appearance of like words, themes, or structures, but on the textual meaning of the author. As Sperber and Wilson explain:

> Our claim is that all human beings automatically aim at the most efficient information processing possible. This is so whether they are conscious of it or not; in fact, the very diverse and shifting conscious interests of individuals result from the pursuit of this permanent aim in changing conditions. In other words, an individual's particular cognitive goal at a given moment is always an instance of a more general goal: maximizing the relevance of the information processed.[65]

In other words, it is the author's responsibility to provide material of maximum relevance so that a desired cognitive goal can be achieved. If this claim of Sperber and Wilson is accepted, then the interpreter must assume a context within which the information provided by the author is of maximum relevance. However, a failure to match the appropriate context with the material that the author provides will ultimately lead to a failure in the cognitive goal. Sperber and Wilson explain this point by stating, "A speaker who intends an utterance to be interpreted in a particular way must also expect the hearer to be able to supply a context which allows that interpretation to be recovered. A mismatch between the context envisaged by the speaker and the one actually used by the hearer may result in a misunderstanding."[66] However, this statement raises three issues.

First, a failure in understanding is either a failure in the author's ability to convey the most relevant material or it is a failure in the reader's ability to recognize the appropriate context within which the material provided is of maximum relevance. It is possible that an author could be so poor as to fail in providing the most relevant material to his intended reader necessary for reaching the cognitive goal. More commonly, however, the conveyance of the cognitive goal fails because of the reader's failure to recognize the appropriate context within which the material given by the author is of maximum relevance.

Second, the issue of context must be addressed. According to Sperber and Wilson:

> The set of premises used in interpreting an utterance . . . constitutes what is generally known as the context. A context is a psychological construct, a subset of the hearer's assumptions about the world. It is these assumptions, of course, rather than

---

65. Sperber and Wilson, *Relevance*, 49.
66. Sperber and Wilson, *Relevance*, 16.

> the actual state of the world, that affect the interpretation of an utterance. A context in this sense is not limited to information about the immediate physical environment or the immediately preceding utterances: expectations about the future, scientific hypotheses or religious beliefs, anecdotal memories, general cultural assumptions, beliefs about the mental state of the speaker, may all play a role in interpretation.[67]

Therefore, the potential contextual settings are more numerous when dealing with an initial utterance. However, when additional utterances are added, the contextual possibilities begin to narrow so long as the added utterance is relevant to the hearer's context. If they do not begin to narrow, then the hearer must seek a new context within which the utterances can be understood.

Third, the issue of relevance must be addressed. According to Sperber and Wilson, "an assumption is relevant in a context if and only if it has some contextual effect in that context."[68] Conversely, if an assumption has no contextual effect on a context, it is regarded as irrelevant. Sperber and Wilson explain:

> There are ... three types of case in which an assumption may lack contextual effects, and be irrelevant, in a context.... (1) the assumption may contribute new information, but this information does not connect up with any information present in the context.... (2) the assumption is already present in the context and its strength is unaffected by the newly presented information; this newly presented information is therefore entirely uninformative and, a fortiori, irrelevant.... (3) the assumption is inconsistent with the context and is too weak to upset it; processing the assumption thus leaves the context unchanged.[69]

This does not mean however, that the information must be literal to be relevant. Instead, a statement is relevant if it shares some of the logical properties with the cognitive goal. Sperber and Wilson explain:

> [F]or the time being we are concerned only with resemblances of a very restricted type: logical resemblances among propositional forms (where two propositional forms resemble each other if and only if they share logical properties). We will show that the identification of these resemblances, like every other aspect of comprehension, is governed by the principle of relevance. Let

---

67. Sperber and Wilson, *Relevance*, 15.
68. Sperber and Wilson, *Relevance*, 122.
69. Sperber and Wilson, *Relevance*, 121.

us say that an utterance, in its role as an interpretive expression of a speaker's thought, is strictly literal if it has the same propositional form as that thought. To say that an utterance is less than strictly literal is to say that its propositional form shares some, but not all, of its logical properties with the propositional form of thought it is being used to interpret. From the standpoint of relevance theory, there is no reason to think that the optimally relevant interpretive expression of a thought is always the most literal one. The speaker is presumed to aim at optimal relevance, not at literal truth. The optimal interpretive expression of a thought should give the hearer information about that thought which is relevant enough to be worth processing, and should require as little processing effort as possible. There are many quite ordinary situations where a literal utterance is not optimally relevant: for example, where the effort needed to process it is not offset by the gain in information conveyed. There are many situations where a speaker aiming at optimal relevance should not give a literal interpretation of her thought, and where the hearer should not treat her utterance as literal.[70]

Applying Relevance Theory to Literary Allusions

The importance of Sperber and Wilson's theory of relevance for the present discussion should be readily apparent at this point.[71] As an author begins to write for the purpose of conveying his intended meaning (i.e., cognitive goal), each additional statement is given because it is of maximum relevance in conveying his intended meaning. In doing so, the author is effectively developing and refining his meaning.

Liken this process to a sculptor who begins with a lump of clay. With each impression of his fingers and each movement of his hands, he moves closer to his intended finished product. In sculpting the artist has at his disposal certain tools to assist him in the creation of his desired sculpture. Likewise, the artist also has at his disposal certain literary devices to assist him in the conveyance of his intended meaning. One of these is literary allusion. An author chooses an allusion to something in another text because its contextual effects in his developing context are large. The point that he wishes to make in his developing context has a meaningful relationship to something in another text. While the author could take the time and effort to

---

70. Sperber and Wilson, *Relevance*, 233.

71. For a recent but brief discussion of the relation between intertextuality and relevance theory see Smith, "The Use of Criteria," 142–54.

spell out the point in laborious detail, alluding to the thing in the other text can be more efficient and effective so long as the relationship between the author's text and the thing being alluded to can be readily accessed. However, if the reader fails to recognize the author's developing context, or if the reader has a different understanding of the text being alluded to, then the reader's ability to recognize the allusion and derive its intended meaning will fail.[72]

Conversely, as a reader begins to read a text, he is constantly seeking a context within which the intended meaning of the author's statements can be apprehended. However, the reader does not begin as a blank state. Instead, he has already made contextual choices and assessments before he approaches the author's text. In no area of textual interpretation is this truer than in that of biblical interpretation. Invariably biblical scholars approach a passage in the Bible with rigid preconceived notions about what the text can and cannot say, about how it was and was not crafted, about whether it is true or false, fallible or infallible, divine in nature or human in nature, etc. These choices may either assist the interpreter or hinder the interpreter in his ability to recognize the context within which the author's words have maximum relevance.

As the reader continues to add the new statements of the text to the contextual meaning that is developing in his mind, similar situations, circumstances, and texts are brought to the fore of the reader's mind. However, if the reader is not understanding the textual meaning intended by the author (because of either the author's failure to provide the material of maximum relevance to the reader or the reader's failure to comprehend the context within which the material being provided by the author is of maximum relevance) then situations and texts may be brought to the fore of the reader's mind that are not relevant to the author's intended meaning. In such a case, false associations (i.e., alleged literary allusions) may be made between the two texts and an allusion may be seen where one was not intended.

According to this line of reasoning then, texts are brought to the fore of an author's mind because they are of maximum relevance in the attending development of his textual meaning. It is through this process that events, people, places, concepts, themes, etc. existing in potentially numerous texts that are far off are brought near. Stephanie Ross argues, "I cannot at random choose two objects and declare that one of them alludes to the other. The one must contain some features which can plausibly be said to refer to the other—and, moreover, do so obliquely."[73] The reason that special note needs

---

72. This discussion will serve as much of the focal point in chapter 5 since it is here that the disagreements concerning the presence of a literary allusion in a text arise.

73. Ross, "Art and Allusion," 62.

to be taken of her statement here is because her observation points out the manner in which allusions work. As contextual meaning is narrowed, texts with related textual meaning become more relevant in the mind of the author and reader.

To illustrate this point, see Table 4.1 below. After the textual meaning of the developing text has been narrowed and relevant texts have been brought near via their relevant textual meaning, the author can freely place any of a number of allusive literary markers into his developing context (illustrated in Table 4.1 by the dotted lines) to be recognized by the reader who has followed his meaning by correctly ascertaining the correct context within which the author's statements gain maximum relevance. However, when the reader derives a faulty or errant context (i.e., one different from the one intended by the author), then texts relevant to the reader's context will be brought near in the reader's mind since they are increasing in relevance to the reader's understanding. It is possible that the reader will also see something in one of these texts that causes him to believe that the author has in fact alluded to this text. To illustrate this point, see Table 4.2.

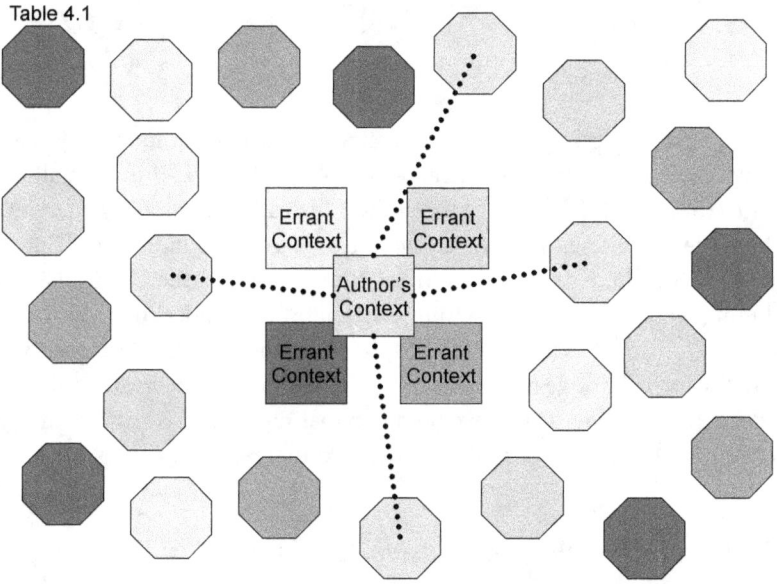

Table 4.1

The problem here is that the reader has found an allusion that the author has not intended. The question then becomes, how can such faulty associations be avoided? This is the question that will be taken up in more detail in Chapter 5. For now, the present discussion must move on to the second issue that has been overlooked in the discussion concerning the identification of literary allusions.

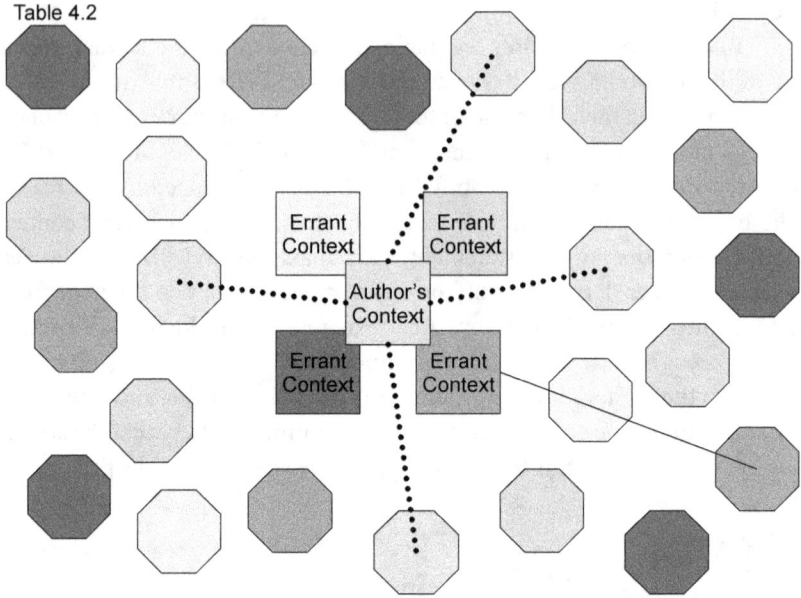

Table 4.2

Finally, the point must be reiterated that it is not the literary markers within a specific poem, narrative, prophecy, etc. that draw the alluded text to the fore of the mind of the author. Instead, it is the relevance of the alluded text to the *developing textual meaning* of the alluding text that establishes the alluded text's "nearness." The literary markers placed in the alluding text are simply those things that allow the reader to recognize the formal attachment to the alluded text. In effect, the literary markers serve to form the formal bridge to the text that has been brought near to the alluding text via the alluding text's developing textual meaning. As this meaning is developing, the relevance of the alluded text increases.

The Impact of Genre on Allusive Textual Markers

Not only has the impact of Relevance Theory been overlooked in the discussion on the identification and validation of literary allusions, but the effect of literary genre on literary allusions has not been adequately recognized either. For example, after citing Robert Alter's observation that Judges 19 is an "elaborate replay" of Genesis 19, Robert Kawashima states, "the allusive plot extends backwards to the preceding scenes: Abraham's gracious reception of the travelers destined for Sodom anticipates the importunate hospitality imposed upon the Levite by his father-in-law."[74] Kawashima correctly points out that characteristics of a certain literary genre can be utilized as allusive textual markers (i.e., in this case, plot).

In the Old Testament several different literary genres are represented. There are the broad categories of narrative literature, poetic literature, prophetic literature, and legal literature. To this list, the New Testament adds the category of epistolary literature. Further, within each of these categories of genre, different forms have also been identified and distinguished by form critics (e.g., myth, sagas, etiologies, festival hymns, royal psalms, thanksgiving psalms, messianic psalms, casuistic law, apodictic law, etc.) While the more specialized forms identified by form critics may warrant more detailed attention, certainly even the broad categories of genre play a part in how literary allusions function.

To begin this discussion, take a hypothetical example of the narrative X. Narrative literature functions through the use of setting, characterization, plot, events, etc. Therefore, narrative Y can utilize any of these distinct characteristics of narrative, along with those enumerated above, to connect it to another narrative X. In other words, the author of narrative Y can use a rhetorical relationship in setting, characterization, plot, events, etc., as the literary markers that signal an allusion to narrative X. However, poetic literature for example does not often utilize many of the characteristics of narrative literature (e.g., setting, characterization, plot, events, dialogue, etc). Therefore, it is not often that these are utilized in poetic literature to signal an allusion. Yet, this does not mean that poetic literature is incapable of alluding to narrative literature. Quite the contrary is true. Instead, it is reasonable to expect poem Z to allude to narrative X in a potentially different way than narrative Y will allude to narrative X since poem Z does not share the same delineating characteristics of genre with narrative X. In other words, in a literary allusion there are always two texts in play: the genre of the alluding text and the genre of the alluded text (see Table 4.3 below).

---

74. Kawashima, "Comparative Literature and Biblical Studies," 336. Kawashima cites Alter, *The World of Biblical Literature*, 111.

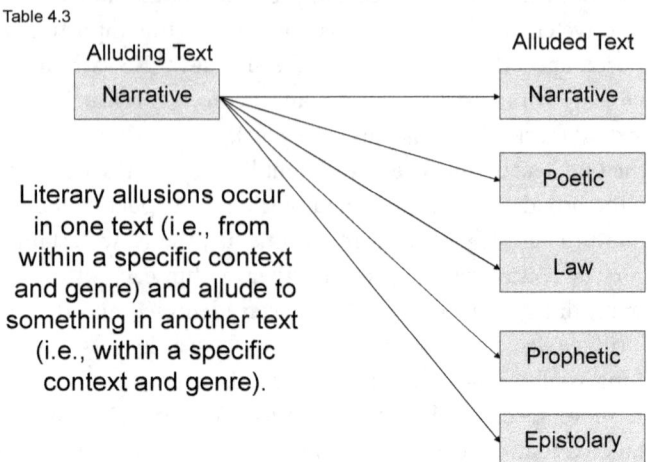

Table 4.3

The literary impact of this reality is that a narrative can allude to narratives, poems, law code, or prophecies, but it must always do so within the framework of narrative literature. This is not to say that poetry, law code, or prophecy cannot be found in narrative. It is to say however, that poetry, law code, or prophecy must appear within the literary framework of narrative literature (i.e., within the storyline, spoken by either a character in the story or the narrator, occur within the events of the story, etc.). Table 4.4 (below) illustrates this point. Similarly, poetry, law code, prophecy, or epistles can allude to things in narratives, poems, law codes, prophecies, or epistles, but it must *always* do so within the framework of its literary genre. This full significance of this point will be made explicit in chapter 6.

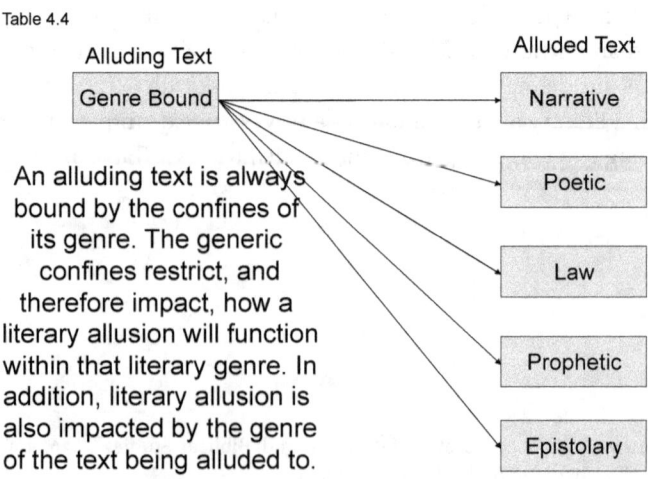

Table 4.4

CONCLUSION

This chapter began by summarizing and evaluating the criteria by which scholars have sought to identify literary allusions. As was pointed out however, these criteria have been unable to produce repeatable and objective results. This situation has prompted scholars to develop a system whereby they can communicate how certain they are that a literary allusion is present in a text. While the intention of this move was to assist in the identification and interpretation of literary allusions, it has only served to make the situation more convoluted since potential allusions are rarely assigned the same level of certainty by different scholars.

The remainder of the chapter explained two of the three key issues concerning the identification of literary allusions that have been overlooked: the relevance of relevance theory and the role of literary genre. The first point of this discussion was to argue that efforts to identify literary allusions via some list of literary markers have failed since they do not take into account considerations of genre. The second point of the discussion was to explain that the association of two texts is made not by the same words, themes, structures, styles, events, settings, etc. (i.e., some literary marker) but by related literary contexts. Of course, the actual linkages may occur through such literary markers. But, the literary markers can only function to connect two texts after the relation of their literary contexts has been established via the relevance of an outside text to the developing context of the alluding text.

5

Validation of and Disagreements over Literary Allusions

IN THE PREVIOUS CHAPTER it was argued that three issues have been overlooked in the discussion on literary allusions. Two of these, the relevance of relevance theory in literary allusions and the role of genre in literary allusions, were discussed in Chapter 4 in terms of being helpful in understanding and identifying literary allusions. The third issue, the identity of the working parts of an allusion, will occupy the focus of this chapter.

VALIDATION OF LITERARY ALLUSIONS

This discussion will now be expanded to account for the working parts of literary allusions for two reasons. The first is that a thorough account of the working parts of a potential literary allusion can serve to either validate or invalidate one's claims to identify a literary allusion. Second, it can serve to surface reasons for disagreement among scholars. This will be an effort to respond to Jon Paulien's charge that "in spite of decades of exploration and discussion, a major commentary on Revelation can be published without any discussion on criteria and with little evidence that anything more than a hit-and-miss application of criteria has been used."[1]

---

1. Paulien, "Criteria and Assessment," 128.

Hermeneutical Considerations

Richard B. Hays makes explicit the inherent difficulty in validating that a literary allusion is present in a text when he explains the five common approaches to such a hermeneutical question:

> (1) The hermeneutical event occurs in Paul's mind. Claims about intertextual meaning effects are valid where it can credibly be demonstrated that Paul intended such effects.
>
> (2) The hermeneutical event occurs in the original readers of the letter. Claims about intertextual meaning effects are valid where it can credibly be demonstrated that the Philippians would likely have perceived such effects.
>
> (3) The intertextual fusion occurs in the text itself. (In this case, we cannot properly speak of a hermeneutical event.) We have no access to the author or to the original readers; we have only the text. Consequently, assertions about Paul's intention are intelligible only as statements about the implied author, and assertions about "the Philippians" are intelligible only as statements about the implied reader. Implied author and implied reader are epiphenomena of the text's rhetoric. Consequently, claims about intertextual meaning effects are valid where it can credibly be demonstrated that they are in some sense properties of the text's own rhetorical or literary structure.
>
> (4) The hermeneutical event occurs in my act of reading. Claims about intertextual meaning effects are valid if I say so. In other words, the perception of intertextual effects has emerged from my own reading experience, and no further validation is necessary.
>
> (5) The hermeneutical event occurs in a community of interpretation. Claims about intertextual meaning effects are valid where it can credibly be demonstrated that they conform to the hermeneutical conventions of a particular community of readers. (Such communities can, of course, be variously composed and disposed: the church, the guild of biblical scholars, the guild of literary critics, the readers of this book—and each of these communities is, of course, fractured into various schismatic schools and subcommunities.)[2]

In these five statements Hays effectively rehearses the three common hermeneutical approaches to texts as he frames his discussion within the context of literary allusions.[3] The first statement applies to those who

---

2. Hays, *Echoes of Scripture in the Letters of Paul*, 26–27.
3. It should be remembered that Hays calls this literary phenomenon "echo" and not

argue that an interpretation is valid only so far as it conforms to the author's intended meaning. Statements two, four, and five reflect the varying reader-response interpretive theories. Finally, statement three reflects the text-centered interpretive approach.

As argued in the first three chapters of this study, literary allusions are a literary device utilized by the author to convey his intended meaning. By definition (see chapter 3) this effectively eliminates statements two, four, and five from consideration since they are based on reader-response interpretive approaches leaving only statements one and three to be addressed. As Hays explains, "option 3 is a heuristic fiction, an attempt to facilitate criticism by bracketing out the messy complications of the history behind the text and the experience of readers encountering the text."[4]

The only statement left for consideration then is the first. What will be explained is how literary allusions do first occur in the mind of the author via the phenomenon of relevance. However, this does not mean that the interpreter must somehow access the thoughts of the author. Instead, the interpreter must simply follow the developing textual meaning. If he is able to do this, and if he is aware of the text that the author has alluded to, then he will recognize the allusion. In order to explain exactly how this occurs, the working parts of a literary allusion must be spelled out in detail.

Prerequisites of Literary Allusion

Before one can argue that one text alludes to another, it must first be demonstrated that such an allusion is even a possibility.[5] This means that a few considerations must first be satisfied before the interpreter begins the process of validation. Each of these considerations is aimed at establishing availability of the text being allegedly alluded to.[6]

"literary allusion." However, this makes no difference in his statements or their relevance.

4. Hays, *Echoes of Scripture*, 27.

5. Chapter 4 made the point that Richard Hays and Michael Thompson categorized these types of considerations as criteria by which literary allusions could be identified. However, it seems better to evaluate these types of questions before seeking to validate one's interpretation that a literary allusion is present in a text.

6. None of these prerequisites is new to the discussion. Instead, each was mentioned in Chapter 4 as criteria by which literary allusions can be identified and therefore only need to be discussed here in brief.

Date

The first prerequisite that must be met concerns the dating of the two texts. While one may wish to argue that one text alludes to another, if the alluded text was *clearly* not written at the time of the alleged alluding text, then the existence of a literary allusion is impossible. Unfortunately, what one scholar assesses to be clear concerning the dating of texts, another sees as unclear. Further, this issue is of particular relevance to Old Testament studies because there is so much uncertainty concerning the dating of many of the Old Testament books. For example, if one holds to a traditional form of the Documentary Hypothesis, then a P text cannot allude to a D text. This point raises two logical questions.

First, is clarity simply a concept that sounds appealing but is ultimately one bound by the chains of subjectivity? Not necessarily. First and foremost, the definition of *clear* must be agreed upon. Per the discussion in the last chapter, it seems that agreement concerning literary allusions is difficult to achieve. However, for something to be *clear*, it is to be *unmistakable*.[7] In this sense then, for something to be clear, it should be clear to all of sound mind. For example, texts found at Qumran set the latest possible date of authorship for some biblical texts. It is clear that these texts were in existence before the texts of the New Testament were written.

Second, does not the reality that the dating of the Old Testament books is in question render this first prerequisite a moot point? Again, the answer is no. If a text can allude only to a text that is in existence, and if an interpretation can be validated whereby it can be reasonably demonstrated that one text is alluding to another, then the alluding text must by necessity precede the text being alluded to. In other words, the validation of an allusion can be used to defend the dating of texts. This point will be expanded upon below.

At this juncture, one final point concerning the identification and validation of a literary allusion can be made explicit that is directly relevant to Old Testament studies. Since allusions work only one way (i.e., the importation of meaning moves only from the earlier alluded text to the later alluding text), then if the dating of two texts is disputed (as most in the Old Testament are) and an interpreter can satisfactorily validate the presence of a literary allusion in a text, he has also provided evidence in support of the alluded text predating the alluding text.[8]

---

7. *Merriam Webster*, s.v. "clear," accessed November 9, 2009, http://www.merriam-webster.com/dictionary/clear.

8. For a good example of such a defense, see Wong, "Ehud and Joab," 403–5.

Region and Language

The second prerequisite that must be considered is that of geography and language. For example, if one is to argue that a text found in one region alludes to a text found in another, the issue of geographical separation and language barriers must at least be considered. For example, is it reasonable to think that an author writing to an audience in one region would allude to a text from another region that was written in another language? If so, why? In such a case, the rhetorical relation between the two texts and the meaning to be imported into the alluding text must help explain or account for this regional and linguistic distance.

Availability

Finally, the text allegedly being alluded to must have been available to the author of the alluding text. In other words, one must ask the question as to whether an alluding author had knowledge of, or access to an alluded text. For example, how could Moses have known about information an Egyptian coffin text that was buried long before he was born and excavated long after his death? While it is possible that some kind of oral tradition could account for such knowledge, the question must still be raised in the mind of the interpreter.

Summary of Prerequisites for Literary Allusions

The prerequisites itemized above are general in nature and therefore would apply to any interpreter of allusion. However, they are admittedly less relevant to the interpreter of Old Testament books. This does not mean however that these considerations should be passed over as irrelevant for consideration when dealing with Old Testament texts. Instead, the interpreter must at least demonstrate that an allusion is possible.

Validation through the Working Parts

One of the problems with ongoing discussions on literary allusion is that there has been little agreement on how one goes about validating one's view that a literary allusion is present in a text. For this reason, claims to the presence of an allusion in a text have remained both difficult to substantiate and interact with. This section will point out that this problem stems from a general failure to delineate exactly how literary allusions function. This section will explain that there are five working parts of a literary allusion. These working parts are (1) the developing textual meaning of the alluding text, (2) the stable textual meaning of the alluded text, (3) the allusive literary markers, (4) the rhetorical relationship between the two texts, and (5) the meaning that is to be imported into the alluding texts. If an interpreter can adequately demonstrate that a suspected literary allusion meets the prerequisites and then explain the five working parts of literary allusion, he has validated his claim that a literary allusion is present in a text. However, if an interpreter cannot adequately demonstrate that a literary allusion meets the prerequisites or if he is unable to explain the working parts, he has likewise failed in his attempt to validate his claim that a literary allusion is present in a text.

For example, when one interprets a literary narrative, he does so via the literary conventions of narrative literature. In other words, he doesn't arbitrarily assign meaning wherever he sees fit. Instead, he takes into consideration the setting, plot, main character's philosophy, the antagonist's philosophy, the rising tension, the climax, the dénouement, etc. In fact, every literary genre must be understood in light of its defining characteristics. Therefore, just as each genre must be understood and interpreted in light of its defining characteristics, so also should allusions be understood and interpreted in light of their defining characteristics or working parts. In other words, when validating the presence of a literary allusion, one must provide an explanation of the five working parts that make up a literary allusion. Thus, if the interpreter is unable to explain how each of the working parts of an allusion are functioning in his interpretation, then he has failed to validate his claim that an allusion is present in the text.[9] In addition, such an approach also provides interpreters who disagree with some objective grounds on which to base their disagreement. That is to say, such an approach will point out exactly where two interpreters disagree.[10]

---

9. It should be noted that this does not mean that the allusion is NOT in the text, only that the interpreter has failed to demonstrate adequately that his interpretation is valid. In response to this realization, the interpreter may return to the texts in question in order to continue to validate his interpretation.

10. This point raises the issue of the validation of an interpretation of a text on a broader scale. Differing interpreters' conclusions about the intended purpose or meaning of a text (or lack thereof) is most often the source of disagreement. Thus, the core of the disagreement is not simply over the presence or meaning of a possible literary allusion in a text, but in the overall meaning or purpose of the two texts (alluding and alluded) themselves.

Developing Textual Meaning of the Alluding Text

The first part of a literary allusion that must be understood and explained is the developing textual meaning of the alluding text (see Table 5.1 below). As explained in the previous chapter, every author has in mind a context within which his assertions are of maximum relevance for conveying his textual meaning (i.e., cognitive goal). An interpreter's failure to ascertain the author's context within which he develops his textual meaning will inevitably lead to a failure to recognize the literary allusions of the author. Further, it may cause the interpreter to see literary allusions in a text that were not intended by the author.

Table 5.1

The goal of the author is to convey his intended meaning. In order to do this, the author provides the reader with statements or assertions of maximum relevance to the author's context in order that his intended meaning can be ascertained.

If the reader fails to correctly understand the author's context, then the reader will likely misunderstand the author's intended meaning.

In order to validate one's interpretation, the interpreter must be able to explain each of the author's statements in order to substantiate his understanding of the author's intended meaning.

Developing Authorial Meaning

This explanation of the author's developing textual meaning should not simply be an explanation of the reader's interpretation, for "a validation has to show not merely that an interpretation is plausible, but that it is the most plausible one available."[11] Ironically Hirsch continues by stating:

> Life is too short and boredom too imminent to demand that every interpreter lay out all the considerations which have led to such a decision, but when interpretive disagreements do occur, genuine knowledge is possible only if someone takes the responsibility of adjudicating the issue in light of all that is known. That

---

11. Hirsch, *Validity in Interpretation*, 171.

few such adjudications exist merely argues strongly that many more should be undertaken. An interpreter is usually deceiving himself if he believes he has anything better to do.[12]

Interestingly, on the one hand Hirsch states, "life is too short and boredom too imminent to demand that every interpreter lay out all the considerations which have led to such a decision" yet on the other he states, "an interpreter is usually deceiving himself" if he thinks that he has something better to do than adjudicate his interpretation.

According to Hirsch, the task validating one's interpretation has been equated with enumerating the pieces of evidence from the text that support the interpreter's conclusions.[13] However, this is very different from what is presented in relevance theory. Sperber and Wilson argue, "every act of ostensive communication communicates a presumption of its own optimal relevance."[14] In other words, every new act (i.e., statement or assertion) that is communicated is assumed to be of maximum relevance to those that precede it. What should be in view then in the validation process is not merely an exercise in proof-texting (i.e., picking out those assertions or statements that agree with or that can be used to defend one's conclusion) but adequately explaining the developing textual meaning in such a way that every assertion or statement is accounted for in the explanation of the author's context.[15] This process of seeking the maximum relevance of each statement not only allows the reader to recognize such things as the intended genre of a text, but also it is the means by which the author's context and developing textual meaning can be understood so that the appropriate conclusions can be drawn.

In *Expository Hermeneutics: An Introduction*, Elliot Johnson makes three statements about the logic of validation and the weight of the evidence. First, Johnson states, "the most accurate interpretation always explains the most evidence that is relevant."[16] However, Wilson and Sperber's

12. Hirsch, *Validity in Interpretation*, 171.
13. Hirsch, *Validity in Interpretation*, 180–96.
14. Sperber and Wilson, *Relevance*, 260.
15. In this sense the validation of an interpretation is similar to being given a set of related variables and being asked to provide a formula that accounts for all of them. While one proposed formula may account for some of the variables, a second formula may account for most of the variables. If it is assumed that all of the variables are of equal importance (i.e., of maximum relevance) and all of the variables are related (i.e., achieve a cognitive goal), then clearly the second formula is to be favored over the first. However, since the second formula does not account for all of the variables, then it must be acknowledged it is still lacking.
16. Johnson, *Expository Hermeneutics*, 288.

relevance theory would cause this statement to be emended. Instead, the most accurate interpretation is the one that best explains how each assertion (i.e., piece of evidence) is of maximum relevance. In other words, it is not the interpreter who gets to determine which statements by the author are of highest importance. Instead, relevance theory assumes that *every* statement of the author is of maximum relevance in contributing to his developing textual meaning. The interpreter then does not assign relevance to an author's statement, but instead explains how it is relevant. In the case of relevance theory, no statement can be excused as irrelevant or inconsequential, but every statement must be accounted for in an interpretation.

Second, Johnson states, "the weight of the evidence is heavier in support of the narrowest statement of the type of meaning."[17] Here the "type of meaning" being discussed by Johnson and Hirsch is equivalent to Sperber and Wilson's context. Relevance theory argues that the narrowest statement of the type of meaning (i.e., context) is derived via explaining how each subsequent statement of the author is of maximum relevance in the narrowing textual meaning of the author. Just because an interpretation provides the narrowest statement of the type of meaning does not ensure that it is more probable. An interpretation can presuppose a context or type of meaning that is very specific yet fail to account for all of the author's statements. Instead, the narrowest possible statement of the type of meaning or context is derived from an adequate explanation of how each statement of the author is of maximum relevance (i.e., highest level of relatedness).

Third, Johnson states, "the weight of the evidence is heavier when the evidence is drawn from the contexts closest to the author's text."[18] However, one must ask how this determination is made. Relevance theory provides the answer in that it argues that evidence drawn from other contexts is relevant only if such a move can be defended via understanding the developing textual meaning of the author. This point is related to the first in that an interpreter is not free to choose where he gathers his evidence. Authors can allude to other texts. When they do, the alluded text is of maximum relevance (i.e., highest level of relevance) to the author's developing textual meaning. Authors can and do talk about the same topics in different texts. However, they also talk about different topics in different texts. Relevance theory argues that statements of the author are not of maximum relevance in many contexts, but in only one context. The context closest to the author's text can be determined only after other contexts are understood (via relevance theory) and then compared to the context of the original text.

17. Johnson, *Expository Hermeneutics*, 288.
18. Johnson, *Expository Hermeneutics*, 288.

Those statements in the immediate context of passage can be summoned as evidence supporting an interpretation only if that interpretation can account for all of the statements of the author.

Therefore, the reader is not assigning a context from only some of the evidence; such an approach is obviously circular, nor is the reader importing meaning from other texts without contextual warrant; this would simply be an exercise in proof-texting. Instead, the reader must explain how he arrived at his conclusions concerning genre, context, meaning, etc. by accounting for every statement or assertion by an author through explaining how each is of maximum relevance. An inability to provide such an explanation for each statement reveals discord with the author's intended context within which his statements are of maximum relevance.[19] Additionally, the failure of an interpreter to validate his interpretation of the developing textual meaning of the text under consideration also causes the interpreter's effort to validate his claim that a literary allusion is present in that text to fail as well.

Stable Textual Meaning of the Alluded Text

The second part of a literary allusion that must be understood and explained in order to validate the claim that a literary allusion is present in a text is the stable textual meaning of the alluded text. As the textual meaning of the alluding text is narrowed by each additional assertion of an author, the relevance of outside texts either remains distant to the developing textual meaning of the author's text or the relevance of outside texts is heightened, or brought near to the author's text (see Table 5.2 below). Since the author is trying to convey his cognitive goal, alluding to these relevant texts is extremely effective and efficient.

For the author then, the recognition of the stable textual meaning and context of the text being alluded to as well as its relevance to his present discussion obviously precedes the placing of literary markers into his text which act as signposts directing the reader to the alluded text.

---

19. Obviously, relevance theory raises several logical questions that Sperber and Wilson address. Of these, two are most relevant to the current discussion: (1) How reliable is the presumption of relevance? (2) Do all communicators at least try to be optimally relevant? To these, Sperber and Wilson respond by explaining that while some communicators are inept or even boring, every communicator wishing to convey something seeks optimum relevance. For the full discussion, see Sperber and Wilson, *Relevance*, 158–63.

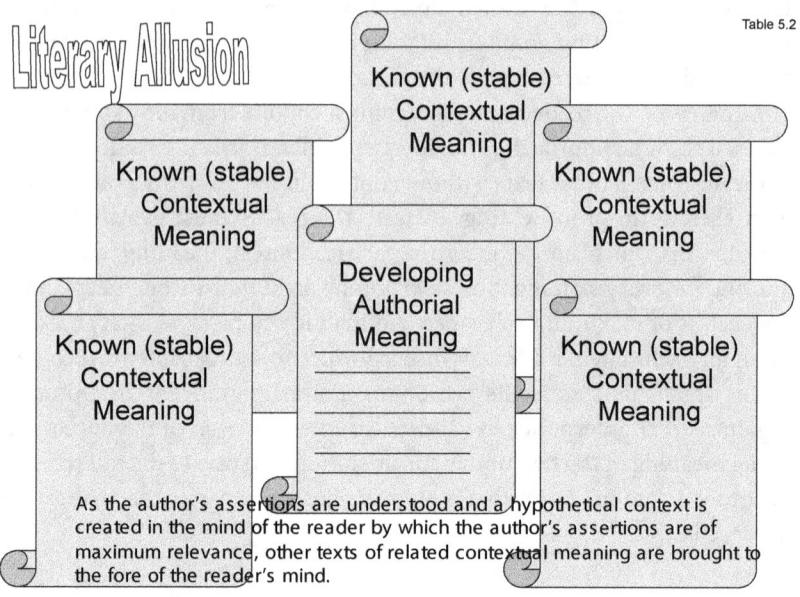

Table 5.2

For the reader trying to ascertain the cognitive goal of the author through his text, the recognition of the context (i.e., narrowest type of meaning) in which each of the author's statements is of maximum relevance allows the signposts to function as the author wishes (i.e., direct the reader to the alluded text). However, the text being alluded to should not be far off in the mind of the reader either since there is some contextual relation between the author's text and the text being alluded to. Surely the interpreter, *after* reading the author's text, could explain how it relates to many texts (i.e., this problem in this story is like the problem in that one, the main character in this story has the same personality as the one in that story, the mood in this psalm is like that in the prophetic utterance, etc.), but this is not the interpreter's job *during* his reading. Instead, the interpreter must wait for the author to speak, for the author to explain his cognitive goal. That is to say, the stable textual meaning of the text being alluded to *precedes* the placing of literary markers for the author of a text. Conversely for the reader, the stable textual meaning of the alluded text is activated by the literary marker and therefore logically follows the literary marker. However, the alluded text has been brought near to the alluding text for both the author and the reader via its relevance to the author's developing textual meaning.

Finally, a couple of points must be emphasized. First, it should be pointed out that the only means by which the reader will likely recognize the literary markers placed in the text by the author is to have correctly comprehended his context and developing textual meaning. The implications of a failure in this regard will be explained below. Second, it should be pointed out that the textual meaning of the alluded text is stable. After all, if the alluded text were in a state of constant flux, being changed by the whim of each reader, then an allusion to it would serve no function. If there is no stable meaning in an alluded text, then there is no reason to appeal to it for assistance in the development of stable meaning (i.e., conveying the cognitive goal of the author). By definition (see Chapter 3) this is what allusions do.

Therefore, an interpreter wishing to argue (i.e., validate his interpretation) that an author has alluded to an outside text must not only be able to explain (i.e., validate his interpretation of) the developing textual meaning of the alluding text, but also the stable textual meaning of the alluded text. Further, the interpreter must be able to explain how the thing being alluded to in the alluded text is situated in that specific textual meaning. Only then can the rhetorical relationship between the alluding text and the thing being alluded to be explained. A failure on behalf of an interpreter to validate the stable literary meaning of the alluded text also results in a failure to validate his claim that an allusion is present in a text.

Allusive Textual Markers

The third part of a literary allusion that must be identified and explained is the allusive textual markers in the alluding text (see Table 5.3 below). For the author of a text, the allusive literary markers are those intentionally placed connectors that serve as signposts to direct the reader to the appropriate text containing the allusion. The exact nature of the allusive literary markers is limited by genre and the author's creativity.

Table 5.3

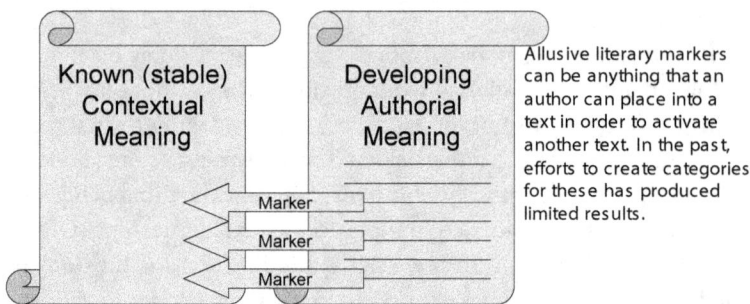

As the author's assertions are understood and a hypothetical context is created in the mind of the reader by which the author's assertions are of maximum relevance, other texts of related contextual meaning are brought to the fore of the reader's mind. However, these texts are only activated in the mind of the reader when allusive textual markers are detected by the reader. If the reader has correctly understood the author's developing textual meaning, then it is quite possible that these textual markers were intended by the author.

Allusive literary markers can be anything that an author can place into a text in order to activate another text. In the past, efforts to create categories for these has produced limited results.

However, the two principles of relevance theory should be remembered. First, the allusive markers should be identifiably relevant. In other words, if an interpreter has correctly understood the developing textual meaning, they should be readily identifiable to him. Second, the effort required to identify the allusive literary markers should be small. In other words, the literary markers of allusion should be fairly straightforward since they are to serve as signposts that direct the reader who has followed the author's context to the appropriate alluded text. If an interpreter is to validate his interpretation of a literary allusion, he must be able to validate his understanding of the developing alluding text and his understanding of the stable alluded text as well as identify and explain how the allusive literary markers connect the two texts. A failure to identify or explain the allusive literary markers will result in a failed effort to validate a claim that a literary allusion is present in a text.

Rhetorical Relationship

The fourth part of a literary allusion that must be understood and explained is the rhetorical relationship between the developing textual meaning of the alluding text and the stable textual meaning of the alluded text (see Table 5.4 below). As explained in Chapter 4, this relationship can take five forms: equal to, greater than, less than, similar to, and not equal to (i.e., ironic opposite).

Table 5.4

Literary Allusion

Once a potential literary allusion has been detected via identifying allusive literary markers in the alluding text that link it to a secondary text, the relationship between the two texts (the developing textual meaning and the thing being alluded to in the secondary text) must be determined.

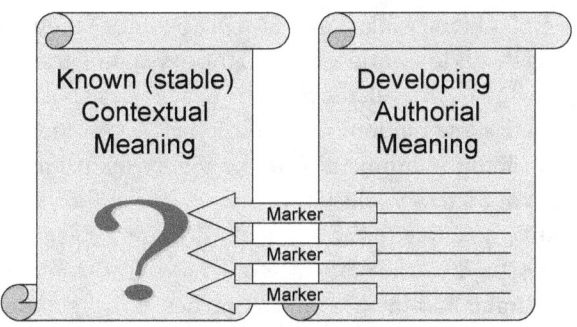

For example, if one were to say, "way to go Einstein!" the statement could not be understood until the context of the developing situation was also understood. Certainly the meaning of a reference to Einstein is stable. Einstein was brilliant. In other words, Einstein functions as a type, a standard bearer for brilliance. However, the allusion to Einstein can be understood only after the rhetorical relationship between the brilliance of Einstein and the developing situation is understood. If the speaker's friend had just discovered the cure for cancer, the relationship between the two can be readily determined. The friend is being complimented because he has displayed true intellectual greatness.

If, however, the speaker's friend had just locked his keys in his car, the relationship between the two is very different. Obviously the speaker's statement is dripping with irony since, while Einstein was a genius, his friend could not even remember to take his keys out of the car before locking the door. In both of these cases, however, there is a clear rhetorical relationship between the subject of the allusion and the object of the allusion. If there is no rhetorical relationship, there is no meaning to be imported into the developing textual meaning of the alluding text. In such a case, the claim that a literary allusion is present in the text is invalid. Instead, it is possible that an echo or literary reference, not an allusion, is present in the text.

Therefore, in order to validate the interpretation of a literary allusion, the interpreter must be able to validate his understanding of the developing textual meaning of the alluding text, his understanding of the stable alluded textual meaning, the identity of the literary markers and to what they direct the reader, and his understanding of the relationship between the alluding text and the thing being alluded to in the alluded text. Failure in any one of these steps invalidates the claim that a literary allusion is present in a text.

Imported Meaning and Rhetorical Function

The fifth and final part of a literary allusion that must be understood and explained is the meaning that is to be imported into the developing text (see Table 5.5 and Table 5.6 below). After all, the purpose of a literary allusion is not simply to demonstrate some random relationship between something in the alluding textual meaning and something in the alluded textual meaning. Rather, the purpose of a literary allusion is to assist the author in the development of his textual meaning to the end that his cognitive goal may be recognized and understood by the reader. In other words, the allusion functionally imports meaning into the text via comprehension of and then contemplation of the rhetorical relationship between the alluding text and the alluded text. This is the exact point that David Mathewson raises in his article, *Assessing Old Testament Allusions in the Book of Revelation*:

> The discussion surrounding the use of the OT needs to move beyond classifying and substantiating allusions based on perceived authorial intention and interpretive confidence in identifying them, to focusing on the interpretive and theological significance of a given allusion or echo in Revelation. What role does an OT allusion or echo play within the discourse of Revelation? What someone might label a conscious allusion might not play a very significant role in John's discourse, or what would appear only to be an "echo" might turn out to be of crucial importance. What difference does postulating this or that allusion actually make in interpreting a given section of Revelation?[20]

In other words, an interpreter cannot simply argue that his interpretation is the author's intended meaning. Instead, an interpreter can operate only on what is comprehensible in the text—on what the author placed there. For the reader, once the developing textual meaning of the alluding text has been understood, the allusive literary markers have been recognized, the stable textual meaning of the alluded text has been recalled, and the rhetorical relationship between the two texts has been understood, the

---

20. Mathewson, "Assessing Old Testament Allusions," 319.

reader must then recognize the meaning that the author intended to be imported into the author's text. This meaning that is to be imported *makes the point* of the allusion; it serves a rhetorical function. While not as specific, this is what Michael Leddy is trying to communicate when he states, "allusion-words typically describe a reference that invokes one or more associations of appropriate cultural material and brings them to bear upon a present context."[21]

Table 5.5

Since the thing potentially being alluded to is situated in a known (i.e., stable) textual meaning, the reader must adequately understand this textual meaning. Only then can the rhetorical relationship between the alluding text and the thing being alluded to be understood. This relationship can take one of five basic forms: equal to, greater than, less than, similar to, or not equal to.

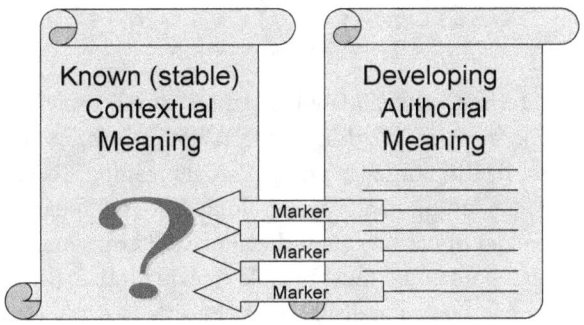

To return to the example just presented, if the speaker's friend had just locked his keys in his car (i.e., developing context) and the speaker states, "way to go Einstein!" then the name Einstein directs the hearer (i.e., allusive marker) to call to his remembrance the brilliant scientist Einstein (i.e., stable context). The rhetorical relationship between the two makes explicit the point that the friend's actions were not brilliant like those of Einstein's (i.e., rhetorical relationship). Finally, the meaning that is to be imported into the developing context by the speaker's words is something like, "Boy, that was a stupid thing you just did! You are certainly no Einstein!" Only after this meaning is imported into the context is the allusion completed.

21. Leddy, "The Limits of Allusion," 112.

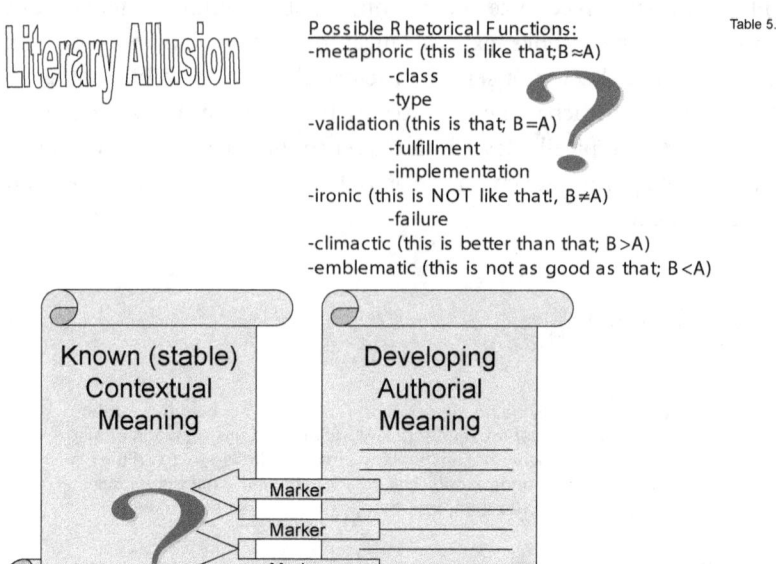

Table 5.6

Therefore, for an interpreter to validate his claim that a literary allusion is present in a text he must do five things (see Table 5.7 below). First, he must validate his interpretation of the alluding textual meaning. Second, he must validate his understanding of the stable alluded textual meaning. Third, he must be able to identify and explain the allusive literary markers placed in the alluding text. Fourth, he must be able to explain the rhetorical function between the two texts. Finally, he must be able to explain the meaning that is to be imported into the author's developing textual meaning by the allusion that both completes the allusion and contributes to the author's textual meaning. This final step then requires that the interpreter not only explain the textual meaning up to the point of the allusion, but also the textual meaning after the allusion as well. Only then can the interpreter explain how the allusion achieves its purpose of assisting the author in the conveyance of his cognitive goal.

Table 5.7

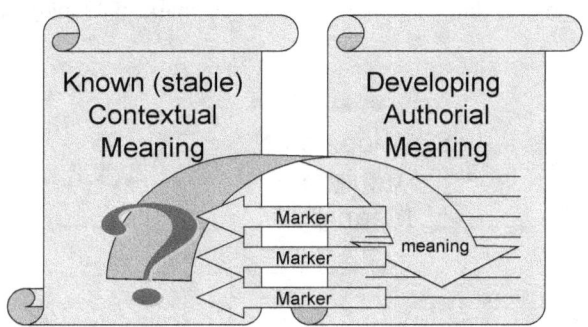

Once the rhetorical relationship between the two texts is determined, the intended meaning that is to be imported into the author's developing textual meaning can be determined as well. Once the meaning has been imported into the alluding text and bridges the gap between the preceding textual context and the following textual context, then the allusion is completed.

Summary of Validation via Working Parts

As was made explicit in Chapter 3, there is little agreement among scholars concerning the identification of literary allusions in the Bible. In response, many have tried to develop a system of categorization whereby they can convey to their readers how certain they are concerning the presence of a literary allusion in a passage. The problem with this approach is twofold. First, what one interpreter argues is a clear allusion, the next claims to be no allusion at all. Second, each interpreter expressing his own opinion does nothing to resolve the fact that they disagree.

The approach to the validation of an interpretation of literary allusion spelled out above suffers from neither of these problems for two reasons. First, this approach to validation exposes the reality that the source of scholars' disagreement is not a specific literary allusion. Instead, their disagreement is present long before any literary allusion is considered. Second, authors either allude or they do not. They do not engage in certain allusions, possible allusions, or doubtful allusions. Therefore, this approach to validation causes the interpreter to first understand and then explain why he believes an allusion is present in the text (see Table 5.8 below).

Table 5.8

Validation of Proposed Allusion Must Include:
-Explanation of the Developing Textual Meaning of the Alluding Text
-Identification of Markers
-Validation of the Known (stable) Contextual Meaning of the Alluded Text
-Explanation of the Rhetorical Function of the Allusion
-Explanation of Meaning to be Imported into Developing Context of Alluding Text

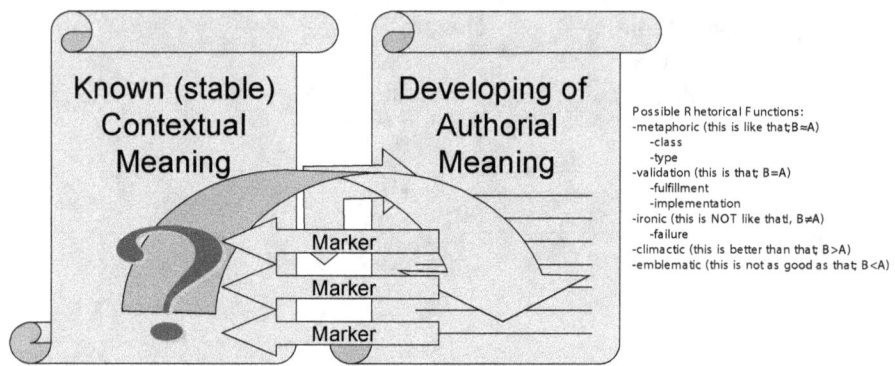

DISAGREEMENTS OVER LITERARY ALLUSION

What this approach will not do is eliminate all the existing disagreements. In fact, it may not eliminate *any* existing disagreements. What it will do, however, is reveal the true source of disagreement between interpreters that lead to their disagreement over the interpretation of a literary allusion.

Context: The Source of Disagreement

The implication of relevance theory on hermeneutics is that it locates all disagreements in interpretation ultimately in differing views of context. The issue then is context, context, context. In biblical studies, there are at least three sources of disagreement that will affect context.

Where Does the Text Begin?

The first source of disagreement concerning context, especially in biblical studies, is over where the text begins. Several factors weigh into such a consideration. First, one's view over whether or not a book is to be understood as a unity will impact one's view of the context of the alluding text. For example, if one considers a book to be an anthology, he will likely have a different understanding of a passage in the book.[22] Second, canonical issues must be addressed. For example, does the literary context of the Bible begin at Genesis 1:1 or somewhere else? One's hermeneutical, philosophical, and critical approaches to the Bible can dramatically impact how one answers this question.

What Does the Context Include?

The second source of disagreement concerning context concerns the place of background material in literary interpretation. In other words, does the context of a passage include all known information about a subject? (i.e., is all available background information relevant to the context of a biblical passage?) Relevance theory would argue that it is not. Instead, background material is relevant only if it explains (i.e., is of maximum relevance to) an assertion or statement of the author.

This is not to say that background material is necessarily irrelevant to the understanding of a biblical passage either. Instead, background information is relevant only when it is textually warranted. It is textually warranted when it becomes of maximum relevance for the understanding of the assertion of the author. Therefore, relevance theory itself assumes the unity of a text. Further, it assumes that each statement of an author is given for the purpose of achieving his cognitive goal (i.e., conveying his intended meaning). Background material may thus assist in the modern reader's ability to comprehend the correct context within which the author is operating to bridge the temporal gap between the ancient author and the modern reader. However, assuming that background material is relevant just because it was written in the same time period or region may in fact hinder the modern reader's ability to comprehend the correct context within which the author is developing his textual meaning.

---

22. See for example, the debate between Lyle Eslinger (Eslinger, "Inner-Biblical Exegesis and Allusion," 47–58) and Benjamin Sommer (Sommer, "Exegesis, Allusion and Intertextuality in the Hebrew Bible," 479–89) over the implications of Michael Fishbane's *Biblical Interpretations in Ancient Israel* is one such example.

Criticisms and Context

The third source of disagreement over context concerns the interpreters' approach to the biblical text. Source Criticism, Form Criticism, Redaction Criticism, Structural Criticism, Rhetorical Criticism, Canonical Criticism, Tradition-Historical Criticism, Narrative Criticism, Reader-Response Criticism, and all of the other forms of criticism will not only cause interpreters to disagree on the context of a passage, they will even serve to dictate which contexts are even a possibility. Most often these forms of higher criticism do not assist in discovering the context within which the author's words have maximum relevance. Instead, they impose on a text the pretext of the interpreter. It is for this reason that most of these approaches do not recover meaning, but create it. Therefore, any discussion over the context of an Old Testament text immediately raises several questions concerning the unity of the text under consideration. In the higher critical method of the past few centuries, it has become increasingly in vogue to reject the unity of Old Testament books in favor of the view that these texts are composite in nature. The effect of this is a potential rejection of the presupposition that there is a developing context of the author.[23]

Context and Meaning: Disagreements over Allusions

There are several sources of disagreement concerning literary context and textual meaning. However, when considering the interpretation of literary allusions, they reveal themselves in four pivotal places: the context of the alluding text, the context of the alluded text, the allusive literary markers, and the meaning to be imported into the alluding text.[24]

---

23. As will be recalled from Chapters 1 and 2, there are even those who reject the notion of an "author" of a text. In such cases, objectivity and validity in interpretation are viewed as hopeless endeavors. Instead, each reader or group of readers has the right to read a text however they wish with no one to tell them that their interpretation is flawed.

24. While there are many examples that could be cited here, the three-way debate between Steve Moyise, G. K. Beale, and Jon Paulien is one case in point. See Moyise, "Does the NT Quote the OT out of Context?," 133–43; Moyise, "The Use of Analogy in Biblical Studies," 33–42; Moyise, "Does the Author of Revelation Misappropriate the Scriptures?," 3–21; Beale, "Questions of Authorial Intent, Epistemology, and Presuppositions," 152–80; Moyise, "The Old Testament in the New," 54–58; Moyise, "Seeing the Old Testament through a Lens," 36–41; Moyise, "Authorial Intention and the Book of Revelation," 35–40; Paulien, "Dreading the Whirlwind," 5–22; Beale, "A Response to Jon Paulien on the Use of the Old Testament in Revelation," 23–34.

Context and Textual Meaning of the Alluding Text

The first potential disagreement concerning the interpretation of literary allusions is the context of the alluding text. If two interpreters disagree over the context of the alluding text for whatever reason, then they will not likely agree on the textual meaning (i.e., the cognitive goal) of the author. Further, disagreement concerning the developing textual meaning of the alluding text will largely determine whether or not two interpreters will agree on the presence of an allusion in a text. Therefore, if two interpreters supply two different contexts for a text leading to two different developing textual meanings, it is inevitable that they will even see different allusions in that text as well. However, in such a case their disagreements are not over the identification and validation of a literary allusion. Instead, their disagreements existed before they began reading. In other words, their disagreements were brought to the text via their preexisting interpretive and hermeneutical grid.

Surely every interpreter must supply or quickly develop some sort of context within which the author's words gain maximum relevance. If, however, the statements of the author are not of maximum relevance in the context within which the reader has supplied, the reader must adjust his contextual understanding to fit the author's words.[25] Unfortunately, herein lies the problem with many higher critical approaches. They impose limitations (predetermined contexts) upon the text via the consideration of individual statements found therein instead of seeking to provide a context within which each of the statements is of maximum relevance. Such an approach inevitably dissects and segments a text in order to make it fit the preordained context within which the text under consideration must operate. Sperber and Wilson's relevance theory presupposes unity (i.e., the speaker or author's cognitive goal). Much of critical scholarship presupposes disunity. Obviously much more can and should be said in regard to this issue. Unfortunately, our discussion must move forward. However, before leaving this issue the words stated in Chapter 1 bear repeating:

> It is for this reason that Christian scholars can no longer sit on the philosophical sidelines and wait for an exegetical discussion over a particular text to arise. Instead, a lack of engagement in hermeneutical theory means that the game has already been played and its outcome determined *before* the text to be interpreted is even considered. This is not an option for the Church. These philosophical hermeneutical issues *must* be settled *before* we approach a text lest what ensues is not the "playing of the

---

25. This is exactly the point set forth concerning context by Sperber and Wilson, *Relevance*, 132–42.

game," but simply the "reading of the box scores"! It is for this reason that, while the primary focus of this study is on validity in the identification and interpretation of literary allusions, much will have to be said about the philosophical theories and conclusions that undergird much of the present day hermeneutical approaches in order to expose and tear down logical fallacies that have undermined the belief that an author, the Author, can speak and be understood.[26]

In summary then, the first step in validating one's interpretation of a literary allusion is to explain how each statement functions to provide maximum relevance to the author's developing textual meaning (i.e., cognitive goal). If the two disagreeing interpreters take this first step, it may become evident that their disagreement is over hermeneutical principles and critical approaches and not over the identification and validation of a literary allusion. However, if the two interpreters are in agreement concerning the author's developing textual meaning via explanation of the author's argumentation, their attention must proceed to the next working part of a literary allusion.

Context and Textual Meaning of the Alluded Text

The second place for potential disagreement among interpreters is over the context of the alluded text. If two interpreters agree on the developing textual meaning of the alluding text, but disagree on the stable textual meaning of the alluded text, they will also disagree on the literary allusion for three potential reasons. First, they may disagree on the identity of any allusive literary markers. Second, even if they were to agree on the identity of the allusive literary markers, they would disagree on the rhetorical relationship between the two texts stemming from their differing understandings of the alluded text. Third, if they disagree on the stable textual meaning of the alluded text, they will disagree on the meaning that is to be imported into the developing textual meaning. Therefore, for one to validate his claim that a literary allusion is present in a text, he must validate his interpretation of the alluding text as well as his interpretation of the alluded text.

Allusive Literary Markers

The third place that two interpreters could disagree concerning a literary allusion is in the presence or identity of any allusive literary markers in the

---

26. See p. 2 above.

alluding text. For example, it is possible that two interpreters could agree on both the developing textual meaning of the alluding text and the stable textual meaning of the alluded text yet disagree over whether or not there are any textual markers in the alleged alluding text that connect it to the alleged alluded text. In other words, if one does not recognize the presence or identity of the allusive literary markers in the alluding text, he will not see a literary allusion. If literary allusions are in fact literary devices utilized by an author to convey his cognitive goal, they should be readily recognizable. However, that an allusive literary marker is readily recognizable does not mean that it must meet some predetermined criteria. There are multitudinous ways in which two texts can be linked. Further, for biblical studies there are certainly several obvious complicating factors such as different languages, different genres, and changing word usage that must be taken into account. In addition, there may well be structural norms that may once have been common knowledge but are now unrecognized (e.g., Robert Lowth's recognition of parallelism in Hebrew poetry). Therefore, if one is to validate his claim that a literary allusion is present in a text, he must validate his interpretation of the developing textual meaning of the alluding text, he must validate his interpretation of the stable textual meaning of the alluded text, and he must explain how the two texts are linked via allusive textual markers.

Rhetorical Relationship and Imported Meaning

Finally, the two interpreters could theoretically agree on the developing textual meaning of the alluding text, on the stable textual meaning of the alluded text, and on the identity and presence of the allusive literary markers. However, they could have some disagreement over the exact rhetorical relationship or the exact meaning to be imported into the alluding text. While this seems to be a much less likely scenario than the first three, the validation of the meaning to be imported into the alluding text would become of utmost importance in settling such a dispute since the imported meaning must be of maximum relevance in continuing the author's literary textual meaning. In other words, the interpreter must not only be able to validate his interpretation of the developing textual meaning of the alluding text, he must also explain how it rhetorically relates to the stable textual meaning of the alluded text and what meaning is then to be imported into the alluding text. Further, the interpreter must demonstrate that the meaning to be imported from the allusion is integral to the developing textual meaning of the alluding text. In other words, the allusion must supply a meaning bridge between what precedes the allusion and what follows it.

Summary of Disagreements

Over the past few centuries literally thousands of works have been written claiming that allusions are present in given texts. Unfortunately, little consensus has been achieved concerning the identification and validation of literary allusions. However, given the plethora of hermeneutical approaches to texts that have been derived over the past few centuries such disagreements are to be expected. The higher critical literary approaches and hermeneutical approaches developed since the Enlightenment have served only to fragment texts and reject the rights of the authors (and Author) to both speak and be heard. It is for this reason that disagreements over the identification and interpretation of literary allusions are often hermeneutical disagreements over the interpretation of texts. In other words, disagreements over the identification and interpretation of literary allusions often reveal a much deeper hermeneutical issue.

First, it has not been acknowledged that allusive literary markers only serve to activate meaning that has been brought close to the developing textual meaning of the alluding text via relevance theory. The fact that two texts use the same words, same themes, or same structures hardly proves the presence of a literary allusion. Same words, structures, themes, etc. cannot link two texts in the mind an author or reader unless they share some textual relation (i.e., the text must be relevant to each other). In other words, there is a logical prerequisite that precedes the possibility of a literary allusion: the two texts must share some relation in textual meaning. It is the closeness or relatedness of meaning that activates the literary allusion. Therefore, in order to identify a literary allusion, texts must be read for their author-intended meaning as, or even before, they are analyzed for their lexical forms, syntactical structures, or any other allusion identifying strategy. This presupposes that the meaning of texts is unified and discernible. That is to say, allusions only function within the interplay of two rhetorically related texts.

Second, any list of allusive literary markers can only be descriptive and not prescriptive in nature. In other words, there are no steadfast rules for how an author can link two rhetorically related texts. Instead, the author is limited only by the conventions of the genres within which he is working. Therefore, before an interpreter can claim that a literary allusion is at work in the text, he must demonstrate (i.e., validate) two things: (1) that the textual meaning of the two texts is related, and (2) that the two texts are linked via textual markers.[27]

---

27. For example, an author may intentionally use such things as wordplay, synonyms, antonyms, and homonyms. He may connect stories with like characters, like events, like plots. He may connect poetry with recognizable features such as alliteration,

Third, recognizing the working parts of an allusion allows the interpreter to slow down and evaluate each step in his interpretive process. Most often, interpreters intuitively know that a literary allusion is present in a text. Recognizing and analyzing the working parts of an alleged literary allusion enable the interpreter to ask himself, "How do I know what I know?" The recognition of the working parts of a literary allusion is nothing more than putting the process of relevance theory in slow motion and asking the appropriate questions along the way. As the reader begins comprehending the meaning of the author's text, he must ask himself if he has accurately accounted for each of the author's statements. (That is, have I understood how each statement of the author is of maximum relevance to the developing textual meaning?) As the reader recognizes textual links (i.e., allusive textual markers) to another text, he must ask himself if such a connection is textually warranted (i.e., Are the textual markers actually there? Is the stable text allegedly being alluded to actually saying what I think it says?). As the reader comprehends the allusion, he must ask himself why the author alluded to this text (i.e., What is the rhetorical relationship between the two texts and what meaning am I to import into the developing textual meaning?). Usually, these five steps are performed so intuitively and quickly that they are often thought of as one unified process instead of several separate steps assimilated into one. However, making each interpretive step explicit will help in the identification and interpretation of literary allusions.

CONCLUSION

In this chapter, Paulien's point was acknowledged that little progress has been made in the area of validating a claim that a literary allusion is present in a text.[28] The reason for this, it was argued, is that there has been a failure to recognize the working parts of literary allusions.[29] If, however, scholars sought to validate their claims that a literary allusion is present in a text via explaining their understanding of the five working parts of allusions, there would be grounds upon which scholars could disagree. In Chapter 3 the point was made that there has been little agreement over the identification and interpretation of literary allusions. If this approach to the validating intertextual claims is followed, scholars will know exactly where they disagree and why.

---

like meter, etc. The possibilities here are limited only by the creativity of the author.

28. A claim that is still true today.

29. It should be pointed out that the rhetorical function of a quotation or citation works in the same way (although more direct). Thus, the five working parts identified above are also helpful in explaining why an author quotes or cites another passage.

6

Illustrations in the Identification and Validation of Literary Allusion in the Old Testament

CHAPTERS 4 AND 5 proposed that three areas have been overlooked in the discussion on the identification and validation of literary allusions.[1] At the end of chapter 5, all three were put together in order to demonstrate a way in which interpreters can proceed in identifying and validating literary allusions in texts.

What follows are four examples of the process of identifying and validating the presence of literary allusions. It is not being suggested that the details provided below must accompany every claim that a literary allusion is present in a text. To do so would require that too much space be taken in published works. Instead, what follows is intended to achieve two ends. First, the examples below will illustrate the steps that an interpreter should go through when considering the possibility that a literary allusion is present in a text since these five "steps" simply walk through the logical progression of any allusion. Further, while the full detail need not necessarily accompany every claim that a literary allusion is present in a text, a brief summation of the interpreter's explanation of the allusion should. Such an approach allows for one's interpretive decisions to be followed. Second, the examples below were specifically chosen in order to demonstrate how

---

1. The three areas were relevance theory, literary genre, and the working parts of literary allusion.

different literary genres effect literary allusions. As will be seen, the largest effect that genre has on literary allusions is the manner in which allusive textual markers function.

Finally, in addition to what was said in chapter 4 concerning literary allusions, a brief word needs to be added about the different genres represented in the Old Testament. Sandy argues for the presence of ten genres in the Old Testament: narrative, history, law, oracles of salvation, announcements of judgment, apocalyptic, lament, praise, proverb, and non-proverbial wisdom.[2] Because of space limitations and the fact that many of these categories can be consolidated because of their similarity, the more general categories of narrative, poetry, law, and prophecy will be considered. In addition, it must be remembered that genre has a potential impact on literary allusions in both the alluding text and the alluded text. Therefore, it is important for the purpose of illustration to select a passage that is potentially alluded to by all of the various genres in the Old Testament so that the impact of genre can be seen. Genesis 19 (i.e., the destruction of Sodom and Gomorrah) is one such passage.

It has been claimed that this narrative passage is alluded to in the Old Testament via narrative, poetry, law, and prophecy.[3] For this reason, a potential allusion to Genesis 19 from each of these four Old Testament genres has been selected in order to illustrate the approach being forwarded in this study: Judges 19 (narrative), Deuteronomy 29:23 (law), Isaiah 1:9–10 (prophecy), Psalm 11 (poetry). By way of final note before moving on, it should be remembered that the steps in validation simply follow the working parts of a literary allusion. However, since the same passage is allegedly being alluded to in all of these examples, Genesis 19 will only be explained once in order to both preserve space and reduce redundancy. Afterward, each allusion will refer back to this initial explanation with additional comment added only when necessary. In addition, it should be pointed out at this juncture that literary allusions made within the same literary genre contain more potential points of contact than is possible when alluding to a different genre.[4]

2. Sandy, *Cracking Old Testament Codes*.

3. In addition, Gen 19 is alluded to in the New Testament as well in Matt 10:15; 11:23–24; Luke 10:12; 2 Pet 2:6; Jude 1:7; Rev 11:8.

4. As will be seen below, the Judges 19 allusion to Genesis 19 is quite extensive. However, the Isaiah 1 and Psalm 11 allusions to Genesis 19 will be more direct. When allusions cross genre lines, they tend to employ much stronger literary markers. (cf. Deut 32:32; Isa 3:9; 13:19; 30:33; Jer 23:14; 49:18; 50:40; Lam 4:6; Ezek 16:46, 48, 49, 53, 56; 38:22; Amos 4:11; Zeph 2:9; Hos 11:8 for examples of potential allusions in the Old Testament that utilize either "Sodom," "Sodom and Gomorrah," "Admah and Zeboiim," or "fire and brimstone" to refer/allude to Genesis 19.

ALLUSION IN NARRATIVE: GENESIS 19 IN JUDGES 19

The first allusion to be considered is the potential allusion to Genesis 19 in Judges 19. This alleged allusion has been chosen as a starting point for three reasons. First, this allusion is widely acknowledged.[5] Second, this allusion serves as one of the best examples for demonstrating how one narrative passage can allude to another narrative passage. Third, working through the process of validating this potential allusion may help make sense of the textual meaning of Judges 17–21.

Prerequisites of Literary Allusion

Before turning to Judges 19, it must be considered whether or not such an allusion is possible. With the dating of Old Testament texts constantly in a state of flux and often varying from scholar to scholar, there is certainly no consensus opinion over the date of authorship for the book of Judges or the book of Genesis.[6] However, only in the case of the most radical dating of the Old Testament texts can it be argued that Judges 19 precedes Genesis 19 in authorship.[7] Not only does Niditch argue for the chronological priority of Judges 19, she also argues, "Each version . . . is best regarded as a variation on a theme, used for specific purposes in each context. The international folktale pattern involves weary travelers who seek succor but instead are treated with virulent hostility, thereby casting their 'hosts' as the quintessentially antisocial 'other.' The Greek tales of the Cyclops and the Lestragonians provide comparable examples."[8] In other words, these two

---

5. At least as widely as is possible with a biblical allusion. As Lasine points out, while some textual relation between these two passages is widely acknowledged, "there is no agreement about the significance of that similarity. Some commentators are unable to decide whether the Gibeah outrage is dependant upon the Sodom story, or whether the reverse is the case" (Lasine, "Guest and Host in Judges 19," 38). For further discussion on this issue see Culley, *Studies in the Structure of Hebrew Narrative*, 58–59; Niditch, "The 'Sodomite' Theme," 375; Rad, *Genesis*, 218; Jüngling, *Richter 19-Ein Plädoyer für das Königtum*, 289.

6. For a good discussion on developments to the documentary hypothesis, see Rendtorff, "What Happened to the Yahwist?," 39–66. For a discussion on the dating of the Book of Judges, see Block, *Judges, Ruth*, 44–50.

7. For example, Niditch argues that Judges 19–20 predates Genesis 19 (Niditch, *Judges*, 376–78). Also see Penchansky, "Staying the Night," 77–88, and Brettler, *The Book of Judges*, 80–91, who come to the same conclusions. In addition, Van Seters argues that the J document was a product of exilic times. Depending upon how one dates authorship of the Deuteronomic history, such a move could place the Patriarchal narratives after the book of Judges (Seters, *Abraham in History and Tradition*).

8. Niditch, *Judges*, 192.

passages are similar not because of Judges 19 alluding to Genesis 19 or vice versa, but because they simply share the same "tale type."⁹ However, if it can convincingly be demonstrated that Judges 19 is specifically interacting with Genesis 19, then Niditch's argument is overturned. At this point then, per the potential dating of these texts, it is certainly possible that Judges 19 alludes to Genesis 19.

Developing Textual Meaning of Judges 19[10]

The Deuteronomic History and the Book of Judges

Since Noth's assertion that Joshua–Kings was the work of a Judean historian called the Deuteronomist and therefore part of the Deuteronomic history, the Book of Judges has been commonly understood in light of the Book of Deuteronomy.[11] However, exactly *how* Joshua through Kings should be understood in this light remains an issue of discussion.[12] Merrill explains, "It is commonplace to refer to Joshua through 2 Kings as the Deuteronomic History, a term that suggests that these books constitute a theological history written with a view to Deuteronomy and to the extent to which Israel (and Judah) conformed to or departed from the covenant principles of that book."[13] However, per the discussion below it seems that even the structure of Joshua through Second Kings could be a result of the book of Deuteronomy

It was argued in chapter 5 that the presence of an allusion must be validated via explaining the alleged allusion's working parts.[14] Further, per the principles set forth in Wilson and Sperber's relevance theory, information provided by an author is of maximum relevance only in a particular

---

9. Niditch, *Judges*, 192.

10. While there are many theories concerning the composition of the Book of Judges, the possibility that the Book of Judges can be understood as a unity is not ruled out a priori. For a discussion on the critical approaches to the Book of Judges, see Harrison, *Introduction to the Old Testament*, 680–90.

11. This has been the standard approach to the book of Judges since Noth's argument that Joshua–Kings was the work of a Judean historian called the Deuteronomist, see Noth, *The Deuteronomistic History*.

12. See Campbell and O'Brien, *Unfolding the Deuteronomistic History*.

13. Merrill, *Everlasting Dominion*, 413.

14. The first working part of an allusion is the developing textual meaning of the alleged alluding text. The second is the stable meaning of the alluding text. The third is the allusive literary markers of the alluding text. The fourth is the rhetorical relationship between the two texts. The fifth is the meaning that is to be imported into the alluding text.

context.¹⁵ Therefore, the closer the interpreter gets to providing the correct interpretive context for an assertion or set of assertions (i.e., the context within which the author working), the greater the probability that understanding will be achieved. In the specific case of literary allusion, the closer the interpreter gets to providing the correct interpretive context, the greater the probability that an intended literary allusion will be understood (i.e., the literary allusion will "make the point" via bridging the gap between what precedes the allusion and what follows it). However, the problem that immediately presents itself when considering Judges 19 is that scholars have struggled to make sense of the "epilogue" of Judges (chs. 17–21).¹⁶ Therefore, if Judges 19 really is an allusion to Genesis 19, and if Judges 19 is meant to bridge the meaning gap between what precedes the passage and what follows it, then validating this allusion will also assist in the understanding of the epilogue of the book of Judges.

Developing Textual Meaning and the Epilogue of Judges

The book of Judges begins with a prologue (1:1–3:6). Judges 2:11–23 explains the cycles of judgment that occurred when וַיַּעֲשׂוּ בְנֵי־יִשְׂרָאֵל אֶת־הָרַע בְּעֵינֵי יְהוָה "The sons of Israel did evil in the eyes of the LORD."¹⁷ When the sons of Israel became "severely distressed," the LORD would raise up judges to deliver them. However, the nation would not listen to the judges and when the judge died, the sons of Israel would return to their sinful ways. For this reason, the anger of the LORD burned against the nation and would therefore no longer drive out the nations before Israel in order to test them to see if they would walk according to the word of the LORD (i.e., do what was right in the eyes of the LORD).¹⁸ Instead of the Israelites eradicating the Canaanites in the land, the Israelites intermarry with them and eventually

15. The term "author" has been intentionally chosen simply to convey the presumption of unity necessary for understanding. Amit correctly explains, "the reader of biblical literature who is aware of the complex processes of transmission and editing needs to assume, in one way or another, that he is confronting an unified work." Amit, *Reading Biblical Narratives*, 22. For his full discussion, see pp. 1–24.

16. For example, O'Connell identifies 17:1—18:31 as Dènouement-A and 19:1—21:25 as Dènouement-B (O'Connell, *The Rhetoric of the Book of Judges*, 297–303). Moore entitled this section as "Two Additional Stories of the Times of the Judges" (Moore, *A Critical and Exegetical Commentary on the Book of Judges*, 365). Soggin regards the section as an "appendix" (Soggin, *Judges*, 261). For a good review of the various approaches to these chapters see Brettler, *The Book of Judges*, 80–91. Boling regards chapters 16–21 as "Supplementary Studies" (Boling, *Judges*, 245–96).

17. See for example Judges 2:11; 3:7.

18. Judges 3:5–6 provides a summary of this introductory section.

serve their gods. Thus, the actions of the Israelites are in direct violation of Deuteronomy 7:4-5. This point, calling specifically for the destruction of the Jebusites, plays a significant rhetorical role in Judges 19-20.

After the prologue to the Book of Judges, chapters 3-16 detail the downward spiral of the nation by chronicling the increasing rebellion of the sons of Israel that is paralleled by the increasing failure of Israel's judges to establish righteous judgment in the land.[19] The downward spiral of the judges culminated with Samson, the last judge presented in the book, who acted in accordance with what was right in his own eyes (cf. Judg 14:3, 7) rather than according to what was right in the eyes of the LORD.[20] The point here should not be overlooked—every man in Israel, *even the judges*, was doing what was right in his own eyes. Certainly the book has shown the downward spiral of the judges. By this point the Israelites are no longer crying out for deliverance and the judges are no longer providing it

The repeated conclusion of the book is straightforward as well—there was no king in Israel, every man was doing what was right in his own eyes. While this repeated refrain has been variously understood, what cannot be denied is that there is a connection between there being no king in Israel and the Israelites rebellion against the LORD.[21]

---

19. Several have pointed out this parallel. For a good chart illustrating this, see Block, *Judges, Ruth*, 146-47. For an extended discussion on this point, see O'Connell, *The Rhetoric of the Book of Judges*, 19-57.

20. Israel was to operate according to the word of the LORD. That is to say, they were to operate according to what was "good" and "right in the eyes of the LORD" instead of what was "evil in the eyes of the LORD." In Deuteronomy 12:8, 28, a contrast is established between every man in Israel doing what was "right in his own eyes" (אִישׁ כָּל־הַיָּשָׁר בְּעֵינָיו) and the nation doing what was "good and right in the eyes of the LORD" (כִּי תַעֲשֶׂה הַטּוֹב וְהַיָּשָׁר בְּעֵינֵי יְהוָה אֱלֹהֶיךָ). Olson argues that the statement אִישׁ כָּל־הַיָּשָׁר בְּעֵינָיו ("every man did what was right in his eyes") is the same as וַיַּעֲשׂוּ בְנֵי־יִשְׂרָאֵל אֶת־הָרַע בְּעֵינֵי יְהוָה ("The sons of Israel did evil in the eyes of the LORD"). See Olson, "The Book of Judges," 864.

21. Some argue that God was Israel's king. Therefore, the Israelites were rejecting God (Boling, *Judges*, 293–94). Block understands the point being made differently and argues that the passage is illustrating the fact that Israel was capable of sinning even before they had a king to lead them in their sin (Block, *Judges, Ruth*, 475–76). Thus, Block does not see the king as a solution to the problem. Block explains, "rather than lifting up the kings as an ideal above the confusion of the period, the addition of 'everyone did as he saw fit' in 17:6 and 21:25 reduces the population to the moral and spiritual level of Israel's kings in later years" (Block, *Judges, Ruth,* 59). However, the key phrase in Block's argumentation is "in later years." It was not supposed to be that way— the judges, priests, kings, and prophets were to ensure it. Further, the kings were later evaluated with the same language (cf. 1 Sam 15:19; 2 Sam 12:9; 1 Kgs 15:26, 34; 16:25, 30; 22:53; 2 Kgs 3:2; 8:18, 27; 13:2, 11; 14:24; 15:9, 18, 24, 28; 17:2; 21:2, 20; 23:32, 37; 24:9, 19). When the king failed, the result was that Israel sinned. However, if the judges, priests, and kings had carried out their responsibility to establish righteousness in the

For Niditch, "Judges 19, like the two previous and two subsequent chapters, departs from the judge-centered format of the tales in chapters. 3–16 and lacks the frame of the theologian that now introduces the tales of the judges."[22] Further, she argues, "the tale as told also emphasizes the ways in which women, the mediating gender, provide doorways in and out of war."[23] In other words, she fails to see how chapters 17–21 fit together with chapters 3–16, and therefore rejects them as a continuation of the same narrative.[24] Certainly Niditch is not alone in failing to see how Judges 17–21 serves to connect Judges 1–16 to the book of 1 Samuel.

While Niditch rejects the assertion that an allusion to Genesis 19 is present in Judges 19 on the claim that they both borrow from a common "weary traveler" tale type, others like Soggin provide a different context to Judges 19 for source critical reasons leaving the text fragmented. For example, Soggin sees no reason why the man being identified as a Levite is relevant when he states, "the fact that the young man is a Levite is unimportant for the purpose of the narrative."[25] However, while Soggin and other source critics see no relevance in the fact that the man is a Levite, it will be argued below that this is in fact the very point of the whole section.

If one is to argue that the book of Judges is not only pointing out the failure of the judges (i.e., the local officials in every town), but also the need

---

land, then every man in Israel would not have been reduced to doing what was right in his own eyes. Satterthwaite correctly sees the point. Israel needed an obedient king to establish righteousness in Israel (Satterthwaite, "No King in Israel," 87–88). Also see O'Connell, *The Rhetoric of the Book of Judges*, 268–304. In addition, O'Connell provides an extensive bibliography of those who also hold this view on pp. 268–69n2.

Up to this point in the discussion over the nature of the statement "there was no king in Israel, every man did what was right in his own eyes," each side in the discussion has been able to gather evidence to support their view. However, none of these views has explained how their understanding makes sense of Judges 17–21. What will be argued below is that there is an intentional movement at work in the book of Judges that is pointing out the failure of the appointed leaders of the nation (Deut 16:18—18:22) to establish righteousness in the land. Judges 3–16 makes the failure of the local judges explicit; Judges 17–21 makes the failure of the Levites explicit. First Samuel 1–7 makes the failure of the high priest explicit. What is needed is the ideal king.

22. Niditch, *Judges*, 191.
23. Niditch, *Judges*, 193.
24. Thus, such an understanding must be evaluated in light of other interpretations (i.e., process of validation of interpretations). To this point it seems that few if any have been able to explain why chapters 17–21 are present in the book of Judges. However, if an interpretation can be presented that satisfactorily explains why these chapters are needed and how they contribute to the overall meaning and movement of the narrative, then such an interpretation should be favored over competing interpretations that cannot.
25. Soggin, *Judges*, 284.

for a righteous king to appear (i.e., one leader to judge the nation), then one logical question remains—how are Levitical priests failing? Is it possible that after demonstrating the failure of the judges to establish מִשְׁפַּט־צֶדֶק "righteous judgment" (cf. Deut 16:18) in the land, a failure that resulted in every man in Israel doing what was right in his own eyes, the focus of the book of Judges turns to the Levitical priesthood (Judg 17–21)? An initial consideration of the lexical evidence seems to suggest that possibility.[26]

Deuteronomy and the Offices of Judge, Priest, King, and Prophet

The introduction to the office of the judge is in Deuteronomy 16:18. In fact, from Deuteronomy 16:18—18:22, it was the duty of the judges, priests, kings, and prophets to establish righteousness in the land.[27] Two key questions arise when considering the relationship between the book of Deuteronomy and the book of Judges. First, are the judges introduced in the book of Deuteronomy the same as those who are raised up by the LORD to deliver Israel from their enemies? Second, is there a discernible relationship between the offices of judge, priest, king, and prophet introduced in Deuteronomy 16:18—18:22?

Concerning the first question, several factors should be considered. First, the same term (שֹׁפְטִים) is used in Judges 2:16–18 and Deuteronomy 16:18 (also see Deut 17:9, 12; 19:17–19; 21:2; 25:1–2; 1 Sam 7:15–17; 2 Sam 15:4; 1 Kings 3:9, 28).[28] Second, Deborah is fulfilling the same function (i.e., administering judgment in a legal sense) as those set forth in Deuteronomy

---

26. Block correctly points out, "In both accounts (chs. 17–18 and 19–20) the crisis was precipitated by the actions of a nameless Levite" (Block, *Judges, Ruth*, 474). Additionally, in Judges 3:7—16:31 there is no mention of either a "priest" or "Levite." However, in chapters 17–21 the picture is very different. Instead, כֹּהֵן occurs repeatedly in chapters 17–18 (cf. 17:5, 10, 12, 13; 18:4, 6, 17, 18, 19, 20, 24, 27, 30), and לֵוִי occurs repeatedly in chapters 17–20 (17:7, 9, 10, 11, 12, 13; 18:3, 15; 19:1; 20:4). Further, Judges 18:30 identifies Jonathan, son of Gershom, son of Moses as the Levitical priest leading the tribal idolatry in Dan and Judges 20:27–28 places Phineas, son of Eleazer, Aaron's son in the center of the controversy ending the book. Finally, there is no use of the root שפט in *any* form in chapters 17–21.

27. It is common among commentators to divide the text along these lines. For example, see Tigay, *Deuteronomy*, 159; McConville, *Deuteronomy*, 278–306; Merrill, *Deuteronomy*, 217.

28. For a full explanation of the uses of שפט in biblical Hebrew, see Niehr, "שפט" 15:411–31. The Ugaritic term *tʿft* appears in the sense of judge, king and ruler. See Lete and Sanmartin, *A Dictionary of the Ugaritic Language in the Alphabetic Tradition*, 926.

16:18 and 17:8–9.²⁹ Third, by way of deduction the judge was the logical choice to fulfill the role of deliverer. In the days before there was a king in Israel, only the offices of judge, Levitical priest, and prophet had been established. Since the Levites were not men of war, it is reasonable to conclude that the LORD would not raise up Levites to deliver Israel from their enemies.³⁰

Concerning the second question, there appears to be an ascending order to these offices. Deuteronomy 16:18 explains that local Judges (שֹׁפְטִים) were to be appointed בְּכָל־שְׁעָרֶיךָ אֲשֶׁר יְהוָה אֱלֹהֶיךָ נֹתֵן לְךָ "in all the towns which the LORD your God is giving you" for the purpose of judging the people in מִשְׁפַּט־צֶדֶק "righteous judgment" (16:18). However, if a case was too difficult to be decided at the local level, then וּבָאתָ אֶל־הַכֹּהֲנִים הַלְוִיִּם וְאֶל־הַשֹּׁפֵט אֲשֶׁר יִהְיֶה בַּיָּמִים הָהֵם "You shall come to the Levitical priest or judge who is *in office* in those days" (Deut 17:9). As McConville explains, "The day-to-day responsibility for the rule of Torah falls . . . to the judges in the cities of Israel, who are appointees of the assembly (16:18), and to a high court at the main sanctuary, consisting of a judge (or judges) and priests (17:8–13)."³¹ Therefore, there is an ascending authoritative relationship between these two offices (i.e., the local judge and the Levitical priest/judge occupying the higher court).³²

The next office in the hierarchy was that of the king (Deut 17:14–20).³³ While the kings in the ANE had no restriction on their power, McConville points out, "It is the limitations placed on the king (17:16–20) that make

---

29. However, not all agree with this conclusion. Block sees the action of Deborah as one of providing prophetic oracles. See Block, *Judges, Ruth*, 195–97; Spronk, "Deborah, a Prophetess," 236.

30. Deborah was the first after the book of Deuteronomy to be called a prophet (or in this case prophetess). Further, she was both a prophet and a judge. Interestingly, *she* didn't deliver Israel. Instead, she commissioned Barak to deliver Israel. Therefore, Deborah prophesies about Barak's deliverance of Israel (i.e., exercises the office of prophet) rather than undertake the deliverance of Israel herself (i.e., act as judge in the same manner as the others in the book).

31. McConville, *Deuteronomy*, 305. Part of the Levite's role in Israel was to administrate the word of the LORD (i.e., render verdicts concerning the law). The penalty for not listening to the judgments of the Levite was death (cf. Deut 17:8–9).

32. The ascending authority structure between these two offices is widely acknowledged. See Craigie, *Deuteronomy*, 251–53; Driver, *A Critical and Exegetical Commentary on Deuteronomy*, 206–9; Christensen, *Deuteronomy 21:10—34:12*, 371–77; Tigay, *Deuteronomy*, 163–64; Merrill, *Deuteronomy*, 261–63.

33. As noted above, one of the roles of the king was to judge. Thus, he was to be the supreme judge in the nation in that he was superior in rank to the local judge or Levite. For a good discussion on the role of the king in Israel, see McConville, *Deuteronomy*, 278–306.

the laws on the administration of Israel so radical."[34] McConville goes on to state, "The king is emphatically subject to the real authority, the Torah, which is administered by the assembly, and watched over by the prophet."[35] However, it would be a mistake to conclude that the king had no authority over the judge or Levite in Israel (cf. 1 Kgs 2:26-27, 35; 2 Chr 19:5-6).

The final office is that of the prophet. McConville explains, "As the final section in 16:18—18:22, it completes the laws about Israel's institutions. Following the laws concerning judge, priest and king, we now have the law of the prophet, or, better, about the true way of hearing the voice of Yahweh. The climactic final position of this section stresses the primacy in Israel's affairs of the divine word."[36] In other words, the judge, Levitical priest, and king were to render judgments according to the word of the LORD. However, this word of the LORD came from the prophet who was not chosen by the people but raised up by God. Christensen goes so far as to argue, "The law of the king (17:14-20), together with the law of the prophets (18:9-22), stands at the structural center of the book of Deuteronomy–as a frame around the law of the Levitical priest (18:1-8). This fact suggests that a primary concern of the book of Deuteronomy, and perhaps the Pentateuch as a whole, is the matter of leadership of the people of God."[37]

The implication for a hierarchy in relation to the book of Judges is readily apparent. If the order of offices is ascending, does the Deuteronomic history (i.e., Joshua—2 Kings) follow the same outline? In other words, is the *whole book* of Judges explaining Israel's movement toward a king. If this is the case, then the books of Samuel and Kings continue the progression from the failure to establish righteousness in the land of Israel that began with the judges (Judg 3:7—16:22) and continues through the Levites (Judg 17—1 Sam 8), and kings (1 Sam 9—2 Kgs 25). If this is the case, then Samuel is functioning not only as the last judge (1 Sam 1-7, especially 7:7, 15-17), but more importantly the prophet (1 Sam 9:9, 11, 19) who introduces the kingship in Israel.[38] While all of this may sound good in theory, does Judges 17-21 support such a conclusion?

---

34. McConville, *Deuteronomy*, 283.
35. McConville, *Deuteronomy*, 305. Also see Psalm 72.
36. McConville, *Deuteronomy*, 285.
37. Christensen, *Deuteronomy 1:1—21:9*, 381.
38. Not only does the literary movement seem to support this, but the repeated phrase "There was a man" (פֶּסֶל וּמַסֵּכָה) begins each of these main sections (cf. Judg 13:2; 17:1; 19:1; 1 Sam 1:1; 9:1)—the last of which introduces the first king in Israel.

Judges 17–18

While some separate chapters 17–18 into three parts, it seems better to regard them as one story in three parts (Micah, Judg 17:1–6; the Levite, Judg 17:7–13; and the tribe of Dan, Judg 18:1–31) since the scene's conclusion (Judg 18:30–31) condemns Micah, the Levite, and the tribe of Dan. In other words, a Levite and direct descendant of Moses, was leading the whole tribe of Dan in an idolatrous rival cult.[39] The evil of the Danites wasn't rejected by the Levite, but led by him. The first part of this passage (17:1–6) tells of a man named Micah from the hill country of Ephraim who steals eleven hundred pieces of silver from his mother and then returns them to her only after she pronounces a curse on the thief.[40] A portion of the returned silver pieces is then used to make פֶּסֶל וּמַסֵּכָה, "a graven image and a molten image" which remains throughout the story.

The second part of the passage (17:7–13) introduces a Levitical priest for hire (i.e., taking bribes) who is setting up graven images, and leading the Danites in outright rejection of the LORD's allotment of land (cf. Josh 19:40–48) by moving north to overtake the city of Laish and set up a rival idolatrous cult.[41] Surely everyone, even the Levites, is doing what is right in their own eyes. Moreover, the literary effect of keeping the identity of this Levite from the reader until the very end of the pericope serves to highlight

---

39. While the Hebrew text identifies the Levite as "the son of Manasseh" (with the nun suspended), a few medieval Hebrew manuscripts and Greek witnesses read "the son of Moses." This reading helps explain the suspended nun. For more information on this issue, see Burney, *The Book of Judges*, 434–35; Moore, *A Critical and Exegetical Commentary on the Book of Judges*, 401–2; Weitzman, "Reopening the Case of the Suspiciously Suspended Nun in Judges 18:30," 448–60.

40. Interestingly this passage begins with וַיְהִי אִישׁ "Now there was a man . . ." This phrase is used to introduce several passages relevant to the present discussion (e.g., Judg 13:2; 17:1; 19:1; 1 Sam 1:1; 9:1). These transition points will take the story from the last judge in the book of Judges (Samson), through the failure of the Levites (17:1; 19:1), to the prophet Samuel (1 Sam 1:1) who introduces Israel's first king. Moreover, Samuel remains in the story until David (presented as a Deut 17 ideal king). Block agrees: "The introductory 'Now there was a man' hints at a new focus. In the following chapters the narrator will offer the reader a series of glimpses at how ordinary Israelites fared in the dark days of the 'judges' (governors)" (Block, *Judges, Ruth*, 474). However, after the Samson narrative (chs. 13–16) the judges are not mentioned again in the book. In fact, the Hebrew root word שפט is not used again in the book in any form. Finally, Block does point out that one of the commonalities between chapters 17–18 and chapter 19 is the presence of Levites in both (Block, *Judges, Ruth*, 474–75).

41. Block explains that the Levite in Judges 17–18 is a "parody on Moses' instructions regarding Levites in Deut 18:6–9" (Block, *Judges, Ruth*, 486–87). Moreover, taking bribes was specifically addressed in Deuteronomy 16:19 (וְלֹא־תִקַּח שֹׁחַד כִּי הַשֹּׁחַד יְעַוֵּר עֵינֵי חֲכָמִים וִיסַלֵּף דִּבְרֵי צַדִּיקִם).

just how serious the situation in Israel has become. Even more appalling, however, is the fact that the Levite who was leading the Danites in their worship of a graven image was Jonathan, the son of Gershom, the son of Moses (cf. Judg 18:30). By the beginning of chapter eighteen, just when the reader believes that the rebellion against the LORD could get no worse, it does.

Judges 19:1–27

After the repeated refrain אֵין מֶלֶךְ בְּיִשְׂרָאֵל "there was no king in Israel" in 19:1 (cf. 17:6; 18:1; and 21:25), the narrative will now tell of the depths of depravity and rebellion that the nation has reached. In 19:2, the reader is introduced to another Levite. While the actions of the first Levite led to the idolatry of the whole tribe of Dan, so also will the actions of this Levite lead to civil war and the near annihilation of the tribe of Benjamin.

Leaving the father's house in the evening, the Levite intentionally passes over Jebus stating, "We will not turn aside to this city of foreigners who are not sons of Israel, we will travel on to Gibeah (19:12)."[42] Upon arriving in the city of Gibeah, the small band of travelers were not met with a welcome reception.[43] Instead, they sat in the town square with no one inviting them into their home to spend the night. Finally, an old man who was a temporary resident in Gibeah came in from the field briefly questioned them and invited them to spend the night in his home.[44] The old man warned the Levite not to stay in the open square.[45] After arriving at the old man's house, they ate and drank and were having a good time when the men of the city, sons of Belial, surrounded the house and demanded that the Levite be turned over to them.[46] However, the old man went outside to

---

42. The fact that the Jebusites were still in the land points to the failure of the Israelites to obey the word of the LORD. Per Deuteronomy 7:1–5, they were to be utterly destroyed. Moreover, the sons of Israel were not to intermarry with them. Ironically, this whole scene (chs. 19–21) will leave Gibeah, not Jebus, going up in smoke like the city of Ai; and, it will lead to the Israelites not giving their daughters to the Benjamites, instead of the Jebusites.

43. This is in contrast to the reception they received by the concubine's father in Bethlehem of Judah (19:3–9).

44. It is at this point in the story where the events begin to become reminiscent of the story recorded in Genesis 19. It should be emphasized that the "old man," like Lot, was only a temporary sojourner in the city. This point is being made so that the reader begins to identify the roles that each of the participants will play in the story. Here, the old man is playing the role of Lot.

45. Notice that similar language is used by the old man here (i.e., 19:20, רַק בָּרְחוֹב אַל־תָּלַן) as was used by Lot (cf. Gen 19:2, לֹא כִּי בָרְחוֹב נָלִין).

46. The phrase "sons of Belial" (בְּנֵי־בְלִיַּעַל) is not only used here (19:22) and again

plead with them in order that they would not do such an evil act against the Levite and instead offered them his virgin daughter and the Levite's concubine. The Gibeahites rejected the old man's plea and offer.⁴⁷ The Levite then seized (חזק) his concubine and caused her to go out (יצא) to them (אליהם)).⁴⁸ The men then raped the concubine and brutalized (עלל) her until morning. After the men were finished with her, they sent her (שלח) away. As the day began, the concubine came (בוא) and fell at the door (פתח). The Levite, her master, arose early the next morning to find the results of his judgment. As the Levite was leaving the house the next morning, he discovered his concubine lying at the doorway and commanded her to arise (קוּם). When there was no answer, he took (לקח) her home, cut her into twelve pieces and sent her throughout the territory of Israel.

Stable Textual Meaning of Alluded Text: Genesis 18:16—19:29⁴⁹

Context and Interpretation of Genesis 18:16—19:29

The deliverance of Lot and the destruction of Sodom and Gomorrah begins in Genesis 18:16 and continues through 19:29. Genesis 18:16–33 records Abraham's intercession on behalf of Lot for his deliverance from Sodom.⁵⁰ Sodom and Gomorrah were to be destroyed by the LORD because

---

in the next chapter (20:13) in describing the men of Gibeah, but it is also used of Eli's sons (1 Sam 2:12). Eli is condemned because of the rebellion of his sons. Moreover, because he refused to discipline them, the LORD put his sons and him to death. This phrase serves to connect these two passages by pointing out that Eli the high priest was unwilling to judge evil.

47. What is missing here when compared to the Genesis 19 story is that there is no threat made to the old man (cf. Gen 19:9). The explanation for this can be accounted for by the fact that the angels in Genesis 19 went to Sodom, at least in part, to deliver Lot (the one being threatened). Interestingly, in Judges 20:5, the Levite recognizes only the threat to him.

48. While the Hebrew is unclear as to the identity of the "man," it is clearly the Levite for several reasons. First, the old man's virgin daughter is not put out with the concubine. Second, the third person pronominal suffix points to the Levite. Third, the Levite is very vague and deceitful on the exact details of what happened in the next chapter (Judg 20:4–7). Lasine correctly points out that the actions of the Levite in Judges 19 are to be understood in contrast to those of the angel in Genesis 19 (Lasine, "Guest and Host in Judges 19," 52n5). As will be seen below, it is these actions that serve to condemn the Levite. Not only does the Levite fail to play the role of the Angel, his actions are directly opposite theirs.

49. The most common mistake among those evaluating this allusion is that they confine the allusion too narrowly in both Genesis 19 and Judges 19.

50. Cf. Gen 18:16–33; 19:27–29.

Illustrations in the Identification and Validation of Literary Allusion in the Old Testament 167

of their wickedness.[51] However, Abraham intercedes on behalf of the צַדִּיק; "righteous" arguing that they should not be destroyed along with the רָשָׁע "wicked." Chapter 18 ends with the LORD and Abraham in agreement that the righteous will not be swept away along with the wicked.

Chapter 19 begins with the two angels' entrance into Sodom and Gomorrah in the evening as Lot was sitting in the gate of Sodom.[52] As they came near, Lot immediately rose to meet them and bowed to the ground. Lot then urged the two angels whom he assumed were travelers to spend the night with him. When they refused, Lot urged them strongly warning them not to spend the night in the town square.

After the two angels agreed to Lot's invitation and entered Lot's house, he prepared a meal for them and they ate. However, before they went to bed, the men of the city, both young and old, surrounded the house and called out to Lot to bring the two men out so that they could have relations with them. After Lot entreated them not to act wickedly and they persisted, he offered the men of the city his two virgin daughters so that the men could do to them whatever was right in their eyes (וַעֲשׂוּ לָהֶן כַּטּוֹב בְּעֵינֵיכֶם). However, this was not a satisfactory substitute for the men of the city and they began to press hard against Lot and the door. It is at this point that the two angels sent forth (שלח) their hands and brought (בוא) Lot back into them (אליהם). The angels then struck (נכה) the men of the city with blindness leaving the Sodomites wearying themselves to find the door (פתח).

It is at this point in the narrative that the two reveal both their identity and their intentions—to destroy (שחת) the city. Lot responded by pleading with his sons-in-law to take their wives and flee the city because the LORD was about to destroy it, but they refused him. In the morning the angels urged Lot to arise (קום) and take (לקח) his wife and family lest they be swept away in the judgment of the city. However, Lot hesitated so the two angels seized (חזק) Lot, his wife, and his two daughters and brought them out (יצא) of the city. The next morning Abraham rose early, went to the place where he had stood before the LORD, and saw the judgment of the LORD that was poured out on the city through the angels: fire and brimstone had rained down from heaven leaving smoke rising up from the land like smoke from a furnace. Interestingly, Genesis 19 ends with "the smoke of the land going up like the smoke of a furnace" (עָלָה קִיטֹר הָאָרֶץ כְּקִיטֹר הַכִּבְשָׁן). Ironically however, the wording of the Judges 20:40, recording smoke rising from the city (לַעֲלוֹת מִן־הָעִיר עַמּוּד עָשָׁן), calls to mind the destruction of Ai as

---

51. The Hebrew of Genesis 18:20 reads: כִּי־רַבָּה וְחַטָּאתָם כִּי כָבְדָה מְאֹד.

52. It should be noted that the angels' visit to Sodom was twofold: to deliver "righteous" Lot (cf. 2 Pet 2:7) and to bring destruction upon the cities.

recorded in Joshua 8:21, "the smoke of the city ascended" (עָלָה עֲשַׁן הָעִיר), not the destruction of Sodom and Gomorrah. Israel was not destroying the Jebusites as was instructed in Deuteronomy 7:1–5. They were utterly destroying themselves!

Literary Markers in Alluding Text

Two areas need to be evaluated in order to identify the literary markers in Judges 19: the structure of the narrative and the language of the narrative. Once evaluated in this manner, what will be seen below is that the allusion to Genesis 19 actually extends from Judges 19:14—20:48.[53]

Narrative structure

Westermann asserts, "There is much agreement in sentence structure and word usage, and complete agreement in structure."[54] By "complete agreement in structure," Westermann is referring to the events of the narrative (see Table 6.1)

Table 6.1[55]

	Gen.	Judg.
arrival and reception	19:1–3	19:15–21
attack and repulse of attack	19:4–11	19:22–25
attack, demand to hand over	19:4–5	19:22
offer by householder	19:6–8	19:23–24
rejection and threat	19:9	19:25a
repulse of attack by guests	19:10–11	19:25b

As Block correctly states, "Anyone familiar with the narratives of Genesis will hear in this account (i.e., the Judges 19 passage) remarkable echoes of the depravity at Sodom and Gomorrah in Genesis 19."[56] However, the

---

53. This type of analysis is necessary in order to evaluate all of the elements available to the author since both passages are narrative literature.

54. Westermann, *Genesis 12–36*, 297.

55. Westermann, *Genesis 12–36*, 297.

56. Block, *Judges, Ruth*, 532. The reason for the truth of Block's statement in this instance is not only that the context (i.e., type of meaning) is the same (i.e., the wickedness of men in a city), but that the *same events* take place in both narratives. Thus, while there are surely lexical connections that can and should be made, it is the likeness of

question is not whether there is an echo present in Judges 19, but whether there is an allusion in Judges 19 in that there must be a rhetorical relation between the two passages as well as meaning that is to be imported into the alluding passage.[57]

Since both Genesis 19 and Judges 19 are examples of narrative literature, the author of Judges 19 has available to him all of the components of narrative literature from which to draw. At its most basic level, narrative literature is made up of characters and events.[58] In these two passages, the characters in Judges 19 play the same "roles" as those in the Genesis 19 passage. Obviously the role of the Sodomites is played by the Gibeahites. The role of Lot, the sojourner of Sodom, is played by the old man "from the hill country of Ephraim, and he was staying in Gibeah" (Judg 19:16). This leaves the role of the angels to be played by the Levite. Finally, the old man's daughter and the Levite's concubine play the role of Lot's two virgin daughters.

The events of the Judges 19 narrative follow those of Genesis 19 up through the setting and tension. However, the resolution to the tension in the two stories is very different. Both stories involve strangers coming to a city. In both accounts a foreigner living temporarily in the city exhorts the travelers not to stay in the open square and instead entreats them to stay in his home. In both accounts the host feeds and cares for his guests. In both accounts the men of the city surround the house of the host and demand

---

events that first alerts the reader to the connection between the two accounts. It should be noted that none of the strongest allusive literary markers typically utilized to allude to the Genesis 19 story are present here (e.g., "Sodom," "Gomorrah," "fire," "brimstone/sulfur," "salt," "overturn," "Lot"). The reason for this can be accounted for by genre. Because Genesis 19 and Judges 19 are both examples of narrative literature, the author of Judges 19 has available to him all of the literary devices and distinctives of narrative literature (e.g., characterization, setting, and plot). Therefore, what Alter and others have titled "type scenes" (see Alter, *The Art of Biblical Narrative*, 47–62) are literary allusions intended to make a point. In other words, narrative literature can allude via a "type scene" (i.e., like events in a narrative) while other genres such as legal documents (e.g., Deut 29:23; 32:32), prophetic books (e.g., Isa 1:9–10; 3:9; 13:19; Jer 23:14; 49:18; 50:40; Ezek 16; 38:22; Hos 11:8; Amos 4:11; Zeph 2:9; Rev 11:8), psalms (e.g., Ps 11:6), gospels (Luke 17:28–29), or epistles (2 Pet 2:7) must, because of genre limitations, be more direct via the utilization of stronger allusive literary markers.

57. In other words, there is a difference between recognizing an allusion and understanding an allusion. Authors utilize allusions to make a point. Therefore, in order to validate an allusion, the interpreter must be able to explain and defend the point being made by the allusion.

58. For an introductory discussion on narrative see Abbott, *The Cambridge Introduction to Narrative*. Here, Abbott uses the term "entities" or "existents" instead of characters (see p. 19); Also, as narrative literature relates to the Bible see Ryken, *How to Read the Bible as Literature*; Alter, *The Art of Biblical Narrative*; Amit, *Reading Biblical Narratives*; Berlin, *Poetics and Interpretation of Biblical Narrative*.

that the travelers be brought out to them so that they can have relations with them. In both accounts the host goes outside to the men of the city to entreat them not to do such a wicked thing offering instead two female substitutes. In both accounts the men of the city reject the offer of the host. Up until this point in the Judges 19 narrative, the old man has played the role of Lot perfectly. Likewise, the Gibeahites have performed their role as the Sodomites according to script.

It is at this point that both the angels and the Levite take action in the stories. However, their actions are very different. The angels act to save Lot and his family while the Levite acts to save himself. The contrast in action between the Levite and the angels is presented in the two tables below (6.2 and 6.3). Table 6.2 points out key lexical connections between the two passages. However, in order to make the connections more readily apparent, Table 6.3 considers just the verbs that present the actions, commands and results of the angels'/Levite's actions. Finally, the contrasting results (presented in red) in the two passages will play a significant role in Judges 20.

Table 6.2

Angels' Actions and Results in Genesis 19	Levite's Actions and Results in Judges 19
The men sent forth (שלח) their hands	The Levite seizes (חזק) his concubine
And they struck (נכה) the men with blindness	outside (חוץ) the house
leaving them wearying themselves to find the doorway (פתח)	The men of Gibeah raped and ravished (עלל) her
Inform Lot of coming destruction Command Lot to arise (קום),	Then they sent her away (שלח)
leave (לקח),	and she came (בוא)
for the destruction (שחת) is imminent.	and fell (נפל)
When Lot hesitates, they seize (חזק) Lot and his family	at the doorway (פתח)
and they caused him to go out (יצא),	Levite wakes up and morning light reveals the results of judgment
And they caused him to rest (נוח)	Command for concubine to arise (קום)
outside (חוץ) the city	When there is no answer, he takes her (לקח) home
Abraham wakes up and the morning light reveals the results of destruction (שחת)	

In Genesis 19, Lot was delivered and given rest (נוּחַ) via the actions of the angels while the Sodomites were struck (נכה) with blindness and Sodom was destroyed (שׁחת). Conversely, the concubine was abused (עלל) and fallen (נפל) via the actions of the Levite who saved himself (cf. Judg 20:5).

What is missing is the destruction and punishment due to the Gibeahites for their actions. Amazingly, all five of these verbs appear in four verses (cf. vv. 42–45) in Judges 20 describing the judgment poured out upon the Benjamites. Further, these verbs appear more broadly in the passage as well and are very carefully assigned.

Because of the wickedness in both camps, the verb (שׁחת) is used to describe the destruction that came upon the Israelites and the Benjamites (cf. 20:21, 25, 35, 42). Instead of receiving deliverance (i.e., rest, Heb. נוּחַ) via the actions of the Levite in the same manner that Lot received rest from the actions of the angels (cf. Gen 19:11), the concubine was abused (עלל) and fallen (נפל). These words appear again in Judges 20 (cf. עלל in 20:45, נפל, 20:44, 46, and נוּחַ in 20:43) are used to describe the retribution due the men of Gibeah for their treatment of the concubine. They were pursued, found no rest (נוּחַ), were caught (עלל), and fell (נפל) (cf. 20:45). In addition, the judgment that was dealt to the men of Sodom by the angel (i.e., being struck with blindness), described by the verb (נכה), is also used of the judgment that came upon the Benjamites (cf. 20:37, 39, 45, 48). Therefore, the retribution and punishment that was due the Gibeahites was poured out in the third battle by the LORD.

Table 6.3

Angels' Actions, Commands, and Results in Genesis 19	Levite's Actions, Commands, and Results in Judges 19
19:10 (שׁלח)	19:25 (חזק)
19:10 (בוא)	19:25 (יצא)
19:11 (נכה)	19:25 (עלל)
19:15 (קוּם)	19:25 (שׁלח)
19:15 (לקח)	19:26 (בוא)
19:16 (חזק)	19:26 (נפל)
19:16 (יצא)	19:27 Levite wakes up and morning light reveals the results of judgment
19:16 (נוּחַ)	19:28 (קוּם)
Abraham wakes up and the morning light reveals the results of judgment	19:28 (לקח)

Rhetorical Relationship of Allusion

In his commentary on the book of Judges, Block states, "there can be little doubt that the narrator was composing this text with Genesis 19 in mind and doing so intentionally that a reader might experience a sense of déjà vu."[59] Per the discussion above, this rhetorical relationship is already becoming readily apparent. Lot and the "old man" are one in the same; the Gibeahites have become the Sodomites and are deserving of judgment; and the Levite has failed to play his role of the angels as judge and deliverer.

However, one question remains: why did the Benjamites *and the Israelites* receive the judgment of destruction (שחת) from the LORD? In other words, if Judges 19, 20 and 21 should be understood as related scenes with one leading to the next, then the judgment that the Israelites received must have been deserved because of the events that occurred prior to first battle. Four points need to be raised in response to this question.[60]

First, the Levite was just as culpable for the destruction of the concubine as the Gibeahites. Before the story began, it was clear that "every man was doing right in his own eyes." Moreover, it had become true of the judges also, being made explicit in the Samson story. Chapters 17 and 18 tell not of a Levite who is following the word of the LORD, but of one who was leading the tribe of Dan in rebellion against the word of the LORD. Chapter 19 portrays in tragically ironic fashion that while the Levite was supposed to play the role of the angels of Genesis 19 by standing up against evil and even judging it, his heart is just as evil and callous as the Gibeahites who rape her.[61]

Second, it can easily be argued that the Levite is a "malicious witness" (עֵד־חָמָס [cf. Deut 19:15–21]).[62] Merrill explains:

> In the event there were only one witness, however, and he wished to prosecute the case, he could do so; but he himself would undergo as close a scrutiny as the person he had accused. Such a witness might be reliable, a contingency not addressed here, but more often than not he would be motivated by malice (Heb. Hamas), that is, with intent to do violent harm to an innocent

---

59. Block, *Judges, Ruth*, 534.

60. What is being suggested in these four points is that while the allusion to Genesis 19 is still powerfully at work in Judges 20, allusions and references to other passages are being made in Judges 20 as well (i.e., Joshua 7–9; Deut 17:6–7; 19:15–21; Num 35:30).

61. The actions taken by the Levite in 19:29 highlight this point. The Levite entered (בוא), took (לקח) a knife, seized (חזק) his concubine, cut (נתח) her into pieces, and sent (שלח) her parts throughout the land.

62. See Deut 19:15–21. See Swart and VanDam, "חמס," 2:177–80; Haag, "חמס," 4:478–87.

party. In any case, where a single witness was involved, both he and the one against whom he was pressing charges must appear "in the presence of" the Lord (v. 17). What this means (as in 17:8–12) becomes apparent in the appositional phrase "in the presence of the priests and the judges." These representatives of the Lord (cf. 16:18–20; 17:8–9) acted judicially on his behalf in investigating (lit., "seek thoroughly") and prosecuting the case brought before them. If the result showed the witness to be a liar, he was to suffer the punishment that would have been dealt to the one who he had implicated (v. 19a). Only in this way could the evil . . . be purged . . . from the community (v. 19b; cf. 13:6; 17:7, 12; 19:13; 21:21; 22:21–22, 24; 24:7 for other occurrences of this technical phrase in Deuteronomy).[63]

His testimony serves to exonerate his actions while at the same time condemn those of the Gibeahites. Yet, if he had not seized her and forced her out to them, then they would not have been able to rape and ravish her—at least not before doing the same to him first! His testimony glosses over the fact that *he* was the one who handed her over to them and thus guilty of an offense as well. In addition, the Levite doesn't follow the protocol set forth by the law. Per Deuteronomy 16:18—17:13 the Levite in this story had no authority to act as judge in this case since he was not at that time serving in the "place which the LORD your God chosen."

Third, the case was not handled according the manner set forth in Deuteronomy 17:1–7 or Deuteronomy 19:15–21. While the Gibeahites surely deserved to be put to death because of their actions (Deut 22:22), they were to be put to death on the testimony of two or three witnesses—not one.[64] Further, a witness must be qualified (i.e., not a malicious witness). Ironically, the reversal of roles here is stark. Israel was gathered the witness as one man, וַתִּקָּהֵל הָעֵדָה כְּאִישׁ אֶחָד.[65] In this case, the *Levite* testified the testimony and then commanded the *people* to deliver the verdict (הִנֵּה כֻלְּכֶם בְּנֵי יִשְׂרָאֵל הָבוּ לָכֶם דָּבָר וְעֵצָה הֲלֹם.[66] However, the law set forth that the witnesses were to deliver the evidence and the Levite was to deliver "the word of the judgment" (דְּבַר הַמִּשְׁפָּט).[67] Further, the hand of the witness was to be the first to put a man to death, yet here the "witness" had not seen the crime. Instead, the Israelites had only responded to the malicious witness.

63. Merrill, *Deuteronomy*, 280.
64. Also see Num 35:30.
65. See Judg 20:1. Block makes the point that הָעֵדָה "the assembled group" is derived from the same root as עֵד "witness." See Block, *Judges, Ruth*, 551.
66. See Judg 20:7.
67. See Deut 17:8–10.

Fourth, the judgment of Judges 20 turns into an ironic replay of Joshua 8. While in Genesis 19 the destruction of the LORD leaves smoke (קִיטֹר) going up from "the earth like the smoke of a furnace" (הָאָרֶץ כְּקִיטֹר הַכִּבְשָׁן), the picture in Judges 20 is that of Joshua 8.[68] In Judges 20, smoke (עָשָׁן not קִיטֹר) is going up from the city (הָעִיר), not the land (הָאָרֶץ).[69] In addition, the LORD commands Israel to go up (עלה), for he has delivered (נתן) the enemy into your hands. This occurs only twice after a loss in battle (Josh 8:1; Judg 20:28).

The similarities in these two passages are too unique to overlook. In both passages Israel is defeated in battle. After the two defeats by the Israelites in Judges 20, they implement the same strategy as the one utilized in Joshua 8 to defeat Ai (i.e., draw the enemy away from the city, come into the city from behind, then set the city on fire, and attack the enemy from the front and rear). Further, just as the Israelites' defeat at Ai was because of the actions of one man, so also can the defeat of the Israelites at Gibeah be blamed at least in part on the actions of the Levite.[70] Finally, in Deuteronomy 7:1–5 and Deuteronomy 20:1–20, Israel was to eradicate (i.e., "utterly destroy," הַחֲרֵם תַּחֲרִים) the Canaanites from the land. Ironically, one of their initial failures was not consulting the counsel of the LORD, leading to the Israelites making a vow not to destroy the Gibeonites (Josh 9). In Judges 20, they also failed to consult the LORD at Mizpah, resulting in their plan to make war with the Benjamites and vowing not to intermarry with the tribe of Benjamin.

The Israelites were to utterly destroy the Hittites, Girgashites, Amorites, Canaanites, Perizzites, Hivites or Jebusites as well as not intermarry with them (Deut 7:1–3). However, through their rejection of and rebellion against the word of the LORD they had vowed to spare the Canaanites (Josh 9) and wipe out one of their own tribes (Judg 19–21). Moreover, they had now vowed not to intermarry within their own nation. Apparently they believed that their only way out of their predicament was to violate the law even more (i.e., murder, kidnap, and then blame the LORD for the results, cf. Judg 21:3, 15). Moreover, when they began to conquer the land, smoke rose from the destroyed Canaanite cities (cf. Josh 8:20), but now the smoke is rising from the conquered Benjamite city (cf. Judg 20:38). Their actions

---

68. Compare Gen 19:28 with Judg 20:40 and Josh 8:20.

69. Compare with וְהִנֵּה עָלָה עֲשַׁן הָעִיר, "Behold, smoke going up from the city" (Josh 8:20, 21).

70. For a discussion of the possible reasons for the Israelites' loss in battle see Webb, *The Book of Judges*, 193; Boling, "In Those Days There Was No King in Israel," 43; Olson, "The Book of Judges," 885. Another potential parallel between Joshua 8–9 and Judges 20–21 is the fact that both passages follow victories in battle with foolish vows.

result in the near eradication of the tribe of Benjamin via war and a vow not to give any of their daughters to the Benjamites. The only way that the Israelites are able to avoid Benjamin's extinction is to engage in the same types of actions that caused them to be outraged in the first place.

Imported Meaning into Alluding Text and Conclusion[71]

Block states, "the echo of Genesis 19 in this text is intentional. By patterning this account after the earlier story, the narrator serves notice that, whereas these travelers had thought they had come home, finding safety with their own countrymen, they have actually arrived in Sodom. The nation has come full circle. The Canaanization of Israel is complete."[72] Block's words are absolutely correct. However, the book of Judges not only serves to demonstrate how wicked the nation had become, but also that the nation's wickedness was largely due to the failure of the judges and Levites to establish righteousness in the land. Further, the Israelites were not destroying the Canaanites in the land—they were destroying themselves.

After learning that the nation had ceased to seek deliverance from the LORD and the judges were doing what was right in their own eyes instead of establishing justice in the land (chs. 3–16), the attention of the reader is then directed toward evaluating the priests in order to see how they are faring (chs. 17–21). Upon only brief observation, the reader learns that the situation has gone from bad to worse: the descendants of Moses are taking bribes, perverting justice, and leading the Danites in idolatry (chs. 17–18). Israel had become steeped in harlotry, idolatry, perversion of justice, rape, murder, incest, deceit, and civil war.

The increasing wickedness of the nation and the failure of its judges and Levites introduce a new tension to the Deuteronomic history. The nation needed a king. However, not just any king would do. They needed the righteous king of Deuteronomy 17 to appear and establish righteousness in the land of Israel.

In conclusion, each of the steps for the validation of a literary allusion has been walked through and the claim that a literary allusion to Genesis 19

---

71. One of the main presuppositions of relevance theory is that every statement made by a speaker is of maximum relevance in communicating his cognitive goal. As Eugene Merrill correctly points out, "the Old Testament on close inspection betrays itself for what it really is, a pulsating, life-changing narrative that has a beginning, a plot, a dénouement, and a (at least tentative) conclusion" (Merrill, *Everlasting Dominion*, 2).

72. Block, *Judges, Ruth*, 544.

is present in Judges 19 has been validated. It should be remembered that for an interpretation to be valid does not definitively prove that it is correct. It does, however, serve to establish grounds upon which the interpretation can be compared with other valid interpretations. Moreover, the exact points of disagreement among interpretations can be identified and debated.

ALLUSION IN LAW: GENESIS 19 IN DEUTERONOMY 29:23?

The second possible literary allusion to be considered is that of Genesis 19 in Deuteronomy 29:23. Because of the reference to כְּמַהְפֵּכַת סְדֹם וַעֲמֹרָה "the overthrow of Sodom and Gomorrah," it is clear that the Deuteronomy text refers to the Genesis 19 passage (i.e., literary reference). However, does this reference satisfy the requirements of a literary allusion?[73]

Prerequisites of Literary Allusion

With the dating of the book of Deuteronomy an issue of ongoing debate, coupled with such claims as those of Van Seters that the J documents date to exile with editing occurring in post-exilic times, there is no scholarly consensus concerning the date of authorship for either the book of Genesis or the book of Deuteronomy. Except for the most radical reconstructions of the dating of Old Testament books, and given the nature of the ongoing debates, such an allusion is surely possible.[74]

Developing Textual Meaning of Alluding Text: Deuteronomy 29:23

Context and Interpretation of Deuteronomy 29:23

In his last sermon to the nation before they enter the land, Moses renews their covenant with the LORD and reminds them of the requirements therein. Merrill explains that the book of Deuteronomy follows the basic outline of a Hittite treaty text and divides as follows: The Preamble (1:1–5); The Historical Prologue (1:6—4:40); The General Stipulations (5:1—11:32); The Specific Stipulations (12:1—26:25); The Blessings and Curses (27:1—28:68);

---

73. As explained above in chapter 3 (pp. 75–84), Ben Porat explains a literary reference is "if the process of actualizing the allusion yields no significant additional components, it can be treated as a reference" (Ben-Porat, "Poetics of Literary Allusion," 81).

74. E.g., Seters, *Abraham in History and Tradition* (see 157n6 above).

and The Witnesses (30:19; 31:19; 32:1–43).⁷⁵ However, this outline omits chapter 29 and much of 30. Merrill explains:

> There is general consensus that chaps. 29 and 30 of Deuteronomy (as well as 31:1–8) are not strictly part of the covenant document as such documents were ordinarily crafted. This does not mean, of course, that this section does not serve a covenant function in Moses' own unique creation of the book as a covenant instrument. But even if it doesn't, it is very much at home here as a parenesis that looks to the past, present, and future of the elect nation. It provides a summation of God's past dealings with Israel, restates the present occasion of covenant offer and acceptance, and addresses the options of covenant disobedience and obedience respectively. Finally, it exhorts the assembled throng to covenant commitment. It is most fitting that these summaries and exhortations follow the body of the covenant text and precede the formalizing of the agreement by the Lord and his chosen vassal.⁷⁶

In fact, the context of Deuteronomy 29–30 is quite concentrated as McConville explains: "these two chapters (i.e., 29–30) explore further the implications of Israel's acceptance of the terms of the covenant, and specifically of the curse."⁷⁷ Merrill expands upon this point in discussing 29:22–24 [21–23]:

> Returning to the plural pronoun and thus to the nation as such, Moses looked to the future and the results of divine judgment that would accompany disloyalty to the Lord and the covenant. . . . The only fitting comparison that came to the prophet's mind was the destruction of the cities of the plain in Abraham's day. . . . As they were totally decimated in the Lord's fiery wrath, so Israel would become a barren place of burning sulphur . . . and salt. Crops would no more grow there than along the moonscape-like shores of the Dead Sea.⁷⁸

In discussing 29:23 [22] specifically, Duane Christensen states, "the association of 'brimstone and salt' with the 'overthrowing of Sodom and Gomorrah' in this verse suggests that the curse is something along the lines of the story in Genesis in which 'brimstone [sulfur] and fire' fell out of heaven

---

75. Merrill, *Deuteronomy*, 27–32.
76. Merrill, *Deuteronomy*, 375.
77. McConville, *Deuteronomy*, 413.
78. Merrill, *Deuteronomy*, 384.

on those cities (Gen 19:24)."[79] Further, Craigie explain, "The language employed in v. 22 uses a previous example of God's judgment as a basis for comparison; it is strongly reminiscent of the description of the destruction of Sodom and Gomorrah."[80] For their part, Keil and Delitzsch point out, "the nouns in ver. 23, 'brimstone and salt burning,' are in apposition to the strokes (plagues), and so far depend upon 'they see.' The description is borrowed from the character of the Dead Sea and its vicinity, to which there is an express allusion in the words 'like the overthrow of Sodom.'"[81] That the destruction of Sodom and Gomorrah recorded in Genesis 19 is in view here is readily acknowledged. However, does this verse meet the requirements necessary to be classified as a literary allusion?

Stable Textual Meaning of Alluded Text: Genesis 19

(For the stable meaning of the alluded text, see pp. 167–69 above). Additionally, it should be noticed that while the focus of Deuteronomy 29:23 is the effect of the judgment of Sodom and Gomorrah on the productivity of the land, Genesis 19 makes no mention of the effects of God's judgment upon the land. Instead, it appears that both the destruction of Sodom and Gomorrah, recorded in Genesis 19, and the description of the land before its destruction, recorded in Genesis 13:10, are in view here.[82]

---

79. Christensen, *Deuteronomy 21:10—34:12*, 726.
80. Craigie, *Deuteronomy*, 359.
81. Keil and Delitzsch, *Pentateuch*, 450.
82. I.e., כִּי כֻלָּהּ מַשְׁקֶה לִפְנֵי שַׁחֵת יְהוָה אֶת־סְדֹם וְאֶת־עֲמֹרָה כְּגַן־יְהוָה כְּאֶרֶץ מִצְרַיִם בֹּאֲכָה צֹעַר ("that all of it [the land] was well watered [before the LORD destroyed Sodom and Gomorrah] like the garden of the LORD, like the land of Egypt as you go to Zoar). In the context of Deuteronomy 28, God would not rain down fire and brimstone from heaven, like he did on Sodom and Gomorrah. Instead, he would raise up nations (Deut 28:47–50) who would destroy many and scatter the remaining (Deut 28:63–65). Tigay points out, "Because of the reference to Sodom and Gomorrah at the end of the verse, this curse is sometimes thought to refer to a conflagration like that which occurred when God rained down 'sulfur and fire' on those cities (Gen. 19:24). However, the reference to salt and infertility suggests that this verse refers to soil sterilants. As a severe punishment, conquerors sometimes spread salt on the soil of conquered lands to render it infertile" (Tigay, *Deuteronomy*, 281). Also see, Judg 9:45; Gevirtz, "Jericho and Shechem," 52–62; Honeyman, "The Salting of Shechem," 192–95, who gives a good bibliography on this issue.

Literary Markers in Alluding Text

In this case, the literary markers are quite clear and numerous. First, there are several unique words used in both passages (e.g., גָּפְרִית, מֶלַח, סְדֹם וַעֲמֹרָה, and הפך). In addition, the phrase "as the overthrow of Sodom" כְּמַהְפֵּכַת סְדֹם (Deut 29:22[23]) is present here as well in several passages where the destruction of Sodom is in view (cf. Isa 13:19; Jer 49:18; 50:40; Amos 4:11).

Second, there is the connection of Sodom and Gomorrah (סְדֹם וַעֲמֹרָה) with Admah and Zeboiim (אַדְמָה וּצְבֹיִים) in Genesis 14:2,8 and Hosea 11:8. The only other city mentioned in 14:2 is Bela, that is Zoar, (בֶּלַע הִיא־צֹעַר) which is the city where Lot pleaded with the angels to allow him to flee. Clearly all of these cities were closely related. Further, Admah and Zeboiim must have been destroyed along with Sodom and Gomorrah in Genesis 19 (cf. Hosea 11:8). Third, the type of meaning in Genesis 19 and Deuteronomy 29:23 is the same: judgment because of the LORD's anger. Therefore, there is the presence of unique terms in each passage as well as likeness in theme.

Rhetorical Relationship and Imported Meaning

In addition to the fact that both Deuteronomy 29:22–28 and Genesis 19 are a result of the judgment of the LORD, there are also clear textual markers in Deuteronomy 29:23 that reference the destruction recorded in Genesis 19. Therefore, the first three working parts of a literary allusion can be explained. However, the fourth and fifth working parts are not present in this example.

Once one considers the rhetorical relationship being made by this reference, it becomes readily apparent that an *analogy* is being drawn between the wrath that will come upon Israel and the wrath that came upon Sodom and Gomorrah. However, there is no meaning from Genesis 19 (or Genesis 13:10) that is not made explicitly in Deuteronomy 29:23. Instead, Moses explains exactly the connections that he wants the reader to make between the two texts. That is to say, Moses' words do not ask the reader to make any more unstated connections between the two texts. Instead, he specifically and explicitly limits the connections that are to be made: the relationship between the judgment of Deuteronomy 29:23 and the judgment that fell upon Sodom and Gomorrah is the effect that it will have on the land, leaving it unplanted and unproductive.

In such a case, the only rhetorical relationship between these two texts is the one explicitly made by Moses, and thus no meaning is to be imported into the Deuteronomy passage. Therefore, the five working parts of a literary allusion are not present and hence, no literary allusion is present. Instead, this is a good example of a literary reference.[83]

ALLUSION IN THE PROPHECY: GENESIS 19 IN ISAIAH 1:9–10?

The third possible literary allusion to be considered is that of Genesis 19 in Isaiah 1:9–10. As in the previous example, it is clear that the Isaiah text refers to Sodom and Gomorrah, but again the question must be raised concerning whether or not this reference satisfies the requirements of a literary allusion.

Prerequisites of Literary Allusion

With the dating of the book of Isaiah an issue of ongoing debate, coupled with such claims as those of Van Seters that the J documents date to exile with editing occurring in post-exilic times, there is no scholarly consensus concerning the date of authorship for either the book of Genesis or the book of Isaiah.[84] Therefore, the possibility of an allusion certainly exists.

Developing Textual Meaning of Alluding Text: Isaiah 1:10

Context and Interpretation of Isaiah 1:1–20

Before the conquest of the land, Moses delivered his last sermon to the nation recorded in the book of Deuteronomy. As Merrill explains, the book of Deuteronomy "would serve as the corpus of law and practice for the covenant community from that day forward."[85] Further, this book served as the covenant agreement between the LORD and Israel. If the nation were obedient to the covenant, they would be blessed (cf. Lev 26:1–13; Deut

---

83. The conclusion here disagrees with Keil and Delitzsch's assessment that an allusion is present in Deuteronomy 29:22[23]. However, this point is raised here not for the purpose of arguing that Keil and Delitzsch were "wrong" in their statements about Deuteronomy 29:22[23]. Instead, Keil and Delitzsch's words serve to point out the need for the present study. If the distinction between literary allusion, literary reference, literary citation, literary quotation, literary paraphrase, and echo were being made at the time of their writing, then their choice of wording may have been different.

84. For an excellent (although somewhat dated) summary on the history and development of the documentary hypothesis as well as the dating of Isaiah see, Harrison, *Introduction to the Old Testament*, 3–82, 495–541, 764–94. For an example of the most extreme dating of the biblical sources, see Seters, *Abraham in History and Tradition*.

85. Merrill, *Deuteronomy*, 27.

28:1–14). However, if the nation were disobedient to the covenant, they would be cursed (cf. Lev. 26:14–46; Deut 28:15–68).

Per Deuteronomy 28:15–68, the disobedience of Israel would bring forth judgment from the LORD in the form of plagues, famine, and foreign invaders. As the first chapter of Isaiah makes clear, the nation had revolted against the LORD and broken their covenant (vv. 2–4). The judgment of the LORD had brought disease, sickness, bruises, welts, and raw wounds (vv. 5–6). However, as Oswalt explains, "Israel's ill health is not merely a matter of disease. She has been beaten and smitten. The words occurring in v. 6 describe injuries received in battle."[86] The result of this assault by the LORD has left the land decimated and Jerusalem (i.e., daughter of Zion) standing like a lone shelter in a vineyard (vv. 7–8).[87] Moreover, the language used in the description of the damage done to the land by these foreigners (v. 7, כְּמַהְפֵּכַת זָרִים) is very reminiscent of language used elsewhere to describe the destruction of Sodom (כְּמַהְפֵּכַת סְדֹם, cf. Isa 13:18; Jer 49:18; 50:40; Amos 4:11).

Stable Textual Meaning of Alluded Text: Genesis 19:1–11

(For the stable meaning of the alluded text, see pp. 167–69 above).

Literary Markers in Alluding Text

As mentioned in the previous example, the allusive literary markers available to an author are limited by genre. The result of this reality is twofold. When making a literary allusion to a text of the same genre, more linking literary characteristics are available to the author. However, when making a literary allusion to a text of a different literary genre, fewer linking literary characteristics are available to the author since the author must operate within the confines of the literary genre that he is writing. Here, Isaiah is pronouncing judgment via poetic Hebrew parallelism where there is a premium placed on every word. In verses 9–10 Isaiah artistically and strategically makes his point via the reference to Sodom and Gomorrah. Few textual markers to the

---

86. Oswalt, *The Book of Isaiah*, 89.

87. As John Oswalt explains, commentators assign one of two settings for this passage, "these occasions include the invasion of Israel and Syria in 735 (e.g., Delitzsch), that of Sennacherib in 701 (e.g., Kaiser, Cheyne), and that of Nebuchadrezzear in 586 (Kissane). Few take this last position today" (Oswalt, *The Book of Isaiah*, 84). Considering the fact that Isaiah prophesied from around 740–686 BC (for dates of the reigns of the Kings of Israel and Judah, see Merrill, *Kingdom of Priests*, 320), the situation that best fits this literary context is the invasion of Sennacherib in 701 BC which destroyed all of the northern and southern kingdoms, leaving only Jerusalem standing.

Old Testament are as strong the mention of Sodom and Gomorrah. In fact, they have become synonymous (i.e., function as a type) with the judgment of God upon a nation for wickedness. In addition, the mention of Sodom and Gomorrah in both 1:9 and 1:10 serves to activate the imagery in 1:7 of "your cities are burned with fire." In other words, 1:9 connects the judgment that came upon Sodom and Gomorrah with the judgment that has come upon Israel. Both are from the LORD. Both have brought fire and destruction. Both are the result of wickedness.

Rhetorical Relationship of Allusion

The rhetorical relationship between these two passages is centered on three parallels and one distinct difference. The three parallels are the LORD's grace, the LORD's salvation, and the LORD's judgment. The key difference is the means by which the LORD brought destruction. It was the LORD's grace that saved Lot. It was the LORD's judgment that destroyed Sodom and Gomorrah because of their wickedness.

In explaining verse 9, Oswalt states, "although Zion is little more than a shack in a vineyard, she is at least that. There is hope for her; she is not completely destroyed. That this is so, the prophet makes plain, is God's doing. The clear implication is that God could have made his people like Sodom and Gomorrah—extinct. But he has chosen not to. This is not an act of weakness, for it is the Lord of Hosts who has done this."[88]

Oswalt has picked up on the "clear implication" of the point in verse 9. Although it is not stated, they still exist and the inhabitants of Sodom and Gomorrah do not. This fact makes Isaiah's words in verse 10 all the more impacting; Isaiah addresses the surviving remnant in Jerusalem as the "rulers of Sodom" (קְצִינֵי סְדֹם) and the "people of Gomorrah" (עַם עֲמֹרָה). Even though they have been spared from annihilation via the grace of God, they remain unchanged. With these words in verse 10 comes the threat of the prophet—God spared you from destruction the first time, but if you don't repent you will not be spared again. In verses 11–17, the clear dissatisfaction of the LORD is given. In verses 18–20, the threat made implicit in verse 10 is made explicit: repent and be restored, or reject and be destroyed (vv. 18–20).

What Isaiah is drawing on here is twofold. First, it is the LORD who brings destruction. While the *type* of destruction that came upon Sodom and Gomorrah was different than that which came upon Israel, the result was the same: only a few survived from each judgment. However, Hans Wildberger argues:

88. Oswalt, *The Book of Isaiah*, 92.

Illustrations in the Identification and Validation of Literary Allusion in the Old Testament 183

> It is most surprising to see the comparison with Sodom and Gomorrah, since these cities were actually not destroyed in a war. Above all else, Isaiah's words betray the fact that he knows nothing of the traditions of Genesis. The sinfulness and destruction of Sodom and Gomorrah must have become proverbial (see 13:19; Amos 4:11; Zeph 2:9 and often elsewhere), even being referred to in the NT, where the present passage is quoted in Rom. 9:29 (see also Rev. 11:8). One can explain why the pre-exilic prophets knew of the destruction of these cities, since they are mentioned in connection with the covenant traditions which they knew very well (see Deut 29:22, where Admah and Zeboiim are mentioned in addition to Sodom and Gomorrah). The gloss in 1:7 (emended text) with its use of the formula מהפכת סדם (the destruction of Sodom), the exact phrase used in Deut. 29:22 and Jer. 49:18, shows that this tradition must have been very well known. The phrase appears to be an abbreviation which was repeated in a stylized way: מהפצת אלהים סדם (as when God overthrew Sodom) (Amos 4:11; Isa. 13:19; Jer. 50:40).[89]

In other words, Wildberger is arguing that the writer of Isaiah could not be alluding to the Genesis 19 account because it was unavailable to him. Instead, the author of this passage must have been referring to Deuteronomy 29:22[23]. However, emending the text without any external evidence and then arguing that Isaiah is referring to the emended text can hardly be viewed as anything but circular reasoning.[90] Moreover, one must ask where the book of Deuteronomy got its information?[91] Instead, Wildberger's analysis here misses the point being made by the passage.

As is true with any allusion, the developing textual meaning of the alluding passage must serve as the control mechanism that establishes what

---

89. Wildberger, *Isaiah 1–12*, 31.

90. Wildberger is willing to follow Ewald in reading Isaiah 1:7 as כְּמַהְפֵּכַת סְדֹם rather than כְּמַהְפֵּת זָרִים. To emend the text in this way disregards the parallelism between "Your land is being devoured by strangers" (Heb. אַדְמַתְכֶם לְנֶגְדְּכֶם זָרִים אֹכְלִים אֹתָהּ) with "It is a desolation, as overthrown by foreigners" (Heb. וּשְׁמָמָה כְּמַהְפֵּכַת זָרִים). The focus here is the effect that the invasion has had on the land. Second, the familiar imagery of כְּמַהְפֵּת., typically used in reference to Sodom, helps to introduce the reference to Sodom and Gomorrah in 1:9–10.

91. From the validation of the Judges 19 allusion to Genesis 19 passage above, it seems clear that Genesis 19, Deuteronomy 16–18, and Joshua 7–9 predate Judges 19. Wildberger argues, "the concept of a remnant . . . had a long history before the time of Isaiah. . . . When one searches for sources, this concept also has its roots in the descriptions of holy war; in Josh. 8:22, the Israelites slew the people in Ai . . . until there was left none that survived or escaped" (Wildberger, *Isaiah 1–12*, 28). In addition, is it not possible that the concept of a "righteous remnant" may have gotten its start in the Genesis 19 story?

rhetorical relationships are to be made and thus, what meaning is to be imported into the alluding text.[92] Here the rhetorical relationship focuses not on the means of judgment, but on the reason for judgment (i.e., the wickedness of the people and leaders), the source of judgment (i.e., the LORD), and the effect of judgment (i.e., extinction of the people and the land left in ruins).[93]

Because of the grace of the LORD, Lot escaped the judgment that came upon Sodom and Gomorrah. This is the point being made in Isaiah 1:9. However, 1:10 turns right back around and accuses those who escaped as being unchanged (i.e., still wicked). Thus, they are threatened again with the destruction that Sodom and Gomorrah received.

Imported Meaning into Alluding Text and Conclusion

The meaning to be imported into the text of Isaiah 1:9–10 is that while the LORD has spared a remnant in the land, their character and actions have not changed: they are still wicked in the eyes of the LORD. What the allusion does not answer is why the Israelites are still wicked in the eyes of the LORD. Verses 11–14 spell out the LORD's charge of wickedness against them. The result of their wickedness is that the LORD will not hear their prayers (v. 15). Therefore, they need to respond to the threat of the LORD appropriately or they too will perish (vv. 16–31). In conclusion, Isaiah 1:9–10 can be considered a literary allusion to Genesis 19 since all of the working parts of a literary allusion can be explained.

ALLUSION IN POETRY: GENESIS 19 IN PSALM 11:6?

It was argued above that validation of an alleged literary allusion requires that one explain the working parts of a literary allusion. The first step in this process is providing an explanation of the developing textual meaning of the alluding text. Psalm 11 is one example wherein this endeavor proves difficult because of the textual issues involved.[94] In this short Psalm containing only seven verses in the Hebrew text, there are no less than sixteen textual issues. Thus, the translation of the Psalm and an evaluation of the textual

---

92. It is at this point that the significance of relevance theory and the illustration quoted above (Table 4.1) should be recalled.

93. Also see Williamson, *Isaiah 1–27*, 73.

94. The result of this reality is that many have offered emendations of the text in order to make argue some interpretation or point. Some, such as Sonne, suggest fairly mild changes (Sonne, "Psalm Eleven," 242–43) while others, such as Morgenstern, offer suggestions that emend almost every line (Morgenstern, "Psalm 11," 221–31).

issues must first be performed. In order to best determine the developing textual meaning of Psalm 11, the following translation is proposed.

Psalm 11

1 For the choir director, *A Psalm*[95] of David
In the LORD I have taken shelter. How can you say to my soul,
"Flee[96] *as* a bird to your mountain![97]
2 For behold, the wicked prepare a bow, they put their arrow[98] on the string,
to shoot in the darkness at the upright of heart.
3 When the foundations are destroyed, what can the upright do?"
4 The LORD is in his holy temple; the LORD's throne is in heaven.
His eyes see; his eyes examine the sons of Adam.
5 The LORD examines the righteous, but his soul hates the wicked and those who love violence.
6 May the LORD rain down burning[99] coals and brimstone on the wicked.
A scorching wind will be the portion of their cup!
7 For the LORD is righteous; he loves the righteous; the upright will see his face.

In Luke 17:28–29, Jesus connects the raining of fire and brimstone from heaven on the day of the LORD with the judgment of God that fell upon Sodom and Gomorrah.[100] Likewise, Samuel Terrien says of Psalm 11:6, "The annihilation of those who love evil is sketched in terms that recall the story of Sodom and Gomorrah (Gen 19:24). This may allude to the final theophany and to the Last Judgment."[101] In other words, for Terrien the judgment requested of the LORD to bring down upon the wicked not only looks

---

95. Two medieval manuscripts and LXX add מִזְמוֹר. Here it has been added in italics to assist in translation.

96. Reading נוּדִי with Qere.

97. Reading הרכם per 5/6 HevPsalms with MT.

98. Reading per 5/6 הצם HevPsalms with MT.

99. Delitzsch correctly argues, "Assuming that פַּחִים might be the equivalent to פֶּחָמִים, even then the Hebrew פֶּחָם, according to the general usage of the language in distinction from גַחֶלֶת, does not denote burning, but black coals. It ought therefore to have been פַּחֲמֵי אֵשׁ" (Delitzsch, *Psalms*, 189).

100. "Likewise, just as it was in the days of Lot, they were eating, drinking, buying, selling, planting, building, but on the day when Lot went out from Sodom, it rained fire and brimstone from heaven and destroyed them all" (Luke 17:28–29).

101. Terrien, *The Psalms*, 150.

backward to the total destruction that came upon Sodom and Gomorrah, but looks forward as well. Certainly this view deserves consideration given the appearance of the same language in Ezekiel 38:22.[102] Additionally, Hans-Joachim Kraus says of Psalm 11:6, "His (the Psalmist's) conception of God's intervening legal aid is revealed in v. 6: 'On the wicked he lets fiery coals and brimstone rain down.' The prototype of this conception of the destructive intervention of Yahweh is, on the one hand, the narrative of the destruction of Sodom and Gomorrah (Gen. 19:24) and, on the other, the theophanic tradition as it is expressed, for instance in 18:12ff."[103] In fact, the same phrase, אֵשׁ וְגָפְרִית, appears in Ezekiel 38:22 and Psalm 11:6. However, is this phrase in 11:6 an allusion to Sodom and Gomorrah?

Prerequisites of Literary Allusion

As with the previous three examples, there is little scholarly consensus concerning the relative dating of the two passages in view here. Lussier argues that the setting of Psalm 11 (Psalm 10 in the Latin) seems "strikingly appropriate to the circumstances of David's life when he was at Saul's court (1 Sam., C. 18)."[104] In contrast, Briggs argues, "On the whole the Ps. seems to be subsequent to J, D, and Is.2, and to precede the legal attitude of Ezra and his times. It is best explained as from the circumstances of the feeble community in Jerusalem shortly after the Restoration."[105] However, Kraus explains, "A dating of the psalm is, in accordance with what has been said about its form, hardly possible. There can hardly be any doubt that the formulary belongs to the realm of the temple and the cultic act of the jurisdiction of God. A preexilic origin is possible. But in such a dating the perspective of the history of tradition is not to be curtailed."[106] Thus, the possibility of an allusion surely exists.

---

102. וְנִשְׁפַּטְתִּי אִתּוֹ בְּדֶבֶר וּבְדָם וְגֶשֶׁם שׁוֹטֵף וְאַבְנֵי אֶלְגָּבִישׁ אֵשׁ וְגָפְרִית אַמְטִיר עָלָיו וְעַל־אֲגַפָּיו וְעַל־עַמִּים רַבִּים אֲשֶׁר אִתּוֹ.

103. Kraus, *Psalms 1–59*, 203–4.

104. Lussier, "The New Latin Psalter," 200.

105. Briggs, *The Book of Psalms*, 89.

106. Kraus, *Psalms 1–59*, 202.

Developing Textual Meaning of Alluding Text: Psalm 11

Context and Interpretation of Psalm 11:6

Craigie classifies Psalm 11 as an "individual song of confidence."[107] As he explains, the Psalm has two sections, "(1) the sense of despair (11:1–3); and (2) the restoration of the confidence (11:4–7)."[108] In vv. 1–3, the Psalmist explains that the wicked set out to destroy the righteous. However, the LORD is in his holy temple and sees what is happening. In the end, the righteous will be delivered but the wicked will be destroyed in the judgment of the LORD (vv. 4–7).

While the exact setting and context of Psalm 11 may be unclear or debated because of the textual issues involved, there are some things concerning Psalm 11:6 that are clear. First, the verb מטר appears in the jussive (יַמְטֵר). Thus, the psalmist is requesting that the LORD rain down his judgment upon the wicked. Second, whether one is inclined to argue that what is being rained down is "traps of fire and brimstone" or "coals of fire and brimstone" the source of the imagery of "raining down" and "fire and brimstone" is unaffected (cf. Gen 19:24, וַיהוָה הִמְטִיר עַל־סְדֹם וְעַל־עֲמֹרָה גָּפְרִית וָאֵשׁ). Third, nothing in Psalm 11:6 makes explicit the result of the raining down of fire and brimstone. Instead, the significance of the event is only realized once the LORD's destruction of Sodom and Gomorrah is connected to the psalmist's request.

Stable Textual Meaning of Alluded Text—Genesis 19:1–11

(For the stable meaning of the alluded text, see pp. 167–69 above).

Literary Markers in Alluding Text

There are two possible lexical links between Psalm 11 and Genesis 19. The first possible connection is that when Lot was commanded to flee from the destruction that was coming upon Sodom and Gomorrah, he was told to go to the mountains to seek refuge (cf. Gen 19:17). However, two points militate against such a connection. First, Genesis 19:17 uses a different word (מלט) than does Psalm 11:1 (נוד) for "flee." Second, the command of the angel in Genesis 19:17 is to be regarded as good advice.

---

107. Craigie, *Psalms 1–50*, 132.
108. Craigie, *Psalms 1–50*, 132.

The second, and much stronger connection between Psalm 11 and Genesis 19 is the image of judgment from the LORD being rained down (מטר) from heaven in the form of fire (אֵשׁ) and brimstone (גָּפְרִית). The combination of these three allusive literary markers certainly warrants further evaluation of the potential rhetorical relationship between these two texts.

Rhetorical Relationship of Allusion

In the context of Psalm 11, the point of the author is that the righteous will be delivered but the wicked will be judged. However, the effect of the raining down of fire and brimstone is not readily apparent in Psalm 11. However, once the allusion to Genesis 19 is understood, the implication is readily apparent to the reader. The psalmist is not simply calling for trouble to come upon the wicked. Instead, the psalmist is calling for their complete annihilation at the hand of the LORD.

Imported Meaning into Alluding Text and Conclusion

The confidence of the psalmist is twofold. First, the wicked will be destroyed (v. 6). The allusion to Genesis 19 makes this point. Second, the righteous will be saved (i.e., see the face of the LORD, v. 7).

CONCLUSION

As has been argued above, validity in the identification and interpretation of literary allusions can be achieved via an interpreter validating his argumentation via the working parts of a literary allusion. Once this process is completed, the interpreter can determine whether or not a literary allusion is actually present in a text. Thus, it was argued that Judges 19–20; Isaiah 1:9–10; and Psalm 11:6 are all allusions to the destruction of Sodom and Gomorrah in Genesis 19. Additionally, it was argued that Deuteronomy 29:23, while referring to the destruction of Sodom and Gomorrah, did not meet the qualifications of a literary allusion since the connection between the two passage was made explicit by the author (i.e., no additional meaning was to be imported into the passage from Genesis 19).

It was also argued that literary allusions within the same genre are capable of having more points of intersection (i.e., the allusive literary markers can be more numerous and can take the form of the characteristics of the genre) and thus are capable of being more multi-dimensional in their rhetorical function and meaning (i.e., at least this was demonstrated within the bounds of narrative alluding to narrative). Although not evaluated here, it seems reasonable to suspect that the same phenomenon would take place if one psalm were to allude to another, or one prophetic text were to allude to another. In addition, the converse was also pointed out. Namely, when literary allusions cross genre lines they tend toward utilizing fewer and stronger allusive textual markers (i.e., usually like terms) and being more one-dimensional in their rhetorical function and meaning. Finally, this chapter sought to briefly illustrate the manner in which genre, relevance theory, and the working parts of a literary allusion can assist in the identification and validation of a literary allusion in a text.

7

Conclusion

As explained in the introduction, there has been a need for a more thorough theoretical treatment on the topic of literary allusion. Several possible explanations were posited in an effort to account for this void. However, it was explained that the most probable and troubling reason for the void is that recognition of authorial intention as well as the literary devices that authors use to convey meaning are no longer in vogue in the field of philosophical hermeneutics. This study is an effort to begin to fill that void.

Along the way, several contributions to this ongoing discussion have been made. In Chapter 2, a defense of the author, authorial intention, and literary devices was made. Moreover, the current hermeneutical approaches as well as their philosophical underpinnings were exposed as contradictory and theologically driven.

Chapter 3 began with a search for an adequate definition of literary allusion. Along the way it was explained that one contributing factor to the inconsistent use of literary terms was the fact that no clear categories have been created within which a detailed and theoretical discussion could take place. Therefore, categories were created within which intertextual literary devices such as literary reference, literary citation, literary quotation, literary paraphrase, and literary allusion, and echo could be logically placed. In addition, Chapter 3 provided a clear definition for literary allusion that adequately accounts for all of its components. While this definition is theoretical in nature, and therefore longer than most that have come before it, every effort has been made to avoid common mistakes such as vagueness and inaccuracy.

In Chapters 4 and 5, three key considerations of literary allusion that have been largely overlooked were made explicit: the relevance of relevance theory, the impact of genre on allusive literary markers, and the identification of the five working parts of literary allusion. In addition, it was pointed out that the magnitude of the disagreements over the presence of literary allusions in texts stems from disagreements over one or more of the working parts that create a literary allusion. This acknowledgment allows interpreters to identify exactly where and why they disagree over the presence of a literary allusion in a text.

Finally in Chapter 6, illustrations of an approach to identifying and validating a claim that a literary allusion is present in a text via explanation of the five working parts of literary allusions was presented. These illustrations were not exegetically exhaustive, nor were they intended to be. Instead, they were provided in order to demonstrate how walking through the working parts of a literary allusion in a step-by-step manner can assist the interpreter in his identification and validation of a claim that a literary allusion is present in a text.

Because of space limitations, not every issue that was unearthed in this project was addressed. One major consideration concerning the topic of literary allusion is still in need of study. It was pointed out that genre can and does affect the allusive textual markers in both the alluding text and the alluded text. Further, it was argued that this point, along with the impact of relevance theory, were the two contributing factors in the failure to identify allusions via their textual markers. Still a study needs to be conducted that examines a large quantity of literary allusions in order to provide a descriptive list of genre specific categories that are commonplace.

Bibliography

Abbott, H. Porter. *The Cambridge Introduction to Narrative.* 2nd ed. Cambridge: Cambridge University Press, 2008.
Abrams, M. H. *A Glossary of Literary Terms.* New York: Holt, Rinehart, and Winston, 1971.
Allen, David, and Steve Smith, eds. *Methodology in the Use of the Old Testament in the New: Context and Criteria.* London: T. & T. Clark, 2020.
Allen, Garrick V. *The Book of Revelation and Early Jewish Textual Culture.* Cambridge: Cambridge University Press, 2017.
Alter, Robert. *The Art of Biblical Narrative.* New York: Basic, 1981.
———. *The World of Biblical Literature.* New York: Basic, 1992.
Amit, Yaira. *Reading Biblical Narratives: Literary Criticism and the Hebrew Bible.* Minneapolis: Fortress, 2001.
Aquinas, Thomas, and Tommaso de Vio Cajetan. *Aristotle: On Interpretation.* Translated by Jean T. Oesterle. Milwaukee: Marquette University Press, 1962.
Aristotle. *On the Soul.* In *The Complete Works of Aristotle,* edited by Jonathan Barnes, 641–90. Princeton: Princeton University Press, 1984.
Baden, Joel S. "Literary Allusions and Assumptions about Textuality Familiarity." In *Subtle Citation, Allusion, and Translation in the Hebrew Bible,* edited by Ziony Zevit, 114–30. Sheffield: Equinox, 2017.
Barthes, Roland. "The Death of the Author." In *Authorship from Plato to Postmodern: A Reader,* edited by Seán Burke, 125–30. Edinburgh: Edinburgh University Press, 1995.
Beale, G. K. "Questions of Authorial Intent, Epistemology, and Presuppositions and Their Bearing on the Study of the Old Testament in the New: A Rejoinder to Steve Moyise." *Irish Biblical Studies* 21 (1999) 152–80.
———. "A Response to Jon Paulien on the Use of the Old Testament in Revelation." *Andrews University Seminary Studies* 39.1 (2001) 23–34.
———. "Solecisms in the Apocalypse as Signals for the Presence of Old Testament Allusions: A Selective Analysis of Revelation 1–22." In *Early Christian Interpretation of the Scriptures of Israel: Investigations and Proposals,* edited by C. A. Evans and J. A. Sanders, 421–46. Sheffield: Sheffield Academic, 1997.
———. *The Use of Daniel in Jewish Apocalyptic Literature and in the Revelation of St. John.* Lanham, MD: University Press of America, 1984.
Beetham, Christopher A. *Echoes of Scripture in the Letter of Paul to the Colossians.* Leiden: Brill, 2008.

Bell, David. "Kant." In *The Blackwell Companion to Philosophy*, edited by Nicholas Bunnin and E. P. Tsui-James, 589–606. Cambridge: Blackwell, 1996.

Ben-Porat, Ziva. "The Poetics of Literary Allusion." *PTL: A Journal for Descriptive Poetics and Theory of Literature* 1 (1976) 105–28.

Ben-Porath, Ziva. "The Poetics of Allusion." PhD diss., University of California, 1967.

Berlin, Adele. *Poetics and Interpretation of Biblical Narrative*. Winona Lake, IN: Eisenbrauns, 1994.

Block, Daniel Isaac. *Judges, Ruth*. New American Commentary. Nashville: Broadman & Holman, 1999.

Boda, Mark J. *The Book of Zechariah*. New International Commentary on the Old Testament. Grand Rapids: Eerdmans, 2016.

Boling, Robert G. "In Those Days There Was No King in Israel." In *A Light unto My Path: Old Testament Studies in Honor of Jacob M. Myers*, edited by Howard N. Bream et al., 33–48. Philadelphia: Temple University Press, 1974.

———. *Judges: A New Translation with Notes and Commentary*. Anchor Yale Bible 6A. Garden City, NY: Doubleday, 1975.

Braiman, Jay. "Literary Devices." https://web.archive.org/web/20090926184005/http://mrbraiman.home.att.net/lit.htm.

Brettler, Marc Zvi. *The Book of Judges*. London: Routledge, 2002.

———. "Identifying Torah Sources in the Historical Psalms." In *Subtle Citation, Allusion, and Translation in the Hebrew Bible*, edited by Ziony Zevit, 73–90. Sheffield: Equinox, 2017.

Briggs, Charles Augustus. *A Critical and Exegetical Commentary on the Book of Psalms: Volume 1*. International Critical Commentary. Edinburgh: T. & T. Clark, 1907.

Burney, C. F. *The Book of Judges, with Introduction and Notes, and Notes on the Hebrew Text of the Books of Kings, with an Introduction and Appendix*. New York: KTAV, 1970.

Campbell, Antony F., and Mark A. O'Brien. *Unfolding the Deuteronomistic History*. Minneapolis: Fortress, 2000.

Carr, David M. "Method in Determining the Dependence of Biblical on Non-Biblical Texts." In *Subtle Citation, Allusion, and Translation in the Hebrew Bible*, edited by Ziony Zevit, 41–53. Sheffield: Equinox, 2017.

Christensen, Duane L. *Deuteronomy 1:1—21:9*. Word Biblical Commentary 6A. Nashville: Nelson, 2001.

———. *Deuteronomy 21:10—34:12*. Word Biblical Commentary 6B. Nashville: Nelson, 2002.

Clayton, Jay, and Eric Rothstein. "Figures in the Corpus: Theories of Influence and Intertextuality." In *Influence and Intertextuality in Literary History*, edited by Jay Clayton and Eric Rothstein, 3–36. Madison: University of Wisconsin Press, 1991.

Conte, Gian Biagio. *Memoria dei Poeti e Sistema Letterario: Catullo, Virgilio, Ovidio, Lucano*. Turin: Einaudi, 1974.

———. *The Rhetoric of Imitation: Genre and Poetic Memory in Virgil and Other Latin Poets*. Translated by Charles Segal. Ithaca: Cornell University Press, 1986.

Cottingham, John. "Cartesian Dualism: Theology, Metaphysics, and Science." In *The Cambridge Companion to Descartes*, edited by John Cottingham, 236–57. Cambridge: Cambridge University Press, 1992.

Craigie, Peter C. *Deuteronomy*. New International Commentary on the Old Testament. Grand Rapids: Eerdmans, 1976.

———. *Psalms 1–50*. Word Biblical Commentary 19. Waco: Word, 1983.
Culler, Jonathan. *The Pursuit of Signs: Semiotics, Literature, and Deconstruction*. Ithaca, NY: Cornell University Press, 1981.
Culley, R. C. *Studies in the Structure of Hebrew Narrative*. Philadelphia: Fortress, 1976.
Delitzsch, F. *Psalms*. Translated by James Martin. Commentary on the Old Testament in Ten Volumes. Reprinted ed. Grand Rapids: Eerdmans, 1978.
Dell, Katharine J., and Will Kynes, eds. *Reading Job Intertextually*. New York: T. & T. Clark, 2013.
Dilthey, Wilhelm. *The Formation of the Historical World in the Human Sciences*. 5 vols. Selected Works 3. Princeton: Princeton University Press, 2002.
Driver, S. R. *A Critical and Exegetical Commentary on Deuteronomy*. International Critical Commentary. Edinburgh: T. & T. Clark, 1902.
Eslinger, Lyle. "Inner-Biblical Exegesis and Allusion: The Question of Category." *Vetus Testamentum* 42.1 (1992) 47–58.
Fekkes, Jan. *Isaiah and Prophetic Traditions in the Book of Revelation: Visionary Antecedents and Their Development*. Journal for the Study of the New Testament Supplement Series 93. Sheffield: JSOT Press, 1994.
Feuerbach, Ludwig. *The Essence of Christianity*. Translated by George Eliot. New York: Harper & Row, 1957.
Fish, Stanley. *Doing What Comes Naturally: Change, Rhetoric, and the Practice of Theory in Literary and Legal Studies*. Oxford: Clarendon, 1989.
———. *Is There a Text in This Class? The Authority of Interpretive Communities*. Cambridge: Harvard University Press, 1980.
Fishbane, Michael. *Biblical Interpretation in Ancient Israel*. Oxford: Clarendon, 1985.
Foucault, Michel. "What Is an Author?" In *Textual Strategies*, edited by Josue V. Harari, 141–60. London: Methuen, 1979.
Friedman, Michael. "Descartes and Galileo: Copernicanism and the Metaphysical Foundations of Physics." In *A Companion to Descartes*, edited by Janet Broughton and John Carriero, 69–83. Oxford: Blackwell, 2008.
Gadamer, Hans Georg. *Truth and Method*. 2nd rev. ed. New York: Continuum, 2004.
Gevirtz, Stanley. "Jericho and Shechem: A Religio-Literary Aspect of City Destruction." *Vetus Testamentum* 13 (1963) 52–62.
Gonzalez, Justo L. *The Story of Christianity, Volume 1: The Early Church to the Dawn of the Reformation*. New York: Harper & Row, 1984.
Grayling, A. C. "Epistemology." In *The Blackwell Companion to Philosophy*, edited by Nicholas Bunnin and E. P. Tsui-James, 38–63. Oxford: Blackwell, 1996.
Haack, Susan. "Pragmatism." In *The Blackwell Companion to Philosophy*, edited by Nicholas Bunnin and E. P. Tsui-James, 643–61. Oxford: Blackwell, 1996.
Haag, H. "חמס." In *TDOT* 4:478–87.
Harrison, R. K. *Introduction to the Old Testament: Including a Comprehensive Review of Old Testament Studies and a Special Supplement on the Apocrypha*. Peabody, MA: Hendrickson, 2004.
Haugg, Donatus. *Die Zwei Zeugen*. Neutestamentliche Abhandlungen 17. Münster: Aschendorffschen Verlagsbuchhandlung, 1936.
Hays, Richard B. *The Conversion of the Imagination: Paul as Interpreter of Israel's Scripture*. Grand Rapids: Eerdmans, 2005.
———. *Echoes of Scripture in the Gospels*. Waco: Baylor University Press, 2016.

———. *Echoes of Scripture in the Letters of Paul.* New Haven: Yale University Press, 1989.

Hebel, Udo J. *Intertextuality, Allusion, and Quotation: An International Bibliography of Critical Studies.* New York: Greenwood, 1989.

Hegel, Georg Wilhelm Friedrich. *The Philosophy of History.* Dover ed. New York: Dover, 1956.

Hegel, Georg Wilhelm Friedrich, and J. B. Baillie. *The Phenomenology of Mind.* New York: Harper & Row, 1967.

Heidegger, Martin. *Sein Und Zeit.* 12th unchanged ed. Tubingen: Neimeyer, 1972.

Herder, Johann Gottfried. *Discourse on the Origin of Language.* New York: Unger, 1967.

Hirsch, E. D. *Validity in Interpretation.* New Haven: Yale University Press, 1967.

Honeyman, A. M. "The Salting of Shechem." *Vetus Testamentum* 3 (1953) 192–95.

Howe, Thomas. *Objectivity in Biblical Interpretation.* Altamonte Springs, FL: Advantage, 2004.

Hoy, David Couzens. "Heidegger and the Hermeneutic Turn." In *The Cambridge Companion to Heidegger*, edited by Charles B. Guignon, 177–201. Cambridge: Cambridge University Press, 1993.

Hume, David. *Enquiries concerning Human Understanding and concerning the Principles of Morals.* Oxford: Claredon, 1902.

Husserl, Edmund. *Logische Untersuchungen.* Tübingen: Niemeyer, 1968.

———. *Psychological and Transcendental Phenomenology and the Confrontation with Heidegger (1927–1931).* Translated by T. Sheehan and R. Palmer. Dordrecht: Kluwer, 1997.

Ingraffia, Brian D. *Postmodern Theory and Biblical Theology.* Cambridge: Cambridge University Press, 1995.

Inwood, Michael. "Hegel." In *The Blackwell Companion to Philosophy*, edited by Nicholas Bunnin and E. P. Tsui-James, 607–16. Oxford: Blackwell, 1996.

Irwin, William. "What Is an Allusion?" *Journal of Aesthetics and Art Criticism* 59.3 (2001) 287–97.

Jauhiainen, Marko. *The Use of Zechariah in Revelation.* Wissenschaftliche Untersuchungen zum Neuen Testament. Tübingen: Mohr Siebeck, 2005.

Johnson, Elliott E. *Expository Hermeneutics: An Introduction.* Grand Rapids: Academie, 1990.

Jones, Peter. "Hume." In *The Blackwell Companion to Philosophy*, edited by Nicholas Bunnin and E. P. Tsui-James, 571–88. Cambridge: Blackwell, 1996.

Jüngling, H. W. *Richter 19-Ein Plädoyer für das Königtum: Stilistische Analzse der Tendenzerzählung Ri 19, 1–30a; 21, 25.* Anbib 84. Rome: Pontificial Biblical Institute, 1981.

Kant, Immanuel. *Critique of Pure Reason.* Translated by N. Kemp Smith. 2nd ed. London: Macmillan, 1929.

Kao, Yu-Kung, and Tsu-Lin Mei. "Meaning, Metaphor, and Allusion in T'ang Poetry." *Harvard Journal of Asiatic Studies* 38.2 (1978) 281–356.

Kawashima, Robert S. "Comparative Literature and Biblical Studies: The Case of Allusion." *Prooftexts: A Journal of Jewish Literary History* 27.2 (2007) 324–44.

Keil, Carl F., and Franz Delitzsch. *Biblical Commentary on the Old Testament, Volume 1, Book 5: The Pentateuch.* Grand Rapids: Eerdmans, 1978.

———. *Biblical Commentary on the Old Testament, Volume 5: The Psalms.* Grand Rapids: Eerdmans, 1978.

Kellett, E. E. *Literary Quotation and Allusion*. Cambridge: Heffer & Sons, 1933.
Kelly, Joseph Ryan. "Identifying Literary Allusions: Theory and the Criterion of Shared Language." In *Subtle Citation, Allusion, and Translation in the Hebrew Bible*, edited by Ziony Zevit, 22–40. Sheffield: Equinox, 2017.
———. "Intertextuality and Allusion in the Study of the Hebrew Bible." PhD diss, Southern Baptist Theological Seminary, 2014.
Kowalski, Beate. "Selective Verses Contextual Allusions: Reconsidering Technical Terms of Intertextuality." In *Methodology in the Use of the Old Testament in the New*, edited by David Allen and Steve Smith, 86–102. London: T. & T. Clark, 2020.
Kraus, Hans-Joachin. *Psalms 1–59*. Translated by Hilton C. Oswald. A Continental Commentary. Minneapolis: Fortress, 1993.
Lasine, Stuart. "Guest and Host in Judges 19: Lot's Hospitality in an Inverted World." *Journal for the Study of the Old Testament* 29 (1984) 37–59.
Leddy, Michael. "The Limits of Allusion." *The British Journal of Aesthetics* 32 (1992) 110–22.
Leonard, Jeffery. "Identifying Inner-Biblical Allusions: Psalm 78 as a Test Case." *Journal of Biblical Literature* 127.2 (2008) 241–65.
———. "Identifying Subtle Allusions: The Promise of Narrative Tracking." In *Subtle Citation, Allusion, and Translation in the Hebrew Bible*, edited by Ziony Zevit, 91–113. Sheffield: Equinox, 2017.
Lete, Gregorio del Olmo, and Jaoquin Sanmartin. *A Dictionary of the Ugaritic Language in the Alphabetic Tradition, Part Two: [l-z]*. Translated by Wilfred G. E. Watson. Leiden: Brill, 2004.
Lussier, Ernest. "The New Latin Psalter: Exegetical Commentary. V, Psalms 9;10." *Catholic Biblical Quarterly* 10.2 (1948) 196–202.
Lyotard, Jean-François. *The Postmodern Condition: A Report on Knowledge*. Theory and History of Literature 10. Minneapolis: University of Minnesota Press, 1984.
Mathewson, David. "Assessing Old Testament Allusions in the Book of Revelation." *Evangelical Quarterly* 75.4 (2003) 311–25.
McConville, J. G. *Deuteronomy*. Apollos Old Testament Commentary. Leicester: Apollos, 2002.
Meek, Russell. "Intertextuality, Inner-Biblical Exegesis, and Inner-Biblical Allusion: The Ethics of Methodology." *Biblica* 85 (2014) 280–91.
Merrill, Eugene. *Deuteronomy*. New American Commentary. Nashville: Broadman & Holman, 1994.
———. *Everlasting Dominion: A Theology of the Old Testament*. Nashville: Broadman & Holman, 2006.
———. *Kingdom of Priests: A History of Old Testament Israel*. Grand Rapids: Baker, 1987.
Mihkelev, Anneli. *Vihjamise Poeetika*. Tallinn: Tuglase Kirjanduskeskus, 2005.
Miller, G. D. "Intertextuality in Old Testament Research." *Currents in Biblical Research* 9 (2011) 283–309.
Miner, Earl. "Allusion." In *Encyclopedia of Poetry and Poetics*, edited by Alex Preminger, 18. Princeton: Princeton University Press, 1965.
———. "Allusion." In *The New Princeton Encyclopedia of Poetry and Poetics*, edited by Alex Preminger and T. V. F. Brogan, 38–39. Princeton: Princeton University Press, 1993.

Moore, George F. *A Critical and Exegetical Commentary on the Book of Judges*. International Critical Commentary. Edinburgh: T. & T. Clark, 1895.

Morewedge, Parviz. *The 'Metaphysica' of Avicenna (ibn Sīnā): A critical translation-commentary and analysis of the fundamental arguments in Avicenna's 'Metaphysica' in the 'Dānish Nāma-i 'alā'ī' ('The Book of Scientific Knowledge')*. London: Routledge & Kegan Paul, 1973.

Morgenstern, Julian. "Psalm 11." *Journal of Biblical Literature* 69.3 (1950) 221–31.

Morier, Henri. "Allusion." In *Dictionnaire de poetique et de rhetorique*, 35–40. Paris: Presses Universitaries de Frances, 1961.

Moyise, Steve. "Authorial Intention and the Book of Revelation." *Andrews University Seminary Studies* 39.1 (2001) 35–40.

———. "Does the Author of Revelation Misappropriate the Scriptures." *Andrews University Seminary Studies* 40 (2002) 3–21.

———. "Does the NT Quote the OT out of Context?" *Anvil* 11.2 (1994) 133–43.

———. "The Old Testament in the New: A Reply to Greg Beale." *Irish Biblical Studies* 21 (1999) 54–58.

———. "Seeing the Old Testament through a Lens." *Irish Biblical Studies* 23 (2001) 36–41.

———. "The Use of Analogy in Biblical Studies." *Anvil* 18.1 (2001) 33–42.

Myers, Elizabeth A. "Probability of Intertextual Borrowing." In *Exploring Intertextuality: Diverse Strategies for New Testament Interpretation of Texts*, edited by B. J. Oropeza and Steve Moyise, 254–72. Eugene, OR: Cascade, 2016.

Niditch, Susan. *Judges: A Commentary*. Louisville: Westminster John Knox, 2008.

———. "The 'Sodomite' Theme in Judges 19–20: Family, Community, and Social Disintegration." *Catholic Biblical Quarterly* 44 (1982) 365–78.

Niehr. H. "שפט." In *TDOT* 15:411–31.

Nietzsche, Freidrich. *The Anti-Christ*. In *The Nietzsche Reader*, edited by Keith Ansell Pearson and Duncan Large, 486–99. Oxford: Blackwell 2006.

———. *The Gay Science*. Translated by Josefine Nauckhoff. Cambridge: Cambridge University Press, 2001.

———. *Twilight of the Idols. The Anti-Christ*. Translated by R. J. Hollingdale. Penguin Classics L207. Harmondsworth: Penguin, 1968.

———. *The Will to Power*. Translated by Walter Kaufmann. New York: Vintage, 1967.

Noble, Paul R. "Esau, Tamar, and Joseph: Criteria for Identifying Inner-Biblical Allusions." *Vetus Testamentum* 52.2 (2002) 219–52.

Norton, David Fate, ed. *The Cambridge Companion to Hume*. Cambridge: Cambridge University Press, 1993.

Noth, Martin. *The Deuteronomistic History*. Translated by D. Orton Journal for the Study of the Old Testament Supplement Series 15. Sheffield: JSOT, 1981.

O'Connell, Robert H. *The Rhetoric of the Book of Judges*. New York: Brill, 1996.

Olson, Dennis T. "The Book of Judges." In *The New Interpreter's Bible, Volume 2*, 721–888. Nashville: Abingdon, 1998.

Oropeza, B. J., and Steve Moyise, eds. *Exploring Intertextuality: Diverse Strategies for New Testament Interpretation of Texts*. Eugene, OR: Cascade , 2016.

Oswalt, John. *The Book of Isaiah: Chapters 1–39*. New International Commentary on the Old Testament. Grand Rapids: Eerdmans, 1986.

Paulien, Jon. "Criteria and Assessment of Allusions to the Old Testament in the Book of Revelation." In *Studies in the Book of Revelation*, edited by Steve Moyise, 113–29. Edinburgh: T. & T. Clark, 2001.

———. *Decoding Revelation's Trumpets: Literary Allusions and Interpretation of Revelation 8:7–12.* Andrews University Seminary Doctoral Dissertation Series. Berrien Springs, MI: Andrews University Press, 1988.

———. "Dreading the Whirlwind: Intertextuality and the Use of the Old Testament in Revelation." *Andrews University Seminary Studies* 39.1 (2001) 5–22.

———. "Elusive Allusions: The Problematic Use of the Old Testament in the Book of Revelation." *Biblical Research* 33 (1988) 37–53.

Palmer, Richard E. *Hermeneutics: Interpretation Theory in Schleiermacher, Dilthey, Heidegger, and Gadamer.* Evanston: Northwestern University Press, 1969.

Pasquali, Giorgio. "Arte Allusiva." In *Stravaganze quarte e supreme,* 11–20. Venice: Neri Pozza, 1951.

———. *Pagine stravananti.* Florence: Sansoi, 1968.

Penchansky, David. "Staying the Night: Intertextuality in Genesis and Judges." In *Reading between Texts: Intertextuality and the Hebrew Bible,* edited by D. N. Fewell, 77–88. Louisville: Westminster John Knox., 1992.

Perri, Carmela. "On Alluding." *Poetics* 7 (1978) 289–307.

Perry, Peter S. "Relevance Theory and Intertextuality." In *Exploring Intertextuality: Diverse Strategies for New Testament Interpretation of Texts,* edited by B. J. Oropeza and Steve Moyise, 207–21. Eugene, OR: Cascade, 2016.

Rad, Gerhard von. *Genesis: A Commentary.* Rev. ed. Old Testament Library. Philadelphia: Westminster, 1972.

Raines, John, ed. *Marx on Religion.* Philadelphia: Temple University Press, 2002.

Ree, Jonathon. *Descartes.* London: Lane, 1974.

Rendtorff, Rolf. "What Happened to the Yahwist? Reflections after Thirty Years: A Collegial Conversation between Rolf Rendtorff, David J. A. Clines, Allan Rosengren, and John Van Seters." In *Probing the Frontiers of Biblical Studies,* edited by J. Harold Ellens and John T. Greene, 39–66. Eugene, OR: Pickwick, 2009.

Ricœur, Paul. *Interpretation Theory: Discourse and the Surplus of Meaning.* Fort Worth: Texas Christian University Press, 1976.

Robinson, James M. "Hermeneutic since Barth." In *New Frontiers in Theology, Volume II: The New Hermeneutic,* edited by J. M. Robinson and J. B. Cobb, 1–77. New York: Harper & Row, 1964.

Rosen, Stanley. "Horizontverschmelzung." In *The Philosophy of Hans-Georg Gadamer,* edited by Edwin Hahn, 207–18. La Salle, IL: Open Court, 1997.

Ross, Stephanie. "Art and Allusion." *The Journal of Aesthetics and Art Criticism* 40.1 (1981) 60–70.

Ryken, Leland. *How to Read the Bible as Literature.* Grand Rapids: Academie, 1984.

Sandy, D. Brent, and Ronald L. Giese Jr., eds. *Cracking Old Testament Codes: A Guide to Interpreting the Literary Genres of the Old Testament.* Nashville: Broadman & Holman, 1995.

Satterthwaite, Philip E. "'No King in Israel': Narrative Criticism and Judges 17–21." *Tyndale Bulletin* 44 (1993) 75–88.

Schreiner, Susan E. *Where Shall Wisdom Be Found?* Chicago: University of Chicago Press, 1994.

Seters, John Van. *Abraham in History and Tradition.* New Haven: Yale University Press, 1975.

Smith, Steve. "The Use of Criteria: A Proposal from Relevance Theory." In *Methodology in the Use of the Old Testament in the New: Context and Criteria*, edited by David Allen and Steve Smith, 142–54. London: T. & T. Clark, 2020.

Soggin, J. Alberto. *Judges: A Commentary*. Philadelphia: Westminster, 1981.

Sommer, Benjamin D. "Exegesis, Allusion and Intertextuality in the Hebrew Bible: A Response to Lyle Eslinger." *Vetus Testamentum* 46.4 (1996) 479–89.

———. *A Prophet Reads Scripture: Allusion in Isaiah 40–66*. Stanford: Stanford University Press, 1998.

Sonne, Isaiah. "Psalm Eleven." *Journal of Biblical Literature* 68.3 (1949) 241–45.

Sperber, Dan, and Deidre Wilson. *Relevance: Communication and Cognition*. 2nd ed. Malden, MA: Blackwell, 1995.

Spronk, Klaas. "Deborah, a Prophetess: The Meaning and Background of Judges 4:4–5." In *The Elusive Prophet*, edited by Johannes C. de Moor, 232–42. Leiden: Brill, 2001.

Stanley, Christopher D. "Rhetoric of Quotations." In *Exploring Intertextuality: Diverse Strategies for New Testament Interpretation of Texts*, edited by B. J. Oropeza and Steve Moyise, 42–52. Eugene, OR: Cascade, 2016.

———. "The Rhetoric of Quotations: An Essay on Method." In *Early Christian Interpretation of the Scriptures of Israel*, edited by Craig A. Evans and James A. Sanders, 44–58. Sheffield: Sheffield Academic, 1997.

Swart, I., and C. VanDam. "חמס." In *New International Dictionary of Old Testament Theology and Exegesis*, edited by Willem A VanGemeren, 2:177–80. Grand Rapids: Zondervan, 1997.

Taylor, Charles. *Hegel*. Cambridge: Cambridge University Press, 1975.

Taylor, Mark C. *Deconstructing Theology*. AAR Studies in Religion 28. Chico, CA: Scholars, 1982.

Tenney, Merrill. *Interpreting Revelation*. Reprint, Grand Rapids: Eerdmans, 1988.

Terrien, Samuel L. *The Psalms: Strophic Structure and Theological Commentary*. Eerdmans Critical Commentary. Grand Rapids: Eerdmans, 2003.

Theological Dictionary of the Old Testament. 14 vols. Edited by G. Johannes Botterweck and Helmer Ringgren. Translated by Geoffrey W. Bromiley et al. Grand Rapids: Eerdmans, 1974–2004.

Thompson, Michael B. *Clothed in Christ: The Example and Teaching of Jesus in Romans 12.1—15.13*. Journal for the Study of the New Testament Supplement Series. Sheffield: Sheffield Academic, 1991.

Tigay, Jeffrey H. *Deuteronomy*. JPS Torah Commentary. Philadelphia: Jewish Publication Society, 1996.

Trudinger, Paul. "The Text of the Old Testament in the Book of Revelation." ThD diss., Boston University School of Theology, 1963.

Vanhoozer, Kevin J. *Is There a Meaning in This Text? The Bible, the Reader, and the Morality of Literary Knowledge*. Grand Rapids: Zondervan, 1998.

———. "Pilgrim's Digress: Christian Thinking on and about the Post/Modern Way." In *Christianity and the Postmodern Turn: Six Views*, edited by Myron B. Penner, 71–103. Grand Rapids: Brazos, 2005.

Waltke, Bruce K. *Genesis: A Commentary*. Grand Rapids: Zondervan, 2001.

Watts, John D. W. *Isaiah 1–33*. Word Biblical Commentary 24. Waco: Word, 1985.

Webb, Barry G. *The Book of Judges: An Integrated Reading*. Journal for the Study of the Old Testament Supplement Series 46. Sheffield: Sheffield Academic, 1987.

Weitzman, Steve. "Reopening the Case of the Suspiciously Suspended Nun in Judges 18:30." *Catholic Biblical Quarterly* 61 (1999) 448–60.

West, David. *An Introduction to Continental Philosophy*. Cambridge: Polity, 1996.

Westermann, Claus. *Genesis 12–36*. Translated by John J. Scullion. Continental Commentary. Minneapolis: Fortress, 1995.

Wildberger, Hans. *Isaiah 1–12*. Translated by Thomas H. Trapp Continental Commentary. Minneapolis: Fortress, 1991.

Williams, Bernard. *Descartes: The Project of Pure Enquiry*. Harmondsworth: Penquin, 1978.

Williamson, H. G. M. *Isaiah 1–27*. International Critical Commentary. London: T. & T. Clark, 2006.

Wimsatt, W. K., and Monroe Beardsley. "The Intentional Fallacy." *Sewanee Review* 54 (1946) 468–88.

Wong, Gregory T. K. "Ehud and Joab: Separated at Birth?" *Vetus Testamentum* 56.3 (2006) 399–412.

Wright, David P. "Method in the Study of Textual Source Dependence: The Covenant Code." In *Subtle Citation, Allusion, and Translation in the Hebrew Bible*, edited by Ziony Zevit, 159–81. Sheffield: Equinox, 2017.

Zevit, Ziony, ed. *Subtle Citation, Allusion, and Translation in the Hebrew Bible*. Sheffield: Equinox, 2017.

www.ingramcontent.com/pod-product-compliance
Lightning Source LLC
Chambersburg PA
CBHW070329230426
43663CB00011B/2263